In the Analyst's Co

MW01493703

In *The Bi-Personal Field – Experiences in Child Analysis*, Antonino Ferro devised a new model of the relationship between patient and analyst. *In the Analyst's Consulting Room* complements and develops this model by concentrating on adults. From the standpoint of the "analytic field", Antonino Ferro explores basic psychoanalytic concepts, such as criteria for analysability and ending the analysis, transformations that occur during the session, the impasse and negative therapeutic reactions, sexuality and setting. The author explores certain themes in greater depth, including:

- Ways in which characters that appear during sessions can be interpreted
- Continual indications given by the patient during the emotional upheavals of the field
- The function of "narrator" which the analyst takes on to mark the boundaries of the possible worlds.

Through clinical narrative, Ferro renders Bion's often complex ideas in a very personal and accessible way, making this book invaluable for psychoanalysts, psychotherapists, psychiatrists and psychologists.

Antonino Ferro is the president of the Centre for Psychoanalysis in Milan. He is the author of *The Bi-Personal Field* (Routledge 1999) and has written numerous articles on techniques of psychoanalysis.

In the Analyst's Consulting Room

Antonino Ferro

English translation by Philip Slotkin

First published 2002 by Brunner-Routledge
27 Church Road, Hove, East Sussex BN3 2FA

Simultaneously published in the USA and Canada
by Taylor & Francis Inc
29 West 35th Street, New York, NY 10001

Originally published in Italian as *Nella stanza d'analisi: Emozioni, racconti, trasformazioni*

Brunner-Routledge is an imprint of the Taylor & Francis Group

English Edition © 2002 Antonino Ferro

Typeset in Times by
Keystroke, Jacaranda Lodge, Wolverhampton
Printed and bound in Great Britain by
TJ International, Padstow, Cornwall

Cover design by Liz Bussell

All rights reserved. No part of this book may be reprinted or
reproduced or utilised in any form or by any electronic,
mechanical, or other means, now known or hereafter
invented, including photocopying and recording, or in
any information storage or retrieval system, without permission
in writing from the publishers.

British Library Cataloguing in Publication Data
A catalogue record for this book is available from the British Library

Library of Congress Cataloging-in-Publication Data
Ferro, Antonino, 1947–
    [Nella stanza di analisi. English]
    In the analyst's consulting room/Antonino Ferro; [translated by
    Philip Slotkin].
        p. cm.
    Includes bibliographical references (p.) and index.
    ISBN 1–58391–221–5—ISBN 1–58391–222–3 (pbk.)
    1. Psychoanalysis—Philosophy. 2. Psychotherapist and patient.
    I. Title.
    RC480.8 .F4713 2002
    150.19'5'01—dc21   2001052807

ISBN 1–58391–221–5 hbk
ISBN 1–58391–222–3 pbk

Contents

Figures

Foreword

Antonino Ferro presents a highly original, eminently useful conception of the clinical psychoanalytic process. At the centre of his thinking lies the theoretical contribution of Wilfred Bion. Many colleagues, while fascinated by Bion's ideas, find them abstruse and difficult to apply; but Ferro renders them in very personal terms, making them experience-near and illuminating their clinical utility. Every point Ferro makes is illustrated with case material – pithy vignettes help the reader see how each concept captures an aspect of the interaction between analyst and analysand, and longer presentations allow us to appreciate the interplay of these variables within the complex unfolding of the psychoanalytic encounter.

With delightful candour, Ferro offers us an account of the mind and heart of the analyst at work, showing us how personal transformation for both members of the psychoanalytic couple is the essence of every successful clinical analysis. Not only does he describe in detail his intimate responses to his patients, but he reflects upon the development of his understanding of the work in general over time, upon his own evolution as a psychoanalytic practitioner. Thus, we are given a picture of the bipersonal field longitudinally, as well as in cross section. We might well say about Ferro's exposition that in many respects, the medium is the message.

In Chapter 1, Ferro draws upon the contributions of a number of authors, particularly the Barangers, to define his terms and to lay out his basic theoretical infrastructure. Readers familiar with his book *The Bi-Personal Field* will recognize an elaboration and extension to the analysis of adults of what Ferro has previously written concerning work with children.

Chapter 2 uses the concept of style as a lens through which to examine the analysis of character. Narrative transformation is envisioned as the outcome of an evolving, dialectical interchange.

In Chapter 3, Ferro builds upon the conception of psychoanalytic dialogue that he has established to discuss field theory. Bion's grid, for example, is integrated with the Barangers' conception of transference–countertransference neurosis.

Chapter 4 continues the consideration of transformations in the field and how they occur, leading, in Chapter 5, to a specific discussion of the analytic impact as danger and opportunity.

In Chapter 6, Ferro creates a uniquely valuable analytic tool by taking up sexuality as dialect. He develops a clinical approach which envisions sexual and aggressive concepts as relational vectors, thus pointing the way toward a method for creating analytic opportunity in the midst of what can be the most intense and difficult embroilments between patient and analyst. Similarly, in Chapter 7, he recasts the experience of fear in relational terms, making brilliant use of Freud's concept of the uncanny.

Finally, in his postscript, Ferro adds a coda in which he ties together what he has written in previous chapters through examination of the setting and the ground rules of the clinical psychoanalytic enterprise.

By the end of this engaging and instructive book, the reader comes to know a good deal about Antonino Ferro and the vicissitudes and transformations that have comprised his clinical experience. But even more important, the reader shares in that experience, is enriched by it, and has transformed him- or herself.

Owen Renik, MD

Chapter 1

Criteria of analysability and termination

A radical vertex

[handwritten margin note: images emerge; box labeled "theory" "prepackaged" or circle labeled "field" "personal" α + α]

I should like in this chapter to present some reflections on the particularities of field theories in relation to two key aspects of analysis, namely the decision to begin it and the decision to end it.

I should say from the outset that I am using the term "field" in the widest possible sense, the range of connotations extending from the basic conceptions of Baranger & Baranger (1961–62) and of Baranger, Baranger & Mom (1983) to the complex and sophisticated notions of Corrao (1986).

Corrao's 1986 contribution includes a succinct *specification* of the field as "a function whose value depends on its position in space–time; it is a system with an infinite number of degrees of freedom, resulting from the infinite possible determinations assumed by it at every point in space and at every instant in time". Comprehensive definitions and more detailed information can be found in Bezoari & Ferro (1990a, 1991b) and in Ferro (1993d, 1993f).

At the precise moment when the field takes shape, space–time is affected by intense emotional turbulence in the form of vortices of β elements, which evoke and activate the α functions and thereby begin their process of transformation into α elements – that is, predominantly, into "visual images" (Bion, 1962); the place "where" these images are manifested – whether in the story told by the patient or in the analyst's reverie or countertransference – is immaterial. (Elizabeth Bott Spillius provides a useful summary of Bion's ideas in her Introduction to *The Bi-Personal Field* (Ferro, 1999: x–xii).)

The emergence of images described by Bion is, however, the end-point of complex operations of transformation, which Bezoari and I previously attempted to describe by the metaphor of mills (Bezoari & Ferro, 1992a). I shall summarize this description below.

Two α functions come into play in the analytic encounter. The patient's recounting of anecdotes, facts and memories imposes heavy demands on the analyst's α function, which will be involved in the process of alphabetizing and semanticizing the patient's communication. Let us say that the major part of the work in the analytic field is carried out by two mills, a windmill (for words) and a watermill (for projective identifications). The two mills are fed with large sacks of

[handwritten notes: wind → water / water / water / words (p.1)]

[handwritten notes: β elements (wheat) → / flour (α elements) / + baked (dream thoughts)]

wheat (β elements), which must then be ground into flour (α elements), kneaded and baked (dream thoughts).

Many sacks of wheat are exchanged between the two mills (projective identifications passing back and forth); a larger number of sacks as a rule travel in the direction patient → analyst, unless the analyst is blocked or overloaded, in which case the flow may be reversed (Ferro, 1987; Borgogno, 1992, 1994a).

The communications between the two mills often tend to be in the raw state, so that they need threshing to separate the grain from the straw. The task of the α function in this case is gradually to grind down these elements to a finer consistency. For example, a high proportion of a given patient's communications (which are unelaborated or in the raw state) are conveyed on the manifest level (by language) or underground (projective identifications), whereas a small number have already been transformed by the patient's own α function. As a result of further processing by the analyst, new flour comes into being and the "functional aggregates"[1] produced by the mental work of both parties in narrating what is happening in the field and in the couple will take the stage.

The "character" (the term is used here also in the narratological sense of the main protagonist, so that it may even be an object in the animal or inanimate world) assumes not only the features of a "real external character" or of a "character from the internal world" but also the quality of a "*syncretic narrative node*", which concretizes, contextualizes, shapes and names what is happening in the field, thereby allowing it to be visualized in three dimensions.

This is the way in which the emotional–linguistic text of the session is able to express emotions and affects in a processed form capable of being transformed, narrated and shared.

The basis of this conceptualization is the "*waking dream thought*" – that is, the continuous "dreaming-in-order-to-be-awake" constantly accomplished by the α function when it forms α elements, which are placed in the appropriate sequence, out of all the sensory, perceptual and emotional afferences reaching us at every existential and relational instant (Bion, 1962).

Waking dream thought continuously separates the conscious from the unconscious and prevents us from being captured by the latter, allowing us to live the experiences we are having without being overwhelmed by them, and to metabolize them in real time. Night dreams enable us to view the outcome of an ever ongoing process (Bion, 1962).

We perceive our waking dream thought through the "near narrative derivatives" of the α elements, which are at all times also *signals* of the emotional–linguistic *text* of the session.

The text signals become perceptible whenever our chosen vertex is that of listening to what comes from anywhere in the field (the patient's story or dream, our countertransference, our own dreams, projective identifications, etc.) *as a live renarration of the emotions and movements of the field and of the success or failure of transformations of the field in the only therapeutic direction, namely* $\beta \rightarrow \alpha$.

These *field signals* are like markers that enable us to keep up the tension of $\beta \rightarrow \alpha$ transformation, calling our attention to any departure from this mutative direction as a dysfunction of the field.

The field signals, which are the moment-by-moment resultant of the emotional forces of the field, are a highly significant approximation to the emotional truth of the field (the "O" of the couple); they stem from the mental functioning of the patient and the analyst and from their interaction and vicissitudes.

Of course, these characters can be seen from other vertices present in the field in accordance with alternative models which assign them to external or internal reality. The models in the field are in a state of mutual oscillation and *are self-confirming from every theoretical vertex of observation*.

Let us now consider the phenomena of analysability and termination by an approach that emphasizes the use of field signals.

Analysability or capacity to endure

There is a conspicuous disparity between the abundance of literature on the criteria of analysability and the scant measure of agreement exhibited by the relevant authors.

What strikes one first is the fundamental inconsistency between the development of the models and the broadening of the criteria themselves: the analysts who have contributed most to advancing our knowledge of analysis of serious pathologies are found to have concerned themselves only marginally with criteria of analysability.

It is in my view more useful to invoke the *criterion of capacity to endure*, in the sense that every analyst ought to be conscious of the point to which he feels he can be pushed to analyse, on the basis of his own analysis, mental functioning and tolerance of risk and frustration. This consciousness should take account, too, of the endurance of the analyst's model: there is often a process upstream of repression that permits the construction and formation of the "apparatus for thinking thoughts" (Bion, 1962) before these thoughts can be processed, and sometimes even allows a hitherto seriously deficient α function to develop.

For a re-examination of the principal literature on the subject, it is worth consulting the comprehensive review by Limentani (1972), its later supplement (1988b), and the excellent review by Etchegoyen (1986).

It should, I think, be noted that authors on this topic have substantially tended to transfer their attention from the characteristics of the patient to those of the couple and to the interaction between a given individual patient and a given individual analyst.

At the same time the concept of analysability (understood as the possibility of a cure, seen as the end-point) has been supplemented and largely replaced by those of *suitability* for analysis (based more on the capacity to tolerate being in an analytic setting and to experience a process of transformation) (Limentani, 1972) and *accessibility* to analysis (where the only possible distinction is between readily accessible patients and patients who cannot easily be reached) (Joseph, 1985).

Again, many analysts have a sense of "alarm" at the possibility that an analysis might be *broken off* (as if "analysable" status guaranteed a process that would culminate in the completion of an expected terminal phase); however, the situation ought perhaps rather to be seen in terms of an analysis pursued as far as it can go (by the specific couple at work), in which case the analyst would have to accept, as Bleger (1967) puts it, that one analysis may end successfully whereas others might begin.[2]

Another cause for alarm is interminability, experienced as a defeat rather than indicating that the treatment cannot be ended owing to the particular pathology of the patient and the field – for such an analysis–dialysis may on occasion also be necessary.

I have only twice turned down requests for analysis (assuming that I had a vacancy). In the first of these cases, dating back to the beginning of my analytic career, the patient confronted me with emotional and existential material similar to that which I had only just worked through in my own analysis, which I did not yet feel solid enough to tackle in another person. The second patient, again in the early days of my work as an analyst, was a tall and bulky man who, while "I was following him" as he told his story, informed me that while driving his car he had sometimes felt "followed" and, if his suspicion was confirmed, he had stopped and beaten up his pursuer; this seemed to me sufficient reason "not to follow him".

On other occasions when I have had time, I have never said no to a patient because I felt that he was unanalysable or that his pathology was too severe – even if I have sometimes paid dearly in toil and mental suffering for this decision, which, however, also made it possible to venture beyond already "mapped" territory.

An air of mystery – albeit perhaps slight – surrounds the situation when the analyst says yes despite not having a vacancy:[3] the patient's material happens to dovetail with the analyst's theoretical and often practical interests at the time, so that the analyst too sets off to explore mysterious, obscure or otherwise insufficiently negotiated areas of his own mind (Meotti, 1987).

Alternatively, the analyst may fear a deterioration in the patient's condition. This could indicate that the technique used is inappropriate to the patient's needs or capacity (as demonstrated by psychotic transferences, negative therapeutic reactions and broken-off analyses; cf. De Masi, 1984; Gagliardi Guidi, 1992; Conforto, 1996), or it might be a necessary corollary of efforts to allow slumbering or encapsulated states of mind to be worked through.

Puget & Wender (1987) consider analysis to consist in the activation – often in extreme situations – of a psychoanalytic function capable of facilitating "the understanding and semanticization of what has been unconscious, uncomprehended and unthought up to that moment – a relief to mental pain".

The analyst must, of course, look closely into his own general availability for accepting *a* new patient into analysis, and subsequently for accepting a *given individual* patient; he may find himself saying no to a particular *individual* patient because there is no place for *a* new patient.

As stated above, the opposite may also happen: although the analyst may not have a vacancy for *a* new patient, he may find a place for a particular *individual* patient. From the classical point of view, a thunderbolt of this kind would be a good reason for not taking on a patient who arouses such countertransference feelings, but how can one resist, and why? There will be time enough to regret it during the course of the analysis – just as, conversely, with patients accepted only because one had *a* vacancy, the analysis sometimes turns out to be very exciting. In my view, this only serves to confirm the infinite range of meanings that may be opened up, and of worlds that may be activated, in an analysis.

The first meeting might be imagined as the most neutral of all, taken up mainly by listening to the patient's history or internal world. However, this idea is naive in the extreme: from the time of the first telephone call, or even before, patient and analyst begin to construct "couple" fantasies, which crystallize from the very first meeting (as Baranger & Baranger, for example, say). What is more, the *listening model*, if applied without consciousness, structures the field and ultimately confirms the analyst's theories through a hallucinosis of microtransformations in which theory distorts the patient's communication by the imposition of a single "reading". Interpretative colonization then creates the domain of the non-existent, avoiding the painful and frustrating experience of confrontation with the void of not knowing, of the doubt aroused by prolonged dwelling in PS, pending activation by the field – the "true matrix of possible histories" (in accordance with the emotional genomes of patient and analyst and with their capacities for trans-formation) – of a "history" that cannot so readily be foreseen. From the very first meeting, there is in my view a continuous oscillation between two analytic functions. The first is the analyst's "negative capability" (Bion, 1970), which includes an ability to remain in doubt, in PS, thereby allowing the emergence of an infinite range of potential histories (or meanings). In the second, the analyst opts for the "selected fact". This entails the strong choice of an interpretative hypothesis born of an emotion which aggregates what was scattered in PS into a Gestalt that forecloses certain meanings in favour of a single prevailing one, while unequivocally reorganizing from a specific vertex what has formed in the field; this is an operation that takes place in D and involves mourning for that which is not.

This corresponds to the narratological concepts of the "open work" and of the "narcotization" of possible histories to allow the development of a single history, a practical demonstration of which is Diderot's *Jacques le Fataliste* (Eco, 1979; Ferro, 1992).

Here is a brief example.

Carmen: her orgasm and her school report

Carmen was a young non-Italian woman whose first communication was that she was unable to attain orgasm with penetration. I specifically noticed that this was the first thing she told me during our meeting.

She went on to tell me of her present rather unsatisfying life and of the family she had left behind in a European town. After recounting some stories from her childhood, she described a particular characteristic of hers, which was that she was always "furious". This had been so since a very disappointing experience as a little girl: she had given her father her school report, which was full of bad marks, and had been sure he would get very angry and punish her. She had felt awful and enraged when he had signed the report without even a glance at the marks and hence without comment. She then told of her superficial relationship with her mother and other experiences connected with the political changes in her home country.

How is this first meeting to be thought of? How are the characters to be interpreted? They could of course be seen as substantially historical characters existing in external reality and connected with her own family romance. The sexual problems could then be considered in terms of femaleness, castration anxieties, oedipal and pre-oedipal themes, and so on.

However, the characters can also be understood as the patient's way of recounting in a dialect the emotional facts of her internal world. "Orgasm with penetration" might stand for "deep intimate relationship", while the story of the school report might be the prototype of a disappointing and frustrating relationship, as if Carmen had said from the outset: "This is my problem: intimate and deep relationships are never pleasurable to me, but only cause disappointment and rage"; and the sexual problem may be the vehicle for conveying these even more intimate matters.

But yet another possible level emerges if the characters and history are seen from the first meeting predominantly in terms of relationship. I had in fact already told Carmen on the telephone that I had no vacancy for an analysis and that I could only offer her a consultation; this must inevitably have aroused feelings of rage and disappointment towards someone who showed no particular interest in learning of her "bad marks", and my answer had certainly not given her any pleasure.

Every one of these readings in my opinion represents a colonization of the patient's text. The alternative is to create in the session a model that does not need such theorizings, whereby a name and meaning are assigned for the first time to something unknown that has never been thought before (at least with, and for, Carmen, with me and by me) – something we cannot know until it has actually come into being. This is basically what Bion means by the use of the "model" constructed in the session and by the analyst's being "without memory or desire" (Bion, 1962, 1970). In other words, rather than relying on decoding-type interpretations, the analyst should look to his own "negative capability" (Bion, 1970) and see what transformations this "history", precisely in the "dialect" in which the patient presents it, may undergo by virtue of the mental interaction between patient and analyst in the field they are together creating – the field being understood as a space–time that promotes and activates possible histories, on the basis, of course, of the emotional ingredients brought by the patient.

A significant aspect of this approach is that, whereas the characters of the session may be seen as falling within a spectrum – extending from historical characters pertaining to the patient's internal world or to the relationship on the one hand, to holograms of the field on the other – that admits of *n* different combinations, none of which can be determined *a priori*.

Analysability therefore seems to me to be only an *a posteriori* criterion, in the sense that we do not yet know what "stories" (of the couple, the internal world or the history) will take shape; all we can do is forecast (no more reliably than forecasting the weather) the turbulences that will be activated in the field – so that we should perhaps ask ourselves how far the "α function of the field" and the field's "apparatus for thinking thoughts" will be capable of resisting the loss of their structure and of transforming (rather than evacuating) the β elements of the field.

The only useful approach in my view, although not a criterion of analysability, is to assess the potential for transformation in the sessions from the very first meeting,[4] by observing what capacity to form images, histories and reverie is activated in the couple, so as to allow prediction of the couple's fertility. The absence of such activation might of course be precisely the problem that needs to be tackled.

It will be recalled that Bion assigned row 2 of his grid to "lies", which stand for everything that "protects" us from the unknown – and it is the unknown that terrifies us most, so that we are always inclined to avoid it, exorcise it and map it with false charts. So I believe that every patient who is "difficult" – or unanalysable depending on one's parameters – is simply impelling us towards unknown aspects of ourselves, of himself and of our theories (Gaburri & Ferro, 1988).

Bion's story of the liars (Bion, 1970) springs to mind; and among the false truths we invoke to protect ourselves, I am not averse to counting much of what has been written on the criteria of analysability.

The acceptance of every new patient inevitably entails risks to the analyst's mental life, which, however, are reduced if the analyst adopts the role of "the" patient's archaeologist or decoder of his fantasies.

Seriously ill patients certainly present a risk to the analyst, because the work will involve confronting and metabolizing very primitive and sometimes catastrophic anxieties, which will enter the field in one way or another. The same applies to patients with severe psychosomatic pathology, with whom we must make the journey from the somatic to the mental.

One danger thus lies in the activation of a degree of mental suffering. (Freud himself said that every analyst needed periodic "maintenance", and Bion mentioned patients who damage the analyst's mind.)

Another "danger" has to do with the growth of the analyst's own mind and concerns the suffering caused by the increase in the area of thinkability, concomitant with the expansion of the mind itself. Yet another – this time for the patient too – is that theories (or indeed interpretations) may be erected as defences against thinking.

Termination

The literature on the criteria for termination is of course extremely rich; detailed considerations can be found in the relevant chapter of Etchegoyen (1986), in Preve (1994) and in De Simone (1994).

My earlier comments apply also to termination. If the analysis is considered in "field" terms, the field itself will necessarily become the locus of "signalling" of the termination. The signal of this event may light up anywhere in the field – in the countertransference, countertransference dreams, or characters or narrations produced by the patient – *on the basis not of a predictive theory but of a permissive model* (Bion, 1962).

Theory and model are clearly distinguished by Bion in *Learning from Experience* (1962): theories are highly saturated and abstract, and if used in the session will distort the material, whereas a model is unsaturated, is invented anew every day, and constitutes a provisional discovery made in the session; although it may be organized into theories outside the session, in the session itself it is always unique and unrepeatable.

A further variable arises when the situation is considered in field terms – namely the fact that the field is structured by the mental contributions of both patient and analyst, and by the interaction of their defences, transferences and projective identifications. Hence the termination is specific to each individual situation and couple.

The termination for me always takes the form of an "event" specific to a particular analysis, even if common aspects can often be identified (albeit always *a posteriori*): the crucial element during the analysis has always been its unforeseen and unexpected "signalling" in the field by the emotional–linguistic text of the session.

Later abstraction from the various models tested in the session has in my experience often revealed a signal such as a token of maturation of the "apparatus for thinking thoughts" (Bion, 1962). In other words, we should in my view be thinking in terms of the development not so much of a given content as of what Bion describes by the metaphor of the digestive apparatus.

In addition to the α function (and its capacity to transform β elements into α elements, and hence to lead on to waking dream thought and to thoughts), it will be recalled that Bion postulates the necessity of an "apparatus for thinking thoughts", which, for all its inadequacy in the human species, is nevertheless required for processing, organizing and using thoughts once produced. In the absence of this apparatus, thoughts are evacuated as if they were α elements.

The "apparatus for thinking thoughts" is made up of PS ↔ D oscillations and the ♀ ♂ oscillation. In my view, sufficient introjection of this apparatus is a key aspect of this signalling. It is achieved during analysis not by discoveries or increased knowledge but through the progressive introjection of the analyst's mental qualities – i.e. introjection of his way of treating emerging emotions, passions and thoughts (Bianchedi, 1991).

[handwritten annotation: a way of treating emerging emotions, passions + thoughts]

It is therefore the introjection of this quality that permits autonomy, which is, of course, acquired by dint of prolonged work on the contents, albeit not by their "revelation" or "interpretation", but by the gradual transfer of this function to the other – as Bion says in connection with reverie and the maternal α function. Whenever it operates, not only are emotional contents reclaimed or transformed but also, and in particular, parts of the function itself, of the PS $\leftrightarrow$ D apparatus and of ♀ ♂ are progressively introjected.

The termination is prepared in the very first session, in that the analyst's mental capacities, put to the test day after day and enduring for years on end, are the factor that will allow their "precipitate" to be introjected; the crucial aspects in my opinion are how the analyst's mind has functioned together with his patient's in the analytic field, and what transformations ($\beta \rightarrow \alpha$) have thereby been made possible, regardless of the theories of "interpretative culture" used.

What matters is how far the analyst's mind receives and transforms the patient's anxieties in the present; the extent to which the analyst's theory includes this fact is of little significance. *The essential point is what the analyst does in reality from the standpoint of the microtransformations occurring in the session, irrespective of what he thinks he is doing or of the dialect he thinks he is doing it in.*

This is different from the more superego-oriented criterion of stabilizing the patient in D: Bion has after all taught us to think in terms not of firm anchoring in D but of a continuous PS $\leftrightarrow$ D oscillation. Introjection of the analytic function can, I believe, be seen as the "enzyme" facilitating the reaction towards D, affording the trust and hope that, even at moments when PS is at its most acute, the possibility of mental transformation in the direction of D still exists.

If analysis is regarded as the probe (Bion, 1970) that allows continuous expansion of the field it is investigating, the situation could not be otherwise.

On the question of whether to focus on the analyst or on the couple at work, Preve (1994) reconciles the positions of Grinberg (1981) and of Bianchedi et al. (1991) by affirming that "it is ultimately the analyst who assumes responsibility for the decisions to separate and to fix the date, but these decisions are the fruit of interaction within the couple".

In addition to the indicators from the patient – described by Libermann et al. (1983) in terms of time, movement, detachment and "typical characters" – there are, again according to Preve, also indicators of architectural restructuring.

Great importance attaches in my view to the negative capability of the analyst, whereby he is able to tolerate doubt and not knowing, and hence to admit whatever the emotional text is signalling. I have been surprised by the emergence of one particular signal – *an implement for maintenance of the mind* – in several different analyses.

The forces operating in the field in effect suddenly yield an emotional resultant of this kind, and I see these signals too as "functional aggregates of the couple", which take shape as such out of the emotions of the field, telling, through the characters, of the transformations that have occurred in the field. What is "transformed is the space of the analysis" (Riolo, 1989), with concomitant trans-formations of the patient, the analyst and psychoanalysis itself.

In the same contribution, Riolo emphasizes this point by his statement that the efficacy of an analysis is measurable only by the correlative transformations to which it has given rise in all its components, and that no result, not even only a therapeutic one, is obtained unless the patient has been able in turn to modify the analysis and the analyst, to "inform them" of himself, and to impose his own truth, thereby avoiding the risk that the vacuum he leaves behind will be filled by the analyst with his own thoughts and emotions.

In the view of De Simone (1994) it is the possibility of "reorganizing the events of the past on the basis of new relational experiences and thereby assigning new meaning to them" that accounts, by the mechanism of *Nachträglichkeit*, for the therapeutic efficacy of the symptom-become-story-and-discourse.

Quinodoz (1991) uses the word "buoyancy" [*portance*] to signify the acquisition by the patient of autonomy and the capacity to be alone.

Here, finally, are some clinical examples, the first and second of which concern "thinking equipment".

Loredana's comb

At the end of her analysis, Loredana dreamed that her father had given her a little bag containing everything she needed (combs, brushes, curlers, a hair dryer, etc.) to put her "head in order" whenever her hair was dishevelled. Apart from the obvious introjective connotations, this dream indicated to me how far Loredana had travelled since her terrifying dream of the ghastly head of Medusa with serpents instead of hair at the beginning of the analysis.

Gabriella's household equipment

Gabriella's problem had been to work through what lay behind her need for *lucidity* – which was all the "madness" that terrified her and by which she was afraid of being infected. During the analysis, she had gradually equipped herself to cope with the intense, violent emotions that assailed her.

All this "crystallized" at a certain point, not only in her account of the way she had restructured her house and housework and defined new and separate spaces, but also in a detailed description of the equipment available to her as a housewife for routine and emergency use. Floods in the house, for example, were tackled with the "*scopa di Chiavari*",[5] which was neither too stiff nor too soft (this was the doubly declined relational capacity, "scopa" and "Chiavari", enabling her to cope with emotional floods). But she also had her food mixer, which could beat and homogenize vegetables, meat and the like to make them assimilable (what better description could there be of the α function?), kitchen paper (which she used in a dream to stop the bleeding in a child's cut finger) . . . and her *husband's toolbag* – for she could rely on him.

The third example shows how the patient – one's best colleague – is able at all times to signal his own emotional needs.

Gianluca: his "Ciao" and his "pliers"

At the beginning of Gianluca's long analysis, which I have described elsewhere (Ferro, 1993b, 1993f), this patient had been unable either to sleep or to stay awake, because he was a constant prey to terrible hallucinatory evacuations. After the reconstruction of a mental container, we had gradually succeeded in transforming these into hallucinosis and then into "dream-like flashes in waking life" (Bezoari & Ferro, 1990b, 1994b). Finally, after telling me of a friend who had undergone neurosurgery for tension that caused him to vomit – involving the insertion of a cannula (*tubicino* = *tu vicino*?)[6] for internal relief of the excess tension (introjection of a container) – he began to dream; this period also saw a rearrangement of his emotions, which had now become negotiable, and of his life.

From then on dreams became our main working channel. He thought very highly of the new mechanic, Mr Morini, who discharged his obligations and made a good job of tuning the motorcycles of boys he liked: "He has a well adjusted son, because calm and solid fathers have calm and solid sons." Gianluca now wanted to get his driving licence . . . to come to Pavia without Dad . . . "to close the doors" . . . he was finding it "easier and easier to *prendere il Ciao*"[7] . . . (just as end-of-session rituals and greetings were becoming simpler).

I was moved anew when I heard of Gianluca's plans to open a branch of his father's hand-made furniture business, not in competition but somewhere else . . . and he wanted to call his own establishment "Sofà".[8]

He showed me a photograph of himself from when he was three years old, another at the age of eight, and then four photographs he had just had taken for his driving licence; he told me he could drive well even on three-lane roads – just as he was now moving at ease within the triangular relationship with his parents.

He had bought an "export-model Maratea car"; he was not sure whether to put in for his driving test, but had dreamed that his father had put a "stop" on the accelerator so that he would not go too fast.

At this point "my" anguish over the termination began: was it time, was he ready, or should I apply the "brake"?

Lagging somewhat behind him and telling myself that it was still early days, I spoke to him of the "boy who would be sad when he left me". Showing me his wrists, he told me that they were sturdy and strong, but, owing to my anxiety at the idea of a premature termination and being unable to metabolize my anxiety immediately, I persisted with old ways of communication. For the first time for years, he had a visual flash: "I see a pair of pliers." This time I could not fail to understand, and told him he was afraid that I might now be the one who was unable to let him go and who wanted to detain him beyond his needs.

I began to see him as a young man wishing to take responsibility for his own mental life and felt that I had to give up the fantasy of protecting him; although I thought, as it were on his behalf, that it was a risk to let him go, it was perhaps a necessary risk . . . No sooner had I begun to think in this way than he told me for the first time about what he had been collecting in the last few years: he had all the equipment of Big Jim, the sledge, the camper, the hut and the radiators . . . all the gear bought in the hunting and fishing shop; he also had Big Jack and the terrible Torpedo that meted out punches, but Big Jim was not afraid; it had cost him a lot to buy these things . . .

I told him that these were perhaps the things he had acquired in so many years of analysis and toil; I did not say any more because I felt that discretion was indicated – and indeed it was rewarded. He had shown his Big Jims to his friend Davide, who had looked at them and then played with him, but very carefully, without spoiling anything, just the way he had wanted . . . In this way he was asking for a date to be fixed for the termination – and we kept firmly to this date, the analysis being rung out by the "sad tolling of bells" in a dream reported in the final sessions.

Notes

1   The term "functional aggregate" (Bezoari & Ferro, 1990a, 1991a, 1991b) is an alternative to "personified parts" and allows judgment to be suspended on whether the characters appearing in the session belong to one actor/author or the other, so that they remain in a transitional situation. The term "affective hologram" (Ferro, 1992) takes account of the scenic three-dimensionality of the characters presented in the sessions, when seen not in historical terms or as inhabitants of the patient's internal world but instead as the overall resultant of the functioning of the couple in the field.
2   I recall a long analysis that was extremely wearisome to me and the patient alike owing to the continuous state of emergency in which it was conducted, with the constant risk of possibly violent acting out; after such instances I had wondered whether it had all been worthwhile, but the patient surprised me by saying: "I owe a great deal to the analysis, because it has prevented me from becoming either a drug addict or a murderer."
3   I mean times not normally available for analysis in my weekly work programme.
4   One patient immediately seemed to me to be very seriously ill, which indeed proved to be the case. He was accompanied and was on large quantities of drugs. Once we were alone together, he described his relationship with his mother in extremely persecutory and violent terms, but after a few cautious, welcoming and *textual* interventions on my part, he began to tell me that, well, it was not always the way he had presented it; that the hate arose out of fear; and that when the fear was not so intense, he was able to discern his mother's good aspects too; in fact she was very available and attentive.
5   [Translator's note: There is an untranslatable double meaning here: *scopa* means "broom" and Chiavari is a town in Liguria, known for the quality of its brooms, but both words allude to vulgar terms for sexual intercourse, *scopare* and *chiavare*.]
6   [Translator's note: A play on words: *tubicino* is a cannula and *tu vicino* means "you are near".]
7   [Translator's note: Another double meaning: *prendere il Ciao* means "saying good-bye", but also "taking the Ciao", which is a kind of motor scooter.]
8   [Translator's note: Double meaning: "Sofà" is also a reference to the couch.]

Chapter 2

Exercises in style

The title of this chapter is of course borrowed from Queneau's fine book of the same name.

The material originates from a multi-year study based on group discussions of sessions for which either a verbatim text or a highly detailed account was available. Freud's clinical cases – in particular that of the "Rat Man" (Freud, 1909) – are quite suitable for this purpose. Then there is the extraordinary case of Richard, painstakingly transcribed in detail by Klein (1961). Other accounts that lend themselves to this treatment are Winnicott's *The Piggle* (1978) and "Fragment of an analysis" (1972), as well as Milner's *The Hands of the Living God* (1969). It is, however, not easy to find direct transcriptions of sessions (except those of young colleagues), as most clinical reports are written down in indirect, narrated and excessively filtered form.

Recordings are in my view of limited utility, although they are resorted to by various research groups. A representative example is that of Thomä & Kächele (1985), whose material has to my mind undergone insufficient filtration (it comprises an "as-it-was" verbatim record, which is very poor, with what seem to me quite inappropriate corrective attempts). Considering Bion's comments in *Learning from Experience* (1962) on psychoanalysis as science, I still prefer a classical record set down after the session.[1]

However, I did not think it right to comment on colleagues' sessions, even if reported in print, because that might have given the impression of a critical exercise with no opportunity for defence or appeal by the authors concerned.

My way of resolving this dilemma has been to take some of my own sessions, dating from different periods in my training and development as an analyst, which I present (with changes to protect the patients' identities) accompanied by comments on the relevant models and a retrospective view from the vantage point of today. Of course, the models and approaches claim no allegiance to any particular schools, but are intended merely to show how I understood and applied the technical and theoretical positions in question. The examples show not what I "acquired" from supervisors or working groups but how I personally assimilated the approaches concerned.[2]

I believe that this account of my evolving experience will be useful precisely because, once the time of supervision of candidates or young associates is past, and leaving aside meaningless generic or syncretic jargon, what the analyst does in the consulting room is and remains truly mysterious.

An issue of the *International Journal of Psycho-Analysis* published in 1991 is exceptional in this respect, containing as it does 15 clinical accounts, often with direct transcriptions of sessions and specifying the authors' chosen models. Again, international psychoanalytic congresses are increasingly featuring papers containing directly reported clinical material, as well as contributions on the presentation of such material (Tuckett, 1993).[3] Moreover, the *Journal* now usually includes a section devoted to "clinical cases".

From unconscious fantasies to the field and its narrative transformations

In search of the unconscious fantasy

I shall now attempt to characterize an early period of my work, in which I was convinced of the need to discover the origin of the patient's anxiety by decoding his underlying unconscious (bodily) fantasy. This unconscious fantasy was the focus of my interpretative attention because I regarded it as underpinning the patient's communications at all times.

My basic references were of course the works of Klein and her school, and Isaacs' fine essay "The nature and function of phantasy" (1948).

Discussions of the vast literature on this subject may be found in Hinshelwood (1989, 1993), Spillius (1988), Giaconia (1996) and Schafer (1994).

As stated, I deal here only with the way I applied the model at the time. I present the sessions with the briefest of notes on the patient and the patient's analysis, because the accounts are intended merely as "homework exercises", or rather as a clinical way of narrating understandings or misunderstandings of theory.

Annalisa and foetal life

The patient was an adult woman in the second year of her analysis.

PATIENT: I like to obey, to be told what to do, and then I do it; I don't want to know anything else, the whys and the wherefores; I obey and I am happy when I can do so, but it mustn't be me who has to think and decide; I like to do what I am asked, to be passive and obedient, and to feel warm and protected.

ANALYST: A little girl inside Mummy, warm and protected, who obeys the stimuli of growth that she feels, with nothing to do except to obey.

PATIENT: I am thinking of a girlfriend of mine, who had a "big estate", which she then lost – one of those people who believe in fairy tales and think the nobility have blue blood. She told me about the time when the Germans arrived at the big house where she lived; it was like a myth: the Germans were very aristocratic, stylish and correct in their behaviour; everything was going well, and it was quiet and peaceful. Then, every so often, the SS would come; they were very violent and brutal, dressed in their leather gear; they would come in, but then go away again, and they did not come too often.

ANALYST: The myth is about your mother's pregnancy, you and your big estate, Mummy's womb, your polite and stylish Daddy, but every so often he became an SS man who made love to Mummy, and you saw all this from your vantage point.

PATIENT: But it's funny, I hate my father, who is not aristocratic or stylish, yet I like the SS men and their violence, I like to see films about the Germans, and the more violent they are, the more I like them. But in real life I don't like uniforms, and I don't like military people of any kind.

ANALYST: You have always been fascinated by brutality and violence, there is a whole film here to be discovered, and you find it hard to cast Daddy in the role of a German SS officer. [A silence.] I wanted to tell you that we won't be able to have sessions next Monday and Wednesday.

PATIENT: I don't feel abandoned. I like to obey, in fact I am proud to be able to do what you want.

ANALYST: I too can be the stylish officer or the brutal SS man who subjects you to his commands.

PATIENT: Yes, and I like it; I once said to a male friend: "When shall we see each other?" and he replied: "It's up to me to ask you, not you me; you must only obey". I like it that way, I am proud, I do what you want, and as far as I am concerned it can go on like that for ever.

ANALYST: You are going back to the mythical age, a baby girl in Mummy's belly, obeying and growing and not wanting to know about anything else.

PATIENT: That's right; I just remembered that in the summer a boy asked me for a date and I said to him: "You really mean me?", because I felt that I did not exist, that I was not there.

ANALYST: You were surprised because on the one hand you felt as though you had never been born, but on the other you really were born and boys ask you for dates, just as I am giving you a date after the session we shall be missing.

My idea was that the patient's anxiety would be mitigated if I were to pick up her unconscious fantasies, which I understood as something that "belonged" fully to her and were completely independent of the instant in the relationship, like part of a film sequence belonging to the patient alone, which could be externalized through the transference – *and the fantasies I was picking up were of foetal life and the primal scene.*

It now seems to me, however, that I was actually creating more anxiety and incomprehension in the patient.

My first interpretation was already persecutory: the patient's first reply described in detail how she had experienced it as formally correct but brutal and disappointing.

The second interpretation, too, generated nothing but hate and the eroticization of violence. And so the session went on, to the point that the patient felt unrecognized and non-existent, not because she was functioning with adhesive identifications but simply because what she was saying was not being appropriately received at any point in the session.

I have often wondered why such sessions nevertheless have a healing potential; I believe the reason is that, even if the analyst protects himself in the session with theories or their misuse, he is nevertheless absorbing β elements from the patient and placing them in a narrative context. Even if the resulting narration is somewhat prefabricated (because the analyst is finding something he knows he is looking for – the very antithesis of the "negative capability" mentioned by Bion in *Attention and Interpretation*!), he is nevertheless transforming material from the patient (as well as what he thinks he knows about the patient) into images; and it is at least the case that the patient's projective identifications, beyond the written text, encounter someone who tries, however partially, to alphabetize them.

The analyst uses his own strong dialect to decode what comes from the patient (the basis in other models may be, for example, the history, if deemed real and not mythical), rather than facilitating an open and unforeseeable narrative and transformational development.

The myth of relationship and transference interpretation

Over a long period my early views gradually mellowed: the conviction that the patient was presenting a text to be decoded as a projection on to the analyst gave way to ever more interactive developments in which an oscillation between relationship and transference progressively arose (Bezoari & Ferro, 1991b). The relationship is the specific, new and creative entity that develops there in the analyst's consulting room and transforms the events of the transference (whether repetitions or fantasies) by interpretation of the patient's material in the here and now.

Luigi and the holidays

I reproduce below a dramatic session with a seriously ill adult borderline patient that took place just before the summer break. I had arranged for him to see a psychiatrist, Dr C., during the holidays in case of need.

PATIENT: It is all up with me; I stopped eating today and I cannot work; this therapy has failed, you have got the treatment wrong.

ANALYST: Perhaps what has failed is the idea of my taking charge of you completely.

PATIENT: Stop talking rubbish; at home I hate everyone, my brother, my sister – and I hate you too because you have got the treatment wrong; there is no hope for me, and now I am going to smash up your consulting room and bash your face in.

ANALYST: Perhaps you are afraid that I don't want to have anything to do with you, because yesterday *I did not speak to you on the phone for very long*, but we must clarify the limits of our relationship; I can help you if you will let me.

PATIENT: Stop talking rubbish, I shall kill my family and then you; I'll murder everyone, and now I am going to bash your face in.

ANALYST: I am going to have to ask you to leave.

PATIENT: [He thumps his fist down hard on the table; he is about to jump on me; already I feel that I have been beaten to a bloody pulp; I am afraid, I have trouble breathing, and am trembling inside, but I remain motionless and seemingly impassive.] I am going to kill you because you have got the treatment wrong; I'll kill everyone; I'll vandalize your car; your fate is sealed, because I'm going to kill you now or in a fortnight or within thirty days; the only way out for you is to take care of me, to make me better, otherwise I'll kill you.

ANALYST: You seem upset, full of rage and very frightened; perhaps the visit to Dr C. is also bothering you, and the fact that your aunt had to pay for the consultation with me.

PATIENT: My aunt made it very clear to me that you are an impostor, that you only see me to steal my money, and that you are adding your own complexes to mine; I know you won't want to see me any more now, but it is all over for you because I shall kill you.

ANALYST: I wonder if you are afraid I shall not want to see you because you have got so enraged, but by behaving like this, all you have done is to bring out this aspect of yourself here, which you were afraid no one would ever be able to deal with – and if you think I shall go on seeing you because I am afraid of you, you certainly cannot have any faith in me.

PATIENT: No one can deal with that aspect, but I must get to know it and woe betide you if you don't find it.

ANALYST: You are afraid that the only reason I might treat you is out of fear, and that I might not have any other reason for bothering with you.

PATIENT: The real problem is not here, but at home [crying]. Who can help me in my home town? Perhaps Dr X or Dr Y, or Dr Z?

ANALYST: I wonder if what has upset you is not a kind of jump that you have made: you wanted the analysis to let you see yourself as the victim of your mother, father and siblings, entitled to compensation; but instead you find you have to settle accounts with your own responsibility and work with the tractor and pay me, just as your aunt did, whereas in the past everyone treated you for nothing. You are afraid that the safety net we have built for the summer may not be enough.

PATIENT: All my hopes have gone [crying]. What you have given me is no more than a few drops of water to a man dying of thirst.

This session would be a good basis for discussing criteria of analysability, perhaps corresponding in this case to an analyst's self-perceived endurance limits.

Here I was no longer expecting to discover the underlying unconscious fantasy, but seeking, not always successfully, to "ride the relationship" and as far as possible to follow the patient with interpretations focused on it.

However, even this aim was pursued inappropriately, partly because of inexperience (especially with "seriously ill" patients), so that I often responded harshly and defensively rather than immediately picking up the patient's desperation at being left alone and his feeling of "starving to death", which he expressed from the very beginning.

This example also shows how an excessively active and insufficiently receptive style reinforces negative transference and intensifies psychotic anxieties.

I failed to pick up the suffering concealed behind the aggression, or the way my interpretative style was arousing the patient's ire and stifling him – and, in particular, the self-generation of aggression in the session resulting from my defensive self-protection against his abandonment anxieties ("I have stopped eating").

Liliana and the flying saint

In this session Liliana gave a detailed description of the situation that arose in her town when the *new doctor* arrived: he had immediately aroused the antagonism of the local authorities and been opposed and denigrated in every possible way. She dwelt on the characteristics of these authorities, who were very conservative, out to protect vested interests and those in power – mainly members of the Mafia – and whose ultimate aim was to keep the local situation unchanged and under control. The patient was very worried that the doctor might not be able to cope and might decide to leave.

In this session Liliana, a brunette with an olive complexion, acted out by turning up with flaming red hair, to assert her ability to "rebel against the dull conformism" of the people of her town.

What the patient was telling me seemed perfectly clear, and I interpreted with reference to her internal situation as she had described it to me, in terms of the establishment that held power within her, the gang opposed to the changes the analysis might bring and the way she wanted to change her mentality just as she had changed the colour of her hair, by openly rebelling against the internal clique that had dominated and controlled her.

The patient's account was long-winded and so was my interpretation; time was up and I had had no feedback on what I had said, but I was filled with a sense of satisfaction at having given a "good" interpretation. However, the more I thought about it, the more discontented I felt at the impression of two people talking in parallel without any point of contact, as it seemed to me my patient and I had been doing. I became increasingly puzzled.

After a silence, the patient began the next day's session by telling me that she had found it difficult to come along and felt very angry and very alone, without knowing why. She had seen a film on television about Saint Anthony of Copertino, who had been portrayed with wings, taking to the air every so often and going off on his own.

At this point I thought I understood what had happened and asked the patient whether she had not experienced me precisely as Saint Anthony of Copertino, launching off into a speech she had felt to be abstract, whereas she had been telling me about something very concrete and had wanted me to follow her in it. The patient confirmed that this was correct, that I had asked her to "detach herself" from what she was saying and to think about it so as to understand its meaning; but for her its meaning had been precisely the actual things she had told me and that was all she had been interested in. Finding me very distant, however, she had felt abandoned and not understood, because *I had not been in the same place as she was*.

The issue that was beginning to emerge in this session seems to have been not only the accuracy of the interpretation (being in "K", as I would now say) but also the importance of emotional attunement with the patient (being in "O").

I had basically given her a stock, textbook interpretation based on Rosenfeld's descriptions of destructive narcissism, and the patient had seen through its theoretical "precooked" quality. I note the beginnings of an appropriate use of the countertransference, in which a dawning sense of dissatisfaction is followed by an ability to see the patient's next communication, in the following session, as a "response" to the inappropriateness of the previous day's "textbook" interpretation. These interpretations were still direct and univocal, but to have picked up the underlying movements was already an important step.

Luciano and the cool theories of the cat

The following account features sessions of a 12-year-old boy in his fourth year of analysis, just before the Christmas holidays.

Monday:

PATIENT: [Arriving on time, he takes some tubes of glue out of his pockets as soon as he sits down.] I got one from the model shop in X Street [the street where I – AF – live] and the other two from Mr M. I need them to finish two models, one of an aeroplane made of balsa wood and the other of a ship.

ANALYST: An aeroplane and a ship: that must mean departure, a journey. You need so many tubes of glue to build good ships and planes, because the holidays are approaching.

PATIENT: [Draws a cat in black pencil in the centre of the paper; Figure 1.]

ANALYST: That cat is so alone in the centre of the paper; perhaps you too feel very alone at the idea of going away.

PATIENT: [Begins to draw some lines round the cat . . . He remembers having done the same with a car . . . He draws so many lines that they turn into a circle.]

ANALYST: You felt exposed, and now you are drawing circles – perfect figures that enfold and hide the feeling of loneliness?

Figure 1 Luciano's drawing of a cat.

PATIENT: They remind me of those Russian dolls with their different layers.

ANALYST: Perhaps it is the smaller Luciano who feels alone, covered and protected by older Lucianos.

PATIENT: I thought of another drawing I did, a Christmas tree with a star; I did it with felt-tip pens that slide over the paper easily, with transparent caps.

Wednesday:

I telephone to cancel the session because I have flu.

Thursday:

Luciano telephones to find out whether his session is on. I confirm that it is.

PATIENT: I'm doing a drawing, here it is, it might be a stadium. But it needs to be shortened [he tries to fold the paper]. This is a bone, a vertebra too if it is shortened.

ANALYST: A stadium and a bone, both shortened, perhaps like our week of analysis, which lost one session.

PATIENT: Yes, but both have to do with *calcio*.[4]

ANALYST: I wonder if my phone call felt like a kick to you, and then you got angry.

PATIENT: Well, let us not exaggerate. After all, it was only one day. I was with my friend *Ferrazzano*, who turned up although he was late. Usually I am with *Pedeferri* . . . Yesterday my mother had to go out and I did not have the keys to the house, so I was locked out and had to go with Ferrazzano to my mother's school; he went with me.

ANALYST: I had also locked you out of here, forcing you to take a long walk; but it was Ferrazzano who was with you – which sounds a bit like *Dr Ferro* and a bit like managing on your own so as not to feel my absence.

PATIENT: [Picking up the pencils.] Here is a flight of steps like the one on the Piazza Vittorio [picking up the *town plan*, he draws the Castello cinema]. It's a big square with arches . . . and there is a garden with a flight of steps.

ANALYST: What flight of steps?

PATIENT: One that leads to a fountain [taking the pencils again, he draws a flight of steps that collapses].

ANALYST: Perhaps yesterday the "cat" [our term for Luciano's affective part] felt lost in a big square, without water, and without the flight of steps that had collapsed/the session that was cancelled.

PATIENT: Poor pussycat, drinking cool theories.

ANALYST: You are afraid there are no cool theories even now.

PATIENT: No, because perhaps the water is poisoned.

ANALYST: There is also a distrustful part that tells the cat that if it drinks it will be swindled, like the snake or the dog [another story of ours, in which a snake was fed only to be weakened and overcome, and a dog was looked after but then surreptitiously abandoned].

PATIENT: [Makes railway lines with the coloured pencils, places the black pencil on top of them and blows it forwards.]

ANALYST: I think you are angry; you don't trust me and you want to control me. You want me to depend on your breath, on your words, perhaps because you are afraid that if you do trust me, I will abandon you again.

PATIENT: [Draws a star, tries to pick up a pencil with two other pencils, and builds a tower of pencils that collapses.]

ANALYST: Perhaps the star is hiding the fact that the cat is suffering and falling to pieces at the idea of leaving us.

PATIENT: [As he leaves, the zip on his jacket gets stuck.]

My interpretations here still show an urge to saturate the text immediately, by making what amount to "symbolic equations" (Segal, 1957): aeroplane + train = departure, *necessarily*, and not as one of a range of possible hypotheses.

There was no room yet for the unsaturated, no openness to unknown spaces or possible worlds, nor did the analyst have the negative capability (Bion, 1970) to tolerate doubt and wait for an unsaturated configuration of the "selected fact" (Bion, 1962).

I responded to the patient's second intervention (the cat and the pencil) by again saturating the text (loneliness and departure), thereby truly transforming it into hallucinosis – that is, interpreting it in accordance with my prevailing code or "encyclopaedia" (Eco, 1979), which I took to be the relational and emotional truth.

Thursday's session began tolerably well; the interpretation of anal masturbation was also given in sufficiently acceptable form (Ferrazz-ano,[5] Ferro + managing on his own), but when the patient then spoke of the fountain I failed to pick up the relief, the good that was emerging, and out of guilt at having cancelled the session I went on insisting to the point of causing the session to degenerate into a crescendo of incomprehension and persecution – without noticing how my exaggeration and excessive imposition of myself on him was making him puff and blow, "see stars", and above all preventing him from opening up and separating.

Luisa and the ferry to independence

This is a session from a fairly advanced analysis, dating from a time just before I transferred my consulting room from my home to another apartment.

PATIENT: So many things happened at the weekend; I realized that it is I who need Marcella and not she who needs me, yes, I am the one who needs her . . . even if Marcella is not well . . . Then I was with Giulia and Simone. We went with Simone for a meal at Michele's with a couple – Michele is the boyfriend of Annamaria, who is Claudia's sister . . . I told Marcella all about it . . . Afterwards I dreamed I was committing a murder, and when I woke up I thought that maybe the victim was Marcella . . . Then I thought of the move, and what came into my mind was when my parents moved, from one house to two that were close to each other, a big one for them and a smaller one for me and Marina, whereas Fabrizio and Massimo stayed with them.

ANALYST: You seem able to accept the fact that you need me, and that this is what matters, and not so much how well or ill I am; then there are men and women together – not all women among themselves as in the past.

PATIENT: Yes, but I was always thinking about the move, that you will be different, more detached, more professional; here I hear voices that make me jealous . . . There . . . you will be different.

ANALYST: But then there is a murder, and the victim is the mother who puts the children in one place and stays with Daddy and the privileged brothers in another; perhaps it is jealousy that causes Marcella to get killed.

PATIENT: But I think I shall not be able to have a love relationship any more because love relationships are absolute and it is not like that now for me – like with a mother, all or nothing.

ANALYST: I wonder how much you believe what you are saying. Outside the world of gnomes, no one is everything, everyone matters – even if it is hard to get one's bearings with all those places at table and all those relationships. After all, Daddy is also the husband of Mummy, and your sisters' daddy too.

PATIENT: But will we go upstairs in the new house?

ANALYST: Meaning that you will be growing?

Thursday:

PATIENT: I went to see the front entrance of the block where your new consulting room will be. Then I had some dreams – I had not had such dreams for a while – catastrophes – I hope they are not warnings of things to come. I was by the lake and there was a tidal wave; then I was at Lucia's house and it was like her disco; Marcella's father was there, but not Marcella; then a cardiologist came along to our ward to do the ECGs; I could get to safety with him, but I didn't go; I thought that maybe the catastrophe was when I went back to sleep at Marcella's house last night and was unable to speak; I tried to tell her: "I have my own life and I want to talk to you about it", but Marcella said: "No, I am not ready yet". That was when it dawned on me that, however ill she may be, I am the one who needs her, and not the other way round.

ANALYST: So we have a change that is tantamount to a catastrophe: the move, the earthquake of leaving this room; but there is something else in the dream, a father without his daughter and a doctor who could get you to safety; then in your story there is a sleeping couple who cannot talk to each other yet, and perhaps the fear that our couple too might not be ready to discover the existence of our separate lives.

[A few minutes' silence.]

ANALYST: What I told you has made you go silent.

PATIENT: Yes, I was thinking of a major change and discovering that I am not self-sufficient, that I need you and Marcella – but if that is how it is, how will I tell you that I am going to Venice with Marta at the weekend, and then there are so many things I have not told Marcella about my life – how I put up a bookshelf at home with Luca's help, how I went to Milan to see a film, *Death of the Artists*, by . . . , and this . . . and that . . .

ANALYST: You discover that you need Marcella, and me, but immediately you are afraid that either you need someone and have no independence, or, if you are independent, you cannot have any needs; you feel that you cannot reconcile needing me with having a life of your own that will enrich you, in which I play no part, while I also have a life of my own, in which you play no part;

and I wonder if, as a result of these thoughts, the tidal wave may also be one of jealousy.

PATIENT: But I think pain and suffering are there too: in the past I always spoke in the plural, "we"; it is terrible to be saying "I" and "you" now – every word spoken is a minor earthquake from that point of view. Marcella is quick to say: "I am available, you are a shit."

ANALYST: You are afraid that changing from "we" to "I" and "you" might unleash rage: I might tell you that you are a shit for going to Venice while I stay in Pavia, and you might say that I am a shit for not letting you have your Saturday morning session because of my move.

[A short silence.]

PATIENT: I was wondering if it is really possible to have a relationship with someone without possessing them completely.

ANALYST: . . . And being possessed by them!

Luisa arrives 20 minutes late for the first session in the new consulting room.

[A few minutes' silence.]

ANALYST: Well?

PATIENT: I was thinking that I like it, it is no longer like coming into an egg as it was at Via C., where we were so protected; there is more contact with reality, and I like that, even if it frightens me a bit . . . Today I wanted to have the session, but not to come to Pavia; I got in touch with the doctor who is organizing cancer treatment centres in Nicaragua, but what am I to do with Marcella? I told her, and I asked her if she wanted to come with me, but really just for the sake of saying so; I would rather go by myself.

ANALYST: You seem to be telling me that there is a place that is new and unknown, but that you are no longer a newborn chick: you want to be independent and go by yourself, but you are afraid that someone might disagree and be hurt by it.

PATIENT: I went to the psychiatrist . . . for my work . . . They said they would take me on provided that I undertook to stay as a *psychiatrist*; I don't know if I want to do that.

ANALYST: You seem to be afraid that your choices might not be free, that there is someone who expects things from you, whereas you want independence and freedom.

PATIENT: But the truth of the matter is that I have the problem of Marcella's suffering if I leave her: *I would like to leave her and to live, but I am afraid that she will suffer.*

ANALYST: You want independence, you want to finish your analysis; but there is also the idea that someone might suffer because of this intention; why call that someone Marcella? Isn't it actually yourself?

PATIENT: I thought that separating from you would be very painful, because I feel understood; now I am remembering about when I wanted to go to X in October, when you said that I had planted a time bomb.

ANALYST: I was afraid at the time that you might break off the analysis, but you
   succeeded in going to X and then carrying on with it; is there another time
   bomb now when I finish? The time factor seems to me to enter into it.
PATIENT: Well, if I think of finishing in July, you will not be there any more in
   September . . .
ANALYST: Would that not be too much like a crash landing?
PATIENT: This week too I was in a *disabled persons' unit*; it doesn't suit me.
ANALYST: Maybe you felt held back by what I said: you want to emerge from the
   egg, from this room.

At the beginning of the next session Luisa reports a dream. She is on an island with
Marcella and is already on a ferry to the mainland when she thought she wouldn't
have managed it and there wouldn't be any more. On the road she comes across a
car containing her parents and her little sisters and brother . . . Then she is with
them in a restaurant, and then in bed with a "boring" man who is a communist. She
takes his penis in her hand, but he has scars from an episode of syphilis in the past,
which, however, is now cured . . .

A further change has now taken place in my way of interpreting: I am no longer
obsessed with forced transference interpretations. A space is beginning to form,
and within it "characters" not necessarily saturated with transference interpretations
are moving, acting and meeting each other, providing the breath of fresh air that
will eventually lead on to conceptualizations in terms of the "field".

There are also references to familiar language from the analysis ("the world of
gnomes = a world without differences"), which also help to mitigate the persecution
of the encounter.

But I am still tending to "interpret" (Bonaminio, 1993, 1996) the patient's
communication – i.e. to produce a kind of parallel discourse, because I am not yet
able to construct a new text "with" the patient without excessive interpretative
caesuras, although I am picking up the patient's emotional state at close quarters,
perhaps with an insistence that makes the analyst appear "boring" and also somewhat dangerous, even if the "syphilis" is cured.

Discovery of characters and their vicissitudes in the field

This is the third major "transformation" in my way of understanding the analytical
session. I focus on the deep emotional level of the couple, on which projective
identifications are used to establish the emotional foundation which needs to be
narrated through the characters and transformed by working through, and which
must be shared by way of a story. This model is made up of unsaturated interpretations, narrative interventions, a conception of the characters mainly in terms
of functional aggregates (Ferro, 1992), countertransference anguish, and estimation
of what the patient is capable of "taking on" as a growth factor.

Marcella and the dog with a scarf and pipe

Marcella was an adult patient in the third year of her analysis when I asked her to agree to an increase in my fees. She skipped the next two sessions. Returning for the third session, she told me of the problems she had had: her little girl had fallen ill, she had been unable to start the car . . . then the child had not wanted to have anything to do with her father, had maltreated him, hit him and got angry with him; she had had an episode of *pavor nocturnus* and yelled and screamed when Daddy came . . . Marcella added: "It must be the Oedipus complex" (she was a psychologist). I could not stop myself saying "It must be the increase!", and then felt the need to add an interpretation linking the missed sessions and what she had told me with the increase.

After a short silence she mentioned a film she had seen in which a girl was raped out of revenge by a former boyfriend whom she had given up.

Of course, I realized that I could again interpret in transference terms, but I decided not to do so because it would be too persecutory . . . so I said something to the effect that it must be terrible to be raped, and into the bargain by a person one has had a relationship with in the past . . . After a moment's silence, I added: "But you always had a boyfriend at your side to speak to – someone very kind, who understands you well . . ."

Marcella began the next session by talking about the difference between Mickey Mouse and a real mouse. She went on to tell the story of a night-time film she had seen on TV in which ants were exposed to radiation, grew to enormous size and attacked two people who were fond of each other . . . ; then she returned to her mice. I made conversational comments about the dangers of mice, which transmitted "rabies"[6] . . . and "plague", too, she added . . . and then she told me about a comic strip in which huge ants guided by extraterrestrials invaded the earth . . . and she did not know how to defend herself . . . Finally she brought one of her repeated dreams, in which an enormous ant emerged from a wound in her own body.

A direct interpretation – in terms of the invasion of feelings infesting her mind and the field, from which she did not know how to defend herself and the analysis – would have been easy but at the time too persecutory. So I merely said that there were remedies, a vaccine for rabies and antibiotics for the wound, and that it seemed to me significant that the insects did not come from nowhere but, in the dream, from a wound in her own body, and that "someone" must therefore have hurt her . . . "Well, surely, it must be the increase . . ." – there we are, I thought – ". . . so much for the office I was going to rent: my friend and colleague asked for an exorbitant price plus expenses" (Marcella came from another town).

I asked her whether her friend was so inflexible that she could not talk to her about it again, and this struck a chord.

After a brief pause, Marcella said: "I read in the paper that Superman is dead."

I added: "And perhaps the days of 'Superwoman' are long past, now that you too can be wounded and have economic difficulties" (I was thinking of the emotional cost of the analysis). She answered: "Right, but I'm sure my friend will give me a little more time; I'll definitely talk to her about it next week, when we have arranged to meet here in Pavia."

The following dialogue ensued about a year later.

PATIENT: On Tuesday I felt awful; the thought of leaving the kids by themselves, I just could not do it . . . so I did not come . . .

ANALYST: And then my phone call came on Wednesday.

PATIENT: Yes, I was afraid you had done it to get even with me . . . then I told myself that could not possibly be . . . then I had a dream – I must tell you first that I had seen a TV documentary about pygmies who were very put out about new roads that were going to devastate their jungle; they said in the documentary that they sharpened their teeth with files, so they didn't need knives when they ate meat, but it was very painful, because it cut into the dentine beneath the hard part . . . Well, in the dream my brother came to my house crying and yelling in pain; he had done something to his teeth, perhaps to do with cleaning them, and was suffering terribly; I tried to give him something, maybe aspirin, but it was no use; I supported him for a bit and tried to help him, and then he left.

ANALYST: What does all this put you in mind of?

PATIENT: Well, it's not difficult . . . that I feel pain and suffer for the sessions when we don't see each other . . . at one time I could never have admitted it . . . it is the dependence, if I am suffering so much, how will I be able to do without you one day . . . well, basically I must also tell you that I did not come on Tuesday because I did not want to be told the dates of the holidays . . .

ANALYST: And you felt awful at the idea that *the kids would be left alone.*

PATIENT: I understand what you mean . . . you are right.

ANALYST: What is more, this pain at being left alone can now be acknowledged; you can take care of this pain and seek remedies for it, even if it then becomes intolerable . . . and you go away . . . and I thought that missed sessions, holidays, are like damage to the pygmies' forest . . . and the pygmies remind me a bit of children, *calimeri*,[7] small and black . . . because they are neglected . . . Well, I really must tell you the holiday dates now: from . . . to . . .

PATIENT: [A few minutes' silence.] I have a colleague on the ward, Carla, who is in a rage . . . she cannot stand the chief physician, who is the one who makes the decisions . . . she said that she would leave in six months . . . that she does not want to come any more . . . she was furious because a little girl could not have the analyses she needed, she was foaming with rage . . .

ANALYST: Carla threatens to leave when she feels something unfair – and basically also because she stands up for the little girl that needs the analyses . . . she is sort of taking revenge as you were afraid I had done by cancelling Wednesday's session, after you had missed Tuesday's.

PATIENT: Yes, but Carla is too full of rage, and if she were to go elsewhere the whole thing would start all over again, and so on and so on . . .

ANALYST: Well, Carla's rage, the pygmies' sharp teeth ready to rip the meat apart like knives, I think they are also telling us something about your rage after I'd mentioned the holidays; but let us not forget that sharpening the teeth also involves a lot of pain, as in the dream about your brother . . . and that your tender, affectionate parts are suffering because of all this . . . Carla is receiving support and perhaps also being understood in her rage, and especially in her suffering.

PATIENT: OK, but I have decided to go away for a month and a half in the summer . . . I shall go to Sardinia to get away from my mother; I shall be calmer there . . .

ANALYST: Perhaps you will be killing two birds with one stone: Carla will be pleased to be going far away for a month and a half . . . but "the pulp and the dentine" will be pleased to be in Sardinia, where they imagine I will also be . . .

PATIENT: [Five minutes' silence.] Now at last I can see what it says under that picture: "hand-coloured"; pictures hand-coloured by their authors are nicer and worth more . . .

ANALYST: Oh, the picture . . . that picture has been important to us.

PATIENT: Yes . . . the balconies opposite my house.

ANALYST: And something else as well . . .

PATIENT: While I was trying to get Viviana to do something today, she drew me a picture, of a dog with spectacles, a scarf and a pipe – a friendly detective-type dog, and she put a hand in front of his mouth: I think that is enough for today!

ANALYST: A word is enough to the wise . . .

The relationship, or rather the field, is now understood not as something that must be continuously interpreted but as the medium for operations of transformation, narratives and successive small insights, which do not need to be interpreted but foreshadow other changes. During the course of its exploration, it is the field that undergoes constant enlargement (Bion, 1970), becoming the matrix of possible stories, many of which are "stored away" until such time as they are ready to bud.

    The analyst is seen to be constantly paying attention to the patient's assimilation capacity and taking care not to overburden her α function and apparatus for thinking thoughts, which would merely cause persecution that would promptly be signalled in the text. The patient is not an accused before the court or the subject of an investigation, but is indeed the analyst's "best colleague" (Bion, 1980), with whom unpredictable journeys can be made; if immediate transference explanations are forgone, it becomes possible to "sow" future journeys, in absolute confidence that even what is not immediately interpreted "remains behind" as the very fabric of the field, ready to be developed at the appropriate time.

Cosimo and the gate of the imagination

When I saw Cosimo's mother (his father had avoided coming to the interview pleading pressure of work), I was struck by the concrete, emotionless factuality of her account of her son's problems: he would not study or apply himself to anything, was dreamy and absent-minded and lacked will-power; he could not get involved in anything.

Cosimo was a 13-year-old schoolboy in his second year at middle school and had already failed his exams twice. His mother responded to my attempts to learn more by saying that Cosimo would often rummage in drawers and cupboards looking for something, and that she found this very annoying. I *then* sought to be more circumspect in my enquiries, while sensing that "drawers and cupboards" were firmly closed.

The only information I gleaned was that Cosimo had said that the reason he could not study was because he was disturbed by his little cousin who constantly distracted him with his crying. "He is a liar," the mother added, "because the cousin is at our place perhaps only once a month."

Unable to resist the opportunity she had thus given me, I said: "Well, perhaps he is not such a liar: it might basically be Cosimo's way of telling us that he is very disturbed by something inside himself, that is upsetting him, like a child crying, something distracting him and preventing him from concentrating."

After a moment's silence, the mother added: "Once when I was a girl doing judo, the instructor knocked me off balance and made me fall down badly, leaving me breathless."

Smiling, I of course refrained from showing her how she had been knocked off balance by my unexpected comment about Cosimo's lies and truth.

In the next session, I was surprised to see before me a lifeless-looking but likeable boy. It was I who took the initiative after a silence in which he seemed ill at ease: "Well, your mother told me about your difficulties at school and how worried she is." "Yes, *I am not interested in studying*. Actually, that is not right, there are things that interest me, but not very many." "What things?" "The discovery of America, the Mayas. I would like to be an archaeologist and also a scientist."

I attempted to get closer by taking up the idea of the "discoveries", "hidden and forgotten things", civilizations about which we know little – but this bore very little fruit. Other lines of approach were no more successful. He then told me how he liked to play "flight *simulation*" games on the computer; I thought that there was a simulation in progress, perhaps of normality, and that he in turn had no wish to reveal what was hidden "in the drawers and cupboards". However, I did not know how to gain admission, how to use the "narremes"[8] already in my possession, which, however, seemed to me to be no more than outlines; I sensed that I would ruin everything by trying to use force.

On an impulse, I suggested: "Why don't you draw something while we are talking?" He eagerly took up this idea and began a drawing, upon which I found myself reflecting on his excellent "perspective skills"[9] for his age (Figure 2).

Already expecting to be disappointed and afraid of having manoeuvred myself into another blind alley, I asked him: "What is happening in this house?"[10] He unexpectedly moved up close with his chair and asked: "Why? Are you interested?"

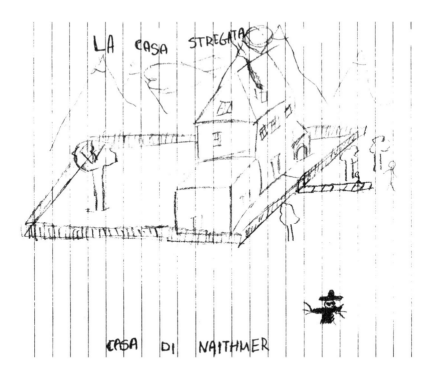

Figure 2 Cosimo's house of *Nightmare*.

"Yes, I am, I'm very interested." "Well, lots of things go on there, some of them incredible." He then launched into a story of great emotional wealth: it was the house of *Nightmare*[11] . . . someone was going into the house, but then the *floor* gave way and they plunged into what seemed to be boilers, but were actually burial vaults . . . it was terrible . . . then along came a monster . . . but something even worse happened to the person . . . what you dreamed had effects in reality . . . he had once dreamed of a dog that bit his arm and when he woke up in the morning he had found his arm bleeding . . . meanwhile he looked at his right arm, on which there was a recent scratch, and said: "Good heavens, just like my arm!" However, he immediately resumed his story: the person had *red eyes* . . . and the curtains were moving . . .

His account continued with more suggestions: stories of other monsters, ghosts, and then the film *Don't Go Into That House*;[12] finally, a secret I had to promise not to betray to his parents: when sitting at the computer he was not playing video games as they thought but had, for more than a year now, been writing a book that filled him with excitement, all about UFOs and extraterrestrials – he was sure they existed . . . he could feel it . . . and he had to know and discover more about *them*.

He was sorry and incredulous when I told him it would be a week before I could see him again.

In the next session Cosimo brought me the book he was writing about the extraterrestrials, which was also the fruit of thorough "scientific" research. Then he told me a dream: he was standing in front of the gate, afraid to go through it, but could not resist the fascination and attraction emanating from what lay behind it. He went through and found himself in a wood, and then in a devastated land full of animals. Suddenly a boy who was with him plunged into a terrible chasm; he tried to rescue him but could not; painful as this was, he had to go on; then he came upon a landscape he could not describe, a kind of Texas canyon, where there were guardians protecting a territory, who might perhaps protect him from falling into it. In fact, all that fell into the vast abyss in front of him was his glasses, which he saw spiralling down as if in slow motion . . . one lens shattered and the other remained intact, but the spectacles did not break on hitting the ground at the bottom of the abyss . . . the scene changed and instead they shattered on the cobblestones outside his house, and he was at his bedroom window watching the scene . . .

I told him he seemed to me to be entering a mysterious world, in which it was possible in one way to get lost, but only up to a certain point, because the guardians were there to protect him from the abyss, and furthermore, just as he was captured by this world, he came out of it again and found himself in his ordinary, familiar reality. "But then that gate is the gate of the imagination, of open-eyed dreams that I see and cannot escape from, which attract and scare me at the same time . . . there, I am having one right now: *I can see a UFO, a spaceship landing on the Ticino, just near here.*" "As if to say perhaps that you feel you are allowing mysterious things – which you knew were there but which had stayed too far away – to land right here and become more familiar . . ."

As the climate became increasingly familiar, all the persecution connected with the new meeting (*Don't Go Into That House*) underwent a kind of collapse that would allow the same contents to be described through something more domestic and familiar. The nightmares and monsters would leave the stage, giving way to the paths in "Ticino Park", on which his house bordered – and from now on there would be the wood, hares, squirrels and little goats, but also wild boar and wolves, foxes and adders. But there would be the "Ticino Park guides" too, accompanying visitors on their modest mopeds and preventing them from getting into danger. And what is more, there were particularly protected areas that might be dangerous, which you could enter only if accompanied.

I decided to take Cosimo into analysis, because of the "excellent perspective/ prospective skills"[13] I had perceived in him.

My object in reproducing these first interviews is to show how unforeseeable developments may be facilitated by a welcoming and containing listening attitude that takes account of the narremes and is able to encourage their activation (without premature interpretative caesuras), and in which a relative degree of unsaturation of the field is tolerated. If force is not applied, the "drawers and cupboards" tend to open up by themselves to the discreet visitor, and what emerges from them will depend not only on the patient's history and fantasy world but also on the quality of the analyst's approach.

Precisely this quality, seen in negative terms as *non-persecution, non-intrusion and non-decoding*, will allow the climate of terror and nightmare to be transformed into the familiar, domestic climate that the patient will be keen to investigate and explore.

In other words, the field that is activated and transformed depends on the mental functioning of the couple, on the freedom of the analyst and on his *negative capability* (Bion, 1963, 1970).

Cosimo's entire story[14] is also the story of how his internal world and fantasies were unknown to him, of how he was bound to be curious about these "unidentified worlds" – which were effectively UFOs which he knew and felt existed, but to which he had never had access owing to the absence of a maternal or paternal reverie. It is the story of protoemotions still too raw to be thinkable or speakable; and furthermore, in stress situations these protoemotional states sometimes broke out of the mental container that usually allows "waking dream thoughts" to exist inside, well separated from consciousness: Cosimo then had what were tantamount to dream-like flashes in waking life, flashes and shreds of waking dream thought that were projected outwards (Meltzer, 1986; Ferro, 1993b).

It would have been possible from the very first session to interpret the terror of the meeting, the uncertainty about what he might have found "in this house and inside himself", and so on. That is how I used to work, and different stories and perhaps silences would have been activated. I now consider it closer-to-life, more creative and useful to the patient to follow him in his account, encouraging and taking a keen interest in it – while remaining *conscious* that there is also another level to the story and that a long road must be travelled over a prolonged period to bring the two levels together and construct a new, original language common to both, without emotional or linguistic colonization of either (Rocha Barros, 1994).

Evolving journeys

This section discusses some journeys still at the stage of exploration, which I have purposely left unsystematized so as not to close off as yet unforeseeable developments. I am as it were presenting notes on current research, which I hope will bear fruit. They are deliberately presented in the form of work in progress, unburdened with excessive bibliographic references.

Rigid-vertex and oscillating-vertex models

"My mother won't take the dog because she has too much work." Out of context, we can undertake some simple exercises on this fragment of communication from a young female analysand.

We can see who the (explicit and implicit) characters are: "my mother", the "dog", "too much work", the "patient telling the story", the "analyst to whom the story is addressed", and so on.

Let us consider some of these characters. "My mother" may be understood as a reference to the *real external mother*, the "dog" to a *real external dog* and the "work" to the *mother's occupation*. The patient's disappointment at this busy mother who has no time for the dog is implicit.

On another level, the characters could be considered in transference terms as parts of the patient, as projected internal images. The "mother" might be a projection on to the analyst of the maternal function, experienced as falling short of expectations; the "dog" the most primitive and animal part of the patient; and the "work" a form of working on the part of the analyst, felt to be inadequate for her most primitive aspects (the dog).

Yet a third vertex is also possible, in which the communication is seen as a story told from the patient's standpoint about the functioning of the analyst and of the patient in the consulting room. The idea here is of an analytic function so far unable to take charge of the most primitive aspects of, let us say, the relationship, because much is still preverbal – namely, emotions that must be worked on by the couple.

However, all three models are equally strong. In the first, the characters are understood predominantly as nodes in a network of historical relations, and the narrated facts in turn give rise to feelings, conflicts and emotional strategies, always vis-à-vis those characters or facts, which, when activated in the present in the intrapsychic dynamic, will be deemed to have virtually taken on an existence "of their own".

In the second model the characters are nodes in a network of intrapsychic relations; the facts narrated are basically a communicable disguise of the patient's internal reality, which, however, is regarded as already "given", pending the presence of an interpreter to clarify its functioning and discover its roots in unconscious fantasies. In this connection it is worth studying Klein's (1961) approach, for example in the analysis of Richard, to understanding the characters emerging in the session or the facts narrated, which she is always able to trace back to unconscious fantasies of her young patient.

In the third model the characters are nodes in an interpersonal, or rather inter-group, narrative network, arising like "holograms" of the present emotional relationship between analyst and patient (Ferro, 1992).

A characteristic feature of these three models is that they are self-confirming owing to the stability of the listening vertices: each listening model validates itself from its own vertex and excludes the others. In other words, we basically have three strong models for decoding a communication. I should now like to present a contrasting fourth model, which is characterized by the instability of the *listening* vertices and therefore includes all the *possible stories* which become narratable on the basis of the patient's statement, and whose freedom of narrative combinations is positively exponential – because "my mother" can be selected in model "a", "b" or "c", and so can the "dog", "work", etc. Message decoding is no longer possible, but only the construction of a story – which will have the characteristic of being necessary to those two minds. This is because what will allow the narration to be organized in one sense rather than another will be the defences of both (or, as we might say, of the field).

This will occur if the analyst allows the emotions arising in the room to pervade him and if, together with his patient, he selects from the emotional noise a narrative harmony that confers order, rhythms and images on what was previously confused, chaotic and preverbal.

This alternative approach will inevitably arouse suspicion and fear, because it dispenses with a definite reading code within which the analyst remains certain of his own role and knowledge, possessing as he does preconstituted truths about himself, his patient and psychoanalysis, to cling to and lean on.

The analyst deploys his own capacities for creation and transformation, accepting the infinite range of possible stories arising in the meeting between two minds, and the need to select a prevailing story in accordance with the deep emotional exchanges and his ability to assume, transform and narrate the "emotional waves" generated in the room.

I do not believe that the analyst is always free and creative enough to work in this way with his patient: there are bound to be moments in which he functions in the first of the modes described above, according to model "a", "b" or "c".

In my view, account must be taken of this oscillation between

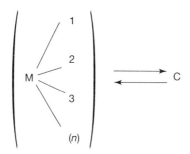

– in other words, between work based on rigid models (M 1, 2, 3, (n)) and genuinely creative work (C).

The analyst will be aware that the boundaries of C are fragile and constantly expanding, because what is C today will necessarily fall into M 1, M 2, M 3 . . . M (n) tomorrow, and may subsequently become a theory.[15]

The patient's "dialect"

"I like to make love with my husband provided that his penis penetrates me by 3 centimetres, not less because I don't feel anything and not more in case it hurts . . ."

What is this patient talking about? About her sex life with her husband and the forms it takes. Or, we may say, about the reliving of forms of breast-feeding in the transference, if we admit a geographical confusion and the difficulty of finding the right gradient of penetration. About the mental functioning of the couple in the analyst's consulting room, in which the analyst's words must penetrate with the right gradient, not less because then they will never reach their destination, and not more in case they are persecutory. However, she is also saying that a container has already come into being and that this container can withstand so much stimulation but no more.

She is saying all these things, and much more besides, if the analyst is able on that particular day to abstain from decoding by his prevailing model and to venture to share the "dialect" used by the patient in telling her story and to learn more about it – what happens in making love; what happens in inadequate or excessive penetration – and to wait for the possible scripts and sets of these penetrations to take shape. The aim will be to allow the analyst–patient relationship to generate an *increase in meaning* rather than leaving the degree of meaning as it was (by translation into another dialect that is more conformable to the analyst) or positively *impoverishing the meaning* (mortification, rigidification or skeletonization of the communication when read by a rigid code – i.e. transformation into hallucinosis).

The more seriously ill the patient, the more necessary it is to increase the degree of meaning ($\Sigma \rightarrow \infty$), for this process is ultimately indicative of the success of the symbolization process (Ferro *et al.*, 1986a, 1986b).

The patients with the severest pathology are, after all, those who cannot tolerate impoverishment of the meaning of their communications. This is one of the stumbling blocks of criteria of analysability: the problem has to do with the defences I must erect in order not to expose myself to excessive suffering. How far am I able to go to meet a patient's emotional demands?

To what extent am I available to receive, transform and renarrate his emotions (as well as mine, as activated by him), rather than defending myself with the lead apron of codified theories – even the most sophisticated ones – of the kind that could be accommodated in column 2 of Bion's grid?

Again, not all patients put us to the test with such primitive needs (criteria of analysability often serve to select patients who confirm our theories to us). Even when, as so often, we misguidedly disregard the patient's dialect and compel him to learn the analyst's (which will be that of repression, part-objects, the unconscious bodily fantasy, the container–contained, etc.), a relative, marginal process of transformational renarration of the patient's emotional states will nevertheless take place (for even if the analyst is unaware of it, these states will pervade him, or else, if blocked off, they will be retold by the patient in their state of not-having-been-received) – woven into a more or less mythical "historical" reconstruction of early or not so early childhood vicissitudes and fantasies.

Of course, where the most primitive parts of the mind are concerned, these unconscious stratagems cannot suffice, and failing a process of symbolization in the here and now mediated by the entire arc of communication (from acceptance of the emotional wave via transformation to subsequent telling-in-a-story) and leading to the formation of α elements – i.e. "thoughts" – the result will be those valuable indicators of a dysfunction in the analytic relationship that we call negative therapeutic reactions, impasse and psychotic transferences, which betoken a mismatch between the analytic instrument – and the minds of the protagonists at that moment – and the analytic task in hand.

This means not that we should expose ourselves to new and greater difficulties, but that we should be aware that we can advance only a little way beyond our own analysis and the theories that underlie it, and that we ought not to shirk this task.

Routine models and creative functioning

At times when I am *not on form*,[16] my transformational receptiveness to the patient's communication is replaced by *interpretation* on the basis of many codes which, having practised for so long, I am bound to have at my disposal.

However, if the *emotional wave* (I prefer this expression to the overused term "projective identification") is not received but instead frozen and photographed by the interpretation, the patient immediately gives notice of the fact. Patients with "severe" pathology in particular signal what has happened forthwith after such an interpretation.

After a routine interpretation from me, 47-year-old Carlo says as if off tune: "Yesterday I could not find all my shirt buttonholes and so I picked up the scissors and cut the shirt . . ." I can of course interpret the failure to meet and respond to his communications, but would then merely be forcing his α function (which Carlo might signal to me as follows: "Yesterday I took my washing along to my mother, but after she had washed it and given it back to me, it was even dirtier and full of lumps of soap; of course I appreciated the trouble she took, but it really wasn't much use . . .!"). So I must make myself available to his narration and, for example, pick up on his level and in his dialect "how infuriating it sometimes is when one cannot find the buttonholes – so much so that one rips the shirt apart" (I forgot to mention that he missed the following day's session!). Carlo might then be able to answer, for instance, "Well, perhaps ruining a shirt out of anger was over the top." This would allow progressive increases in consciousness and would be better than telling him that, because he had not felt that his communication had been received and responded to adequately, he had skipped the session/cut the shirt.

His response to such an interpretation might be: "I cannot bear to go to the office because my boss constantly keeps tabs on everything I do, so I've half a mind to report sick for a while . . ."

At this point the analyst could either persist with decoding-type interpretations to the point of inducing truly psychotic transferences or negative therapeutic reactions (Barale & Ferro, 1992), or be receptive to the patient's emotional demand to be exposed to less interpretative pressure and consequently establish with him the scripts and sets he needs to express what he is experiencing, so as subsequently to allow "emotional transformations" in the field.

CP_1 Stands for a patient's communication that we take to be neutral because *absurd*, bearing no residual relation to the preceding sessions but being merely historical or referring to the internal world.

CA_1 This is followed by the analyst's answer, or communication, or interpretation.

CP_2 The number of buttonholes the patient's buttons have fitted into will be evident only from his subsequent reply (or non-reply, which will also be a reply), and the patient's ability to communicate will continue to develop if sufficient buttonholes have been found; missed buttonholes will be indicated in the patient's communication by characters α, β, γ, and if very few buttonholes have been found, also by $\alpha + \beta + \gamma$.

α, β and γ can be interpreted – and moreover interpreted as belonging to the patient's internal world or history – to the point of generating $(\alpha + \beta + \gamma)^n$ versus psychotic transference/negative therapeutic reaction; or else they may be received as signals of suffering on the part of the emotional text, thereby allowing transformation of the interpretative attitude so that full communication can be restored.

These observations are inspired by the work of Rosenfeld (1987) on communication problems, which he developed in particular in his final contributions, and by Langs (1976), whose intuition about "derivatives" had impressed Rosenfeld. They are important because they take account not only of the *historical world* and the *internal world* but also of the *relational world*, or, better, the *"world of the field"*. While this world of course touches upon the realities of the other worlds, it exists in its own right by virtue of the interaction of the two minds and of the inner groupings both of each protagonist and of the field as articulated in possible narrations.

Narratology (Eco, 1979) can provide us with useful hints, such as the concepts of the rheme, of possible worlds and of the narcotization of elements of the text. However, the analytic situation is much more complex, because it involves the formation of a linguistic–emotional–affective text which not only is generated by the interaction of the two minds but also has the extraordinary capability of itself continuously signalling the narcotizations, suppressions and escape routes – *that is, basically, the defences constantly deployed by the field, which must oscillate with the constitution of meaning if there is not to be an impasse or negative therapeutic reaction or other signal of dysfunction.*

The linguistic–emotional text of the session at all times signals to us the haemorrhages of the text itself, and what ultimately happens will depend on our listening capacity. A complicating factor is that the locus of appearance of the "signal" may be the patient's linguistic or emotional text, or the analyst himself, his reveries and countertransference, or any other "point" in the field. The signal may therefore arise from the complex situation of a new text which, while being generated, indicates the loci of detachment – which it may signal through the text or through acting out (basically as a sign of the accumulation of unthinkable contents) – as with Carlo's cutting his shirt/skipping the session.

Let us consider a theatrical text: "I told my husband that I have had to do all the cleaning myself for too many days on end" (although this might also be the beginning of a session). A wide variety of outcomes and developments are possible depending on the reply given by the interlocutor and by the husband himself – a kitchen smashed to pieces, a quarrel, a scene of domestic tenderness, and so on. How then could an analytic session be less of an open work, unfolding in accordance with anything other than the emotional and defensive attitudes of the two minds concerned?

An analyst's choice of "dialect" (or theory) depends in my view on how much he feels able or otherwise to involve himself in the relationship with his patient. Hence if the analyst believes that "everything will have happened in the history", or that "everything happens in the internal world", or that "everything happens in the relationship", these attitudes betray the analyst's defences, ranging from an extreme need for alienating distance ("everything has already happened elsewhere") to a maximum of confusing closeness ("nothing counts except what is already happening here between us").

Remarks on the characters

I have discussed at length elsewhere the various possible ways of understanding the characters arising in an analytic session, who are characters in the narratological sense and hence significant, not necessarily anthropomorphic, protagonists of the text (Ferro, 1992, 1993f). I have also attempted to describe the main approaches to understanding the characters in the various psychoanalytic models and to compare them with those used in different narratological models.

Having returned to this subject in the previous section of this book, I would merely add that it would be useful to attempt a system of mapping and scoring the characters emerging in a session.

This mapping would allow us to undertake a kind of "regulation by traffic lights" of the various possible worlds arising in a session, as well as a retrospective study of the session and of the implicit models used in it, which would emerge in accordance with the scoring rules; in particular, it would reveal the infinite possible expansions of meaning of a session. The use of "traffic lights" to regulate the infinite number of possible journeys would make it possible for one and not others to be selected. Escher's lithograph *Relativity* (Figure 3) offers a visual image of various models, sections of these models and possible connections between planes and sections within them. Within this complex, chosen journeys valid only at the instant concerned could be activated on each individual occasion.

Besides this simple form of scoring, there could be a more sophisticated one, less abstract than that of Bion's grid and less text-bound than the above. For

Figure 3 Relativity. M.C. Escher's "Relativity" © 2001 Cordon Art
B.V.-Baarn-Holland. All rights reserved.

example, an arbitrary decision could be made to map a session with a maximum of 20 duly identified characters, of whom 10 could be preconstituted because they are the ones who on average "return" most frequently, while 10 could be free, to be invented on each individual occasion. This would allow easy observation over time of the transformations of the characters and their constellations and also enable us to study gradients of their therapeutic effect.

Another possibility would be to attempt to make a grid for each individual character, for example combining the way the character is understood with the interpretative modalities (Figure 4).

An attempt at mapping

The characters in the session – a character being understood as any significant presence in the text – could thus be mapped with identity cards, as in Calvino's *The Castle of Crossed Destinies*, specifying the type of character (Calvino, 1973). Let us consider the "dog".

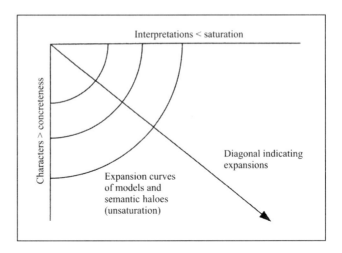

Figure 4 Diagram of characters.

The main characters of the session could be scored in this way; the score would always be rounded down, because they would, if we so wished, be virtually inexhaustible.

Each identity card would then be given a coloured stripe according to how the character is "seen" in the interpretation – let us say red, yellow or green, according to whether the analyst has taken the character concerned as a "character from reality" (red), as a "character from the internal world" (yellow) or as a "relational character" (functional aggregate or affective hologram, green). If the semantic halo of the analyst's interpretations is very wide, yellow plus green or red plus yellow or, in the limit, all three colours could coexist. This would allow the readings of the session to be in effect regulated by traffic lights; the "scoring" could then be quickly understood and it would also be possible to pick up all possible blocked-off worlds, in addition to the acknowledged worlds.

Every interpretation is like a stop sign and at the same time a channel for different histories. An S or a U would be added to the identity cards according to the degree of saturation/unsaturation of the interpretation. I have often drawn a map of this kind, which I have found useful as an indication of how I have scored the various moments in the session and to facilitate discussion with colleagues. A combination of the three systems (identity cards plus colour plus S/U) would also yield the "relationality index" of the field.

Open work

I now present some scattered observations on technique, which, as in the previous section, I do not wish to systematize, precisely so that they can be regarded as still in the process of expansion.

Here and now

Working in the here and now means, not of course that the analyst constantly interprets what is happening in the present situation, but merely that the process of symbolization takes place within the session (Ferro *et al.*, 1986a, 1986b), and that what the patient "brings" (in one of the many ways he may bring it – verbalization, acting out inside and outside the session, projective identification, or evacuation of β elements or screens) must be received in such a way that it can undergo a narrative transformation in the present.

This also entails refraining from "explaining" to the patient what the analyst has understood about him after the session, because the patient would experience this as persecution; true as it might be, it would not be in "unison". Instead, the analyst needs to "work" with the patient, in the "now" of the meeting between the two protagonists, on what is happening in the forming emotional field. This, incidentally, is what Bion means by his famous injunction, whose significance is often lost sight of, that the analyst should work "without memory or desire".

What the patient brings in the present must be listened to, transformed and semanticized with the active participation of the patient himself. Riolo (1989) reminds us of Bion's description of the type of thought that originates from only one of the minds which ought to be in relationship with each other as "lying thought". He goes on: "This is the meaning to be assigned to –K elements, rather than pointing out that something known is 'false' instead of 'true', which would indicate a unilateral knowledge saturating the signifieds of the field with elements taken from the cognitive-affective world of only one of the subjects present."

Gianluca's Mr Parmesan

Gianluca presented me with a large number of communications which I could not metabolize and to which I was able to assign meaning in the "digestive" pause of the post-session period. I felt it important to tell him in the next session about what I had understood, until the appearance of Mr Parmesan and the following communication: "I like fresh cheese, but it has to be today's; there are excellent matured cheeses, which some people might like, but I just find them irritating and rancid.'

Carlo's "bruscia"

With Carlo I had been unable to accept in the here and now a session pervaded with complaint, partly because I was blocked by a sense of guilt at having had to cancel some of his sessions at a difficult time, and so I drew his attention to the sterility of his complaining.

The very next day he brought a dream: the physician in charge was away and he was unable to substitute for him; this was an uncouth man whose education had not gone beyond the fifth year at primary school, whose nickname was "bruscia" (in Italian, an iron brush used to clean up horses that have been wallowing in mud) and who prescribed the wrong medicines. I could not fail to realize how unreceptive and unavailable I had been on the previous day.

However, a situation seen from the point of view of the field can be saved if all the characters who render the functioning of the mind three-dimensional are deemed valuable: the *strigliata*[17] can then be accommodated in a paternal code which Carlo had always lacked, considering his "addiction" to the mother.

In other words, even if my acted-out interpretations of the previous day were responsible, the session had witnessed his allergy to any kind of *strigliata*, even when useful to clean off the "mud" from a horse wallowing in its own self-pitying complaints.

Deep mental states

The whole of a session can be categorized in row "C" of the grid, as a dream generated by the patient's mind about the functioning of the analyst's mind and of the field.

Other forms of categorization are, of course, possible, but are in my view less useful for allowing transformations into "O".

The blocked WC

In one session I had been a good interpreter of the patient's mental state, but had not succeeded in being fully available and permeable to her profound emotional states.

In the next session the patient brought a dream: she had gone to a confined place with a row of WCs that lacked partitions between them; when she eventually found a separate little room the WC itself was missing, and, because there was no hole, "pulling the chain" resulted in the entire floor being flooded.

The dream in effect tells us how the deep exchange of communications had or had not functioned: a confined space in the analyst's mind, little intimacy in the meeting, restricted availability for absorbing the anxieties of the patient, who, if she "pulls the chain", evacuates further anxieties, with the inevitable result of flooding the field.

She also dreamed that her throat was coated with chewing gum which she could not get rid of and which was suffocating her. The "bloody chewing gum" that had risen to her lips at difficult times since she had been very small but which it had never been possible to express, out of fear that there would be no "hole" or "WC" ready to absorb it, was rage.

Even before the dreams, however, I had been alerted by the events of the previous session, which had produced characters such as the "father of Marianna", who in turn did not wish to have anything to do with men she despised, "Stefano", her own brother, who had been swindled so often that he hated other people, and "Licia", her teacher at primary school, a "nun", a woman of virtually non-existent availability, even if the patient loved her passionately.

This *material* can logically be seen from three points of view: as a historical reconstruction of an existential vicissitude (*external reality*); as fantasy, or the functioning of the internal world (*internal reality*); and, in particular, as an expression of the *relational reality* taking shape within the emotional field generated by the couple, which inevitably oscillates with the other two realities, thereby opening up infinite realms of meaning.

Relational truth is the only possible locus of transformations, the other two realities being the locus of knowledge – even if knowledge and transformation are necessarily in a state of mutual oscillation.

The instability of the psychoanalyst's mind – even as regards the capacity to receive the patient's protoemotions (through projective identifications) – is a fundamental instrument of knowledge (and hence also of transformability in the session), whereas stability is an excellent instrument of therapy.

I believe, too, that there is a basic oscillatory type of movement between instability and stability just as there is between the assumption of a role (accumulation of projective identifications?) and the "second look" adduced by Baranger & Baranger (1961–62) as the capacity to metabolize "bulwarks".

Antonia

After a session in which I had felt "mentally absent" and noticed that I was not managing to "hold" her so well, Antonia said that her husband had dropped their little girl on the couch; she had bumped her head and cried so much . . .

Through the characters mentioned, I interpreted the unreliability she might sometimes observe in her husband; the highly available old people's home that had taken in her grandmother then took the stage.

I am becoming more and more aware of the existence of a level on which what counts are not interpretations but "mental facts", the quality of mental functioning, even if liable to damage by the patient's projective identifications – but this too is a problem that must enter into the field if it is to be solved.

The primitive parts of each patient test the analyst's degree of mental availability, perceiving as they do the gradient of projective identifications that the other's mind is available to receive; we are here in the territory of late Rosenfeld's idea of the correct opening of the mind, and of the Bion of the Italian seminars, who tells us that the patient always knows and reflects the quality of the analyst's mental functioning in the session.

Figurative narrations and their resemblance to dreams

This in my view is the type of narration that most readily puts us in contact with the "narrative derivatives" of the α elements. These narrative derivatives partake of the nature of the α element, of which they are a "prose" version, whereas the α element can be known in its "poetry" only during visual flashes.

They of course lend themselves to categorization in row C of the grid. They possess on the one hand the direct inexpressibility of the α element and on the other the expressiveness of a story – as if they were endowed with a twofold specific surface so that they act as an interface between α element and relationship.

The puppies and their container

Here is Luisa's description of the activation of emotions and feelings, which had for a long time been petrified (as in her dream of skyscrapers on a Himalayan mountain) and feared as overwhelming: "I took my little girl to the country and left her free to wander about her uncle and aunt's farmyard; along came lots and lots of puppies and the child was afraid of being overwhelmed by their vitality. So she lay down on the ground on her stomach, as people do when things get dangerous in war films, but then she plucked up the courage to play and amuse herself with them."

The Murano merry-go-round

I should like to present the beginning of a session. Luisa's previous session had been invaded by a "betaloma"[18] (Barale & Ferro, 1992), which had put me in what the patient had described as an "*appartamento*"[19] situation, in that she had at one point began to talk about the mother – a prostitute – of an increasingly psychotic little boy who was interested only in having money with which he would then buy "apartments". I think that what she was describing was the experience of my having withdrawn, setting myself behind the relationship, and in fact setting myself "apart". In the next session the patient began by telling me how, at the motorway toll booth, a lorry had reversed into her car, breaking a headlight and denting the bumper. I did not know whether to interpret or not; however, I thought it important to do so, and suggested that this was perhaps a way of telling me what happened when she noticed that I might be withdrawing rather than being able to feel more in contact and get closer to her.

Smiling, the patient said that this was indeed probably what she felt. Immediately after, however, she mentioned a little girl with a school phobia, who had brought her a "Murano merry-go-round" from Venice; it was made of glass, or rather crystal, with four ponies that fitted on it. She had taken it home, where her own little girl, who was still small and somewhat uncontrollable, immediately picked it up and broke it. At this point I decided to stick to the text and to talk about how it might be possible to mend the merry-go-round, and how children sometimes broke things.

Increasingly we see how characters are born in the sessions as if to reproduce in pictographs the qualities of mental functioning activated in the field.

Notes

1 Again, the entire work of analysis is based on "story-telling", and only this, together with the form in which the story is gleaned, is significant. Recordings put me in mind of the tale of the cartographer who wanted to produce a map on a scale of 1:1. Moreover, who would prefer a faithful recording of facts to Kurosawa's *Rashomon*? What is the most meaningful of the emotional facts of the human mind? For an opposite view, however, see Freni (1996).
2 A further limitation on this exercise is that it allows me to consider only theories which I myself have at some time embraced, so that technical models I have never espoused are disregarded.
3 Further interesting contributions on this subject may be found in Rothstein (1985) and Hunter (1994).
4 [Translator's note: The Italian word *calcio* can mean either "kick" or "football".]
5 [Translator's note: *ano* = anus.]
6 [Translator's note: The Italian word *rabbia* means both "rabies" and "rage".]
7 [Translator's note: Italian television cartoon characters in the form of black birds or chicks.]
8 Subunits of narrations, just as syllables are subunits of words.
9 [Translator's note: *Prospettiva* means both "perspective" and "prospects".]
10 How many possible ways are there of understanding "this house"? To leave the text unsaturated, it is in my view of paramount importance to tolerate the existence of very wide semantic haloes.
11 [Translator's note: In English in original.]
12 The title of a horror film mentioned by Cosimo in our first meeting.
13 [Translator's note: Please see note 9.]
14 It has been noted in connection with this clinical material that "allowing oneself to not understand" is one thing, whereas "allowing oneself to understand and not to say" is another (Manfredi, 1994b). In my view, the second case too may constitute an "understanding" classifiable in row 2 of the grid, not conducive to transformations into "O" (Bion, 1965).
15 The work of Parthenope Bion Talamo (1987, 1991) deserves to be known.
16 I do not believe that the analyst's mind can be regarded as a constant of the field. It is subject to the field's PS–D oscillations as well as to its own intrinsic oscillations (Ferro, 1993f). Nor do I believe that the analyst can be on peak form at all times.
17 [Translator's note: The Italian word *strigliata* can mean either a "currycomb" or a "telling off".]
18 We used this word for a tumour-like "accumulated" agglomeration of β elements.
19 [Translator's note: *Appartamento* can mean either "apartment" or "setting apart".]

Chapter 3

The analytic dialogue
Possible worlds and transformations in the analytic field

The analyst's main concern must be with the material of which he has direct evidence, namely, the emotional experience of the analytic sessions themselves (Bion, 1965).

It will now be clear that I regard an analytic session, from its very beginnings, as open to endless possible developments; what actually happens will depend on the form of interaction between analyst and patient as manifested in the way they talk to each other and, in particular, in the emotional interplay arising between them. In its virtually infinite number of linguistic–emotional articulations, a session inevitably puts us in mind of an "open work" (Eco, 1962), subject, however, to the following fundamental conditions:

(a) In the direction taken, there must be a positive $\beta \rightarrow \alpha$ gradient in favour of the patient.
(b) A "limit" is set to the development of the session in that it must be related to the transference seen both as repetition and as projection of the patient's fantasies.
(c) The session must allow the "story" to develop in a manner useful to the patient rather than in a way designed to confirm the analyst's theories (or, at least, such confirmation must not excessively impede the $\beta \rightarrow \alpha$ process).
(d) It must be accepted that the number of potential "stories" that can be constructed with the patient is infinite, and that each model corresponds to a story in a different dialect – that of infancy, of the internal world, of the current relationship, and so on.

I further believe that it is the patient's response that enables us to choose the correct bearing for the voyage ahead, on the basis of three of its components: (1) an element of transference as repetition; (2) an element of transference as external projection of fantasies; and (3) *the organization of all this by the waking dream thought* (Bion, 1962) *"that dreams" the response to the interpretative stimulus in real time.*

Another important requirement in my view is the capacity to relativize one's own theory, so that the analyst sees it not as the one closest to the truth but as the one whereby he can best function analytically – provided that most of the material used for its construction comes from the patient, the patient's story and the patient's projective identifications.

The narratological idea of "possible worlds" is for me a helpful activator of thoughts. This concept was originally developed in the field of modal logic and subsequently extended to text semiotics by authors such as Petofi (1975), Van Dijk (1976) and Pavel (1976).

Platinga's definition (1974) is "a way the world could have been".

A telling embodiment of these ideas is to be found in Maurizio Nichetti's film *Stefano Quantestorie*, in which a number of stories that might have been assume concrete form and structure according to the prevailing emotional configuration.[1]

The "possible worlds" are also understood as all the expectations the reader has as he engages with a text, and are closely bound up with the encyclopaedias (i.e. his theories) that often distance him from the text and prevent him from following it, so that he constructs possible worlds that have nothing to do with what the text suggests. The prevailing attitude should instead be one of respect for the categories of "economy" of reading and the "right of the text" (Eco, 1990).[2]

The reader's expectation that has "to be discarded" remains the sketching out of other possible stories; in the analytic situation, the development of other stories determined by theory or by different categorizations (Bion, 1965) might be activated.

The analyst's response is therefore not immaterial (still less his mind's disposition to receive projective identifications and allow itself to be traversed by them). Indeed, this response will be the basis for the generation of a wide range of possible stories, including the extremes of the negative therapeutic reaction, impasse, psychotic transferences or the breaking off of the analysis (Barale & Ferro, 1992; Ferro, 1993f, 1994b), or, less dramatically, all the many possible stories – differing according to the interaction of the two minds – within a functioning analysis. From this point of view, the characters will be seen not only in terms of their historical references or the internal world, but as "expressive modalities" of what is happening in the field, the putting of which into words will call for "narrative nodes".

The field concept was anticipated in Gestalt psychology, which was recast by Merleau-Ponty (1945) with the aim of establishing a psychology of man "in his situation", able to observe and understand psychic facts through their meaning in the context of intersubjective relations.

The concept was combined by the Barangers and Mom (Baranger & Baranger, 1961–62; Baranger, Baranger & Mom, 1983) with the fundamental notions of Kleinian psychoanalysis. These authors defined the analytic situation as a bipersonal field, in which all that was knowable was the "unconscious couple fantasy" as structured by the contribution of the patient's and analyst's mental lives, one vehicle of this field being projective identifications.

The patient's pathology as such enters the field only in relation to the person of the analyst, who in turn actively contributes – hopefully to a lesser extent – to the constitution of the *pathology of the field* that will be the concrete object of psychoanalytic working through.

Because analyst and patient form an inextricably linked and complementary couple, the couple's members can be understood only in combination.

Full account is thus taken of the mental functioning of the analyst, who must allow himself to be involved – in effect captured – by the forces of the field, but must then be able to resume his existence as a third entity through interpretation and the "second look" that enables him to stand back from the process which he helps to bring about, while at the same time being capable of discerning and describing its specificity.

If projective identification is not merely the omnipotent fantasy of an individual but something that truly happens between two people (Bion, 1980), it is hardly surprising that it is of decisive importance for the structuring of any couple (Baranger & Baranger, 1961–62).

The adoption of this radically bipersonal model of projective identification also entails important changes in the conception of the dynamics of the transference and countertransference. According to Baranger and Baranger, what is classically defined as transference neurosis (or psychosis) will be seen in field terms as transference–countertransference neurosis (or psychosis) – that is, as a function of the couple.

In the analytic situation, insight occurs when analyst and patient acquire a common understanding of the unconscious fantasies active at a given moment in the field. This coincides with a restructuring of the field itself, because the possibility of thought and communication – both affective and cognitive – extends to areas previously occupied by "bulwarks" – i.e. areas of resistance of the couple, which are thus mobilized and broken down.

Hence the bipersonal field of the analysis is the locus of a dynamic process characterized by the couple's tendency to construct bulwarks – or symbiotic links (in Bleger's sense) – and of the work whereby these experiences are to be transformed into a genuine object relationship. This inexhaustible dialectic imparts to the analytic process what Baranger and Baranger, following Pichon-Rivière, describe as a "spiral" course (Bezoari & Ferro, 1991b; Ferro, 1993f).

Construction of stories

As stated in Chapter 1, at the very moment when the field takes shape through the constitution of the setting, it becomes the space–time of intense emotional turbulence, of vortices of β elements, which evoke and activate the α function and thereby begin their process of transformation into α elements (endowed predominantly with visual qualities); like building blocks in the form of pictographs, these constitute the subunits of waking dream thought, of which we may learn not only by visual flashes (Meltzer, 1982a, 1982b, 1982c) but also through their narrative derivatives (Bezoari & Ferro, 1992a, 1994b; Sacco, 1995b).

I shall now attempt to describe some clinical situations in which projective identifications of not yet thinkable emotions (i.e. protoemotions) came to assume a structure with the potential for transformation.

Mario and the pirate

Describing her son's difficulties at school, Mario's mother told me that he could not yet read and write properly at the age of six, but would always leave "holes" of a few letters in words when both reading and writing.

Mario was portrayed as a quiet, submissive and obedient boy, who liked to be with other children and did not seem particularly bothered by his complicated and unusual family situation.

When Mario came into the consulting room, I showed him that paper and pencils were there for him to use, and he immediately produced a drawing (Figure 5).

It depicted two teachers, "Crisna" and "Snone". These names, I guessed, stood for Cristina and Simone. Without saying anything about the way he had written them, I commented that they seemed to me to be two people with very long legs – "maybe you see them as very tall or perhaps too big for you". He agreed, replying that he would rather be with his schoolmates than with the teachers, and went on to make a second drawing (Figure 6), of a ship he called "Vela" [Sail], a fishing boat, although I noticed what appeared to be beaks on the mainmast; I thought I had better watch what I was saying, as *my words might be the wind that could cause the boat to move in an unpredictable direction*. I asked what the two sailors were doing, and he answered: "They are catching fish and then they eat them." The climate with Mario seemed good, but all at once I became aware of a sudden

Figure 5 Mario's drawing of two teachers.

Figure 6 Mario's drawing of a ship.

anxiety rising within me, which was more like a feeling of annoyance, irritation and rage, as if I had received a blow. In fact I felt a positive pain, a weight "on the stomach", and said to myself: "The climate is fine, yes, but I cannot get my bearings, and everything seems sham and false – and why do I feel so annoyed, positively ill at ease and enraged, just when everything seems to be proceeding calmly?" I was tempted to give an interpretation in terms of devouring anxieties or greed, but barely had time to consider the emotions I had felt, to refocus them internally on what was happening in the room, and to begin saying "Everything seems so peaceful to me . . .", when I was interrupted by Mario: "They may *seem* to be fishermen, but it is a trick: they are really pirates. I always play at pirates, I build ships and mount battles, and what I like most is the cannon the pirates use to fire balls that make *holes* in the enemy ships, and then I enjoy playing with the Robin Hood catapult that makes *holes* in the castle". He quickly drew me the cannon and the catapult (Figure 7).

My anxiety and rage completely disappeared. I became aware of a link between the cannonballs, as projective identifications of not yet thinkable emotions, which had struck me so violently and somatically, and the holes in the words he read or wrote: what had hit me, in the absence of a container available to receive and transform this rage, also hit and "made holes in" the words. Mario was not conscious of these emotions, which were in fact those activated in his very unusual family situation, in which everyone pretended, contrary to their real feelings, that everything was fine.

I kept this interpretative hypothesis to myself; since this was only a consultation, I merely asked him if he also played other games. Yes, he said, he played lots of horror games on his computer: Dracula, Batman, Invaders, etc. (Figure 8). I imagined that these represented some of Mario's very primitive fantasies, which he could handle only by stripping them of their affect through the "computer"; in this way he could distance himself from them, but the energy released in the field turned precisely into the "balls" fired by the cannon and hurled by the catapult.

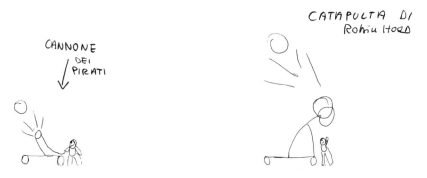

Figure 7 Mario's drawing of a cannon and catapult.

Figure 8 Mario's drawings of characters from computer games.

I confined myself to some minimal comments, which left Mario dissatisfied; in reply, he sadly drew a boy cycling by himself in a courtyard (Figure 9).

I told him that, of course, someone would soon come along to play with the boy he had drawn, that I felt it would be a good thing if he could continue the game we had just begun with someone else, and that I would tell his mother this. "Yes, so long as it is someone who likes pirates," Mario replied, "and above all who is not too afraid."

Figure 9 Mario's drawing of a boy cycling

It is in my view plain that the analyst's refraining from explicit interpretations based on a content-based or symbolic reading of the drawings made it possible to link pictographic and emotional portrayals – the latter having appeared in the countertransference – in a transformational development leading to the appearance of a meaning that could be shared. This made Mario conscious of the emotional reality of the "pirate" and of his need to find a container (and not a target) for his rage and emotional turbulence.

By emphasizing narrative transformations (Corrao, 1991), I have come to see all the dialogue part of a session as more and more like a drawing with the odd characteristic of continuous mobility of all its components, as if it were a living tableau.

It is fascinating in this connection to track a "character" as it enters the session, moves, is transformed and leaves the stage, only to be succeeded, or sometimes supplemented, by another "character" (for example, from an anecdote, memory, story or dream), but always in such a way as to confer shape and colour on what is happening in the couple's mental functioning at the time (Ferro, 1996a; Badoni, 1996).

Each model interacts differently with the "living tableaux" of the sessions; even purportedly more neutral models enter into the construction of the field, partly because interpretations are often the analyst's way of defending against the quantum of mental pain that cannot be assimilated and transformed (Ferro, 1993c).

Modulation of field tensions and emotional pictograms

In clinical situations where the α function is unimpaired, so that the patient is able to make α elements and hence to dream and have waking dream thoughts (Bion, 1962), a possible inadequacy of the "apparatus for thinking thoughts" might result in thoughts being evacuated in the same way as β elements. The same treatment is meted out to the analyst's interpretations whenever they impose intolerable stress on the patient's α function and apparatus for thinking thoughts; interpretations must therefore be given to such patients in doses corresponding to their capacity to accept them. This point is illustrated by the clinical accounts that follow.

Claudia's washing machine: which programme?

Claudia's narcissistic pathology caused her to deny her own suffering and mask her personal need for analysis behind her professional interest as a trainee psychiatrist.

This analysis from the beginning seemed very likely to be broken off, with a high risk of acting out and incipient negative therapeutic reactions, but then a dream led me to realize that "she could not afford *interventions* that were too expensive" (on the emotional level).

While aware of Claudia's need to deny her own suffering, I refrained from making it explicit. I was struck by Claudia's avowed interest in Arabian civilization; before embarking on a career in medicine, she had been on the point of studying oriental languages, and was fascinated by the Arab world with its enormous wealth and great poverty.

I remember how some of my interpretations were followed by the appearance on the stage of a "little boy treated in the resuscitation unit after swallowing nails". Similarly, after direct interpretations I had felt appropriate, "a little girl who almost went blind because she was given too much oxygen in the incubator" took the stage. However, if I noticed and modulated my excessive interpretation dosage, this was received and signalled by the entry into the session of "an oculist who used non-intrusive interventions to help the girl, so that she had good prospects of recovering her sight". Again, if I had been too efficient, she would immediately tell me about the "chief physician who had been on a managerial course and always used the *electronic brain*".

One particular session was very significant for me. Following a direct interpretation of intense rage that had emerged in dreams and which she was now able to experience, which I linked to a deep and painful wound that had always been denied, I was interrupted by a terrified Claudia saying: "What on earth is happening, look, I can see the mask in the picture over there going up . . ."

Of course, the picture on the opposite wall did not depict a mask in motion, or indeed any mask at all.

I realized how the emotions activated by my interpretations were breaking the "container", generating extreme persecution, and giving rise to "dream-like flashes in waking life" (Meltzer, 1982a, 1982b, 1982c; Ferro, 1993b). If I then interpreted this persecution or the feelings generated by my interventions (envy, jealousy, difficulty in being dependent), she would skip sessions or tell me about furious quarrels, or else I would hear of her terrible relationship with her elder sister, characterized by her rejection of and contempt for anything that came from her. It became clear to me that it was impossible to interpret all this in the transference and that I had to modify my usual technique if the analysis was not to be broken off. As a result there appeared "Marcello", her new boyfriend, "who let himself be guided by her and was kind and available".

I accompanied her with interpretations administered in carefully controlled doses in the unfolding of this love story, in which other possible suitors were cast aside: "Claudio", who wanted mainly sex (he appeared whenever I got too close with transference interpretations), and "Sandro", who was capable only of affectionate friendship (he came up when I was too reserved and distant). Marcello seemed to represent the golden mean, and it was not long before they married.

Soon they were expecting a child. The pregnancy enriched Claudia's emotional life, which came to be experienced and narrated through the emotions that were gradually activated and which she discovered in the "child".

For a long time her own separation anxiety was described in terms of the anxiety of her son Marco, who would cry in despair whenever his mother went away; her own jealousy was called "Marco's jealousy on being told of the arrival of a new little brother"; and her own needs were "Andrea's ravenous hunger that bordered on greed".

For a long time, therefore, it was necessary to stay with the story as narrated (*although, of course, I was absolutely convinced that she was speaking and working solely with the emotional and mental facts of the consulting room*), until it became possible to find a more explicit way of allowing Claudia to get close to emotions that could be recognized as her own.

The "lots of medals" from a dream dating from the beginning of the analysis gave way to the "lots of holes" – i.e. "needs" – that had been concealed by medals-as-prostheses in a subsequent dream.

Now began a period of re-owning split-off geographical areas of her own mind: her dreams began to be populated with gypsies, immigrant street vendors and Arabs, who were sometimes as furious as "Marco" – and Marco was so incomprehensible when angry that he seemed to be talking Arabic – and who on occasion asked for asylum . . . Then came faithful "Lassie", who was able to find his own way home.

Next to appear on the stage were the very sick children she was beginning to treat, each of whom also represented the problem we had to deal with (and here again, interpretation had to be by a roundabout route).

We saw "Stella", who had a school phobia because of her fear of an over-demanding mistress (whenever I tried to increase the dosage of my interpretation), or a dessert phobia (actually about the end of the sessions) because the dessert signalled that the meal was at an end and Daddy would be going away; and "Marcella", who was very much in love with the boyfriend who did not look after her as she would have wished; and many, many other characters, each of whom had his or her own "theme".

However, this form of working, which, I believe, had facilitated the working through, metabolization and transformation of Claudia's very primitive emotions, was eventually signalled to me as insufficient by the patient herself in the next session.

I had had to postpone our meeting by one hour.[3]

As Claudia started speaking at the beginning of the session, I noticed that I was distracted by enormous rage at the poor quality of the postal service, as a result of which letters were not being delivered to me punctually and might even have got lost in the post.

When I was able to listen to the patient again, she was telling me about a colour film she had seen and another in black and white. In the first, a girl who was unwanted in a house killed herself and her brother took his revenge by murdering everyone responsible for her death. The second was a sad story set in Pavia, about a doctor's wife who died in childbirth, although her baby girl survived.

It was not difficult for me to devise an exhaustive content-based interpretation (that is, to pick up the presence in the first dream of emotions in "PS", about the loss of the session – rage, despair and revenge – and the appearance in the second of a reworking in "D" of the lost session, albeit coupled with the hope of the new one). However, remembering how the patient had shown that she "did not yet have a place" for interpretations of mine, I offered an unsaturated intervention – of the kind that Bezoari and I (Bezoari & Ferro, 1989, 1994a) have called "weak" interpretations, drawing attention solely to the differing affective tones of the two films.

After a short silence, the patient said: "I am remembering a dream: I was washing some of my sweaters with the extra-delicate programme, which is all right for the very delicate wool, but because the spin programme was also extra-delicate, the sweaters remained saturated with water and I was afraid that they would be too heavy on the washing line."

I asked whether she thought the normal wash might ruin these sweaters: no, she said, because they had now been washed several times with the extra-delicate programme and there was no longer any risk of their being spoilt. She added that she had been thinking of her sister Luisa, whose little blanket had once been hanging up after being washed, but was unusable until it was dry: that had made her cry a lot.

At this point I felt able to give her the normal wash cycle (which was expected and desired), and I brought into the transference the feelings about the first film, the second film, the experiences of the "sister" who could not wait, and her new capacity to contain her emotions.

The patient replied: "Now I understand all the rage I felt yesterday, quarrelling with everyone . . ." – and I in turn understood my own rage at the postmen who did not deliver the mail punctually, which had been my way of receiving the patient's projective identifications.

Basque terrorism

Mimmo came to analysis because of a vague malaise that made him neglect his studies, let himself go, get bored, and often complain.

When I saw him at the door in his grey suit, I thought: "What a boring conformist he must be"; he seemed to me to be the last survivor of another age . . . and then I noticed a kind of unexpected gleam in his eyes, which made me think: "Or perhaps not . . . he looks like a savage . . ."

The beginning the analysis was difficult, with long silences. I myself was afflicted with boredom and sleepiness; I felt that something was being put to sleep, but I was not sure what, nor could I find any opening towards something more living and vital.

So we proceeded, until something very unusual occurred: one winter evening, as a thunderstorm was beginning, the light suddenly went out. I was not equipped to cope with such an eventuality because this had never happened to me before in all my years of practice. Left in the dark, I was invaded by unspeakable terror, which I cannot describe to this day – absolute panic at the terrifying idea that Mimmo might jump on me, kill me, stab me, rip me to pieces. Images of extraordinary violence took possession of my mind . . . meanwhile Mimmo droned on in the same monotonous voice . . . and then the light came back on . . . the session continued . . . but inside me were these scenes that had opened up, but which I did not know how to use. I decided to wait and see, but felt very tense. A few days later, my attention was attracted by a *basco*[4] that Mimmo had begun to wear to his sessions, which was completely out of keeping with the rest of his attire, and when it fell on the floor once as he was leaving, I found myself "picking up his *basco*".

At this point I had an intuition that enabled me to connect what I had experienced, as well as a tendency I had noticed for my interpretations to be insufficiently modulated, with what was happening, and I said to myself: "It is indeed the *Basco* that needs to be picked up". In the next session I cautiously allowed this character to take the stage: perhaps the *basco* that had fallen down, and which it was perhaps up to me to pick up, might be a *Basco* of which I had never heard.

From then on there developed a whole story about the Basques, the importance of the *ferro*[5] mines to their economy, and the particular explosiveness of their character – even if a young Basque had recently married a cousin of his of whom he was very fond; he had even conceived an interest in their language, which appeared not to belong to any known family . . . and then there were the bombs . . . the Basques' need for independence . . . the crushing of the Basque identity . . . and then, in successive sessions, via accounts of films, the American bison . . . the wild animals from a recent trip to Africa, where his father had unexpectedly started an import–export business . . . and ultimately the drama of the Albanians and their needs.

Let us briefly consider the characters. At first they had been lumped together in my mind, probably on the basis of Mimmo's projective identifications. First there had been the Savage, the "Ripper", and then his communicative acting out had introduced the "Basco", affording access to parts of his mind that had been split off in lethargy and rendering them thinkable and amenable to transformation.

For a long time, of course, these tales remained in the "places" where the patient put them (Spain, Africa, Albania), until they eventually entered, with their full affective weight, into the emotional field, and hence into our relationship, and finally into his personal story.

Such a case in my view raises two problems: that of *permeability* to the patient's projective identifications, and the consequent need for as much as possible of what comes from the patient to be received; and, no less important, that of the limit of interpretative hypotheses.

In other words, the Basque, Ghana, etc., are entitled to be received as stories and tales that have to do with the patient's emotional truth and history: it is the patient's projective identifications and emotions, and these *alone*, that must enter into stories.

Moreover, whenever this does not happen, the fact will be signalled by the patient, as in the example of Rosa presented below; however, appropriate listening always makes it possible to pick up the textual signals, which may then appear in the patient's actual text, in the countertransference, or in any other place in the field.

Again, the characters, narrations, memories, drawings and the like emerging in the session may be reconceived from a given vertex as "summaries of the functioning" of the couple at a given time, undergoing constant change and transformation in accordance with their interaction and its qualities (Ferro, 1993a; Cancrini & Giordo, 1995).

Concatenations of "selected facts" and signals of the text

In order to weave the fabric of a narration, a whole group of possible stories constantly has to be suppressed, so as to allow the prevalent, most significant ones to take shape and develop.

By the "prevalent and most significant" stories I mean those derived from the transferences and β elements of the field that permit and activate a maximum of narrative transformation (Corrao, 1991). It is ultimately the concatenation of successive narrative vertices (or the sequential interaction of "selected facts" – Bion, 1965) that allows a story to be defined.

This is basically what Diderot reminds us of in *Jacques le Fataliste*: of all the large number of possible stories, many must be forgone so as to permit the coherent and comprehensible development of a story that can be narrated.

It is interesting to reflect that some of the "possible worlds" (Ferro, 1993d) are those to which admission might be gained by a dysfunction of the field (worlds that we ultimately call negative therapeutic reactions, psychotic transferences, impasse, etc.); these worlds are consistent with what is happening, and tell predominantly of the manifestations of exchanges or blockages, or profound breakdowns of communication (Nissim, 1984; Robutti, 1992b; Barale & Ferro, 1992).

Other worlds have been rendered inaccessible – like the novelist Carlo Cassola's "paths that lead nowhere" – owing to defences of the couple or resistances, or, even when everything is in order, because the worlds concerned are less significant in terms of facilitating the generation of sequential chains of "selected facts" (Bion, 1965) for the purposes of transformation.

This concept is known in narratology as "narcotization" and involves limitation of the expansion (n) of possible worlds.

The emotional–linguistic text woven with the patient can also signal when the process is going astray owing to the loss of "transformational resources". This may be due to the emergence, by way of any place and/or time of the field (a dream by the patient, a countertransference dream, a narration of the patient, images of the analyst, acting in, acting out, etc.), of lumps of β elements adrift which cannot be received and transformed, or of anxieties or protoemotional states, which, however, *must necessarily* be received and transformed in order to generate a β → α gradient.

Again, if the unconscious is seen not as a depository but as the wholly dynamic entity described by Bion (the contact barrier made up of α elements, which, in the manner of a zip fastener, constantly opens, separates, distinguishes and structures into unconscious and conscious, continuously resupplying both through transformed emotional–sensory afferences), then the transformations of the history, of recollections and memories, can obviously be much more extensive than with other conceptions, precisely because of this model's extreme intrinsic plasticity.

If we now consider Bion's (1962) postulated distinction between "memories" and "undigested facts" that continue to exert pressure in the present until the cathexis over and above the transformation capacity of the available α functions finds a possible place and way of transformation, of telling and hence of becoming memory (Etchegoyen, 1986; Ferro, 1993f), it becomes clear that the field is replete with events, emotional facts and constructions of meaning – although, of course, this is merely the tip of the iceberg as regards the phenomena waiting to be described.

Let me finally emphasize that what appears as a *conversational truth* arriving in the field as an event (whenever there are no interpretative caesuras but instead the evident mutual construction of a dialogic text) is in fact the fruit of prolonged "work" based on profound mental travail, a vital component of which is the analyst's *negative capability*. Bion defines this in accordance with the quotation from Keats's letter to his brothers that appears at the beginning of the last chapter of *Attention and Interpretation* (Bion, 1970): "Negative Capability, that is, when a man is capable of being in uncertainties, mysteries, doubts, without any irritable reaching after fact and reason."

Rosa and the proliferative disease

An initial interview with Rosa, a 25-year-old philosophy teacher, was devoted to the feasibility of a proposed analysis, which might have to be postponed for several years because I had no time.

At this first meeting, Rosa succeeded in telling me of something very dramatic that had happened to her on a journey; although it would be a long time before she could commence her analysis with me, she was very determined and had decided to wait for me, because she had unexpectedly managed to talk to me about "that particular episode", of which she had never before been able to tell anyone; I in turn gave up the idea of not accepting her for analysis owing to the long waiting time involved, and accepted her proposal. The following stories appeared at the second meeting. After our talk, she had "very regretfully" had to leave the school where she had felt good. Then a relationship had flared up with Marco, another teacher at the school, who *had lost his head* and become terribly involved. Meanwhile she had also had an affair with another colleague, Aurelio, which she described as a relationship "*the way you want me*", in which she liked to support him in everything. Then there was the boyfriend who guaranteed her a secure and reliable position, but did not satisfy some of her requirements. Finally, she produced the younger sister with a "proliferative disease", who had an urgent need for appropriate treatment.

How were these "*characters*" to be thought of?[6] One possibility might be to accept them according to their prevailing reference, as characters from external reality whose importance lay in the emotions and feelings they activated in the patient.

Alternatively, they could be seen as characters who combined and saturated valencies of Rosa's internal world, thus immediately permitting the step from the external reference to a theory (of internal objects), and hence to Rosa's internal groupings and their organization. In other words, the characters presented in specular form would have to do with Rosa's internal objects, unconscious fantasies and fantasy formations.

It soon became possible to recognize these fantasy formations in the transference and in the relationship that had arisen from the very beginning of the first interview; these "figures" could be seen from a variety of viewpoints – as transference entities, which were thus projected, or as anticipated visions of the transference relationship in the analysis (in terms of transference based on repetition, transference based on externalization, relationship in the form of something unique and specific to the two minds in the here and now, which was a function not only of the transferences but also of the receiving and transformational capacity of the analyst's mind) (Di Chiara, 1983; Ferro, 1992; Folch-Mateu, 1986; Manfredi Turillazzi, 1985).

These aspects could – or could not – be *interpreted* in accordance with a whole complex of technical considerations.

From another vertex, however – *one in a state of necessary oscillation with the others* – these characters could be seen as the syncretic and pictographically narratable expression of the emotional facts occurring in the consulting room, in the mutual fantasy formations activated in the bipersonal field (Baranger & Baranger, 1961–62), or rather in the two-group field arising, which had *three principal emotional modalities* and narratable stories that could assume concrete form according to the interaction of the protagonists' minds. The entity called upon to modulate this interaction was the analytic and transformational function of the analyst's mind (Hautmann, 1981) – its function as a transformational stronghold, the activator of possible stories).[7]

Of course, different interpretations will give rise to very differently structured stories, according to whether the code on which they are based emphasizes seduction, adhesive identification, historical reconstruction, and so on.

Instead of decoding-type interpretations (which would then have generated other possible texts), I opted for an open contribution to the narrative development and said that it seemed to me that there were several different stories here, one of them passionate, one erotic and another concerned more with the affects (the relationships with Marco, Aurelio and the boyfriend).

Of course, I saw these as our possible plots or "fabulae", all demanding to be narrated. However, the emotional text-as-duet (Nissim, 1984) has the characteristic of *"being alive" – and hence of "bleeding" or "weeping" at the unnoticed lacerations of meaning.*

After my intervention, Rosa added: "I would have liked to study medicine; I sometimes feel that philosophy is an exciting but masturbatory game." For a moment I felt confused. "Medicine" . . . "philosophy" . . . "masturbation" – where had they come from? I immediately understood that they were a signal of the text; I had opted for three possible stories, but had disregarded the fourth (Cronin, I said to myself, and his stories of doctors and diseases, but also Kronos, the urgency of therapy/analysis, the urgency of not wasting time: the proliferative disease of the sister who was a part of herself, or rather the proliferation of emotions that could not be contained in the emotional field).

At this point the *suppressed but necessary stories were "budding" with a view to re-entering the text.*

I could have given a decoding-type interpretation. There are so many theories: instead of picking up the self-generativity of the emotional text, I could have drawn on the theory of envy, of devaluation, of attack on the link, on –K; or, seizing on the emotional involvement in the here and now, I could have *made explicit the reason for the appearance of this communication* (à la Langs or late Rosenfeld); or, refraining from "Byzantinization" of the text, I could have opted for simplicity of the emotional exchange and emphasized the *weeping of the text*, introducing (without "upstream" interpretation) the concern for the "proliferative disease", "the battle against time", or the "urgency of treatment". The way the text developed would then narrate the appropriateness or otherwise of the intervention.

If due attention is paid to the signals of the emotional/narrated text, stories that need to be told and transformed will not remain suppressed, while all the possible stories not relevant to the current emotion and urgency may then stay concealed (Faimberg, 1989, 1992).

The development of the shared story (Vallino Macciò, 1993) will then constitute the reservoir on which other grouping levels can draw; "the proliferation of emotions already kindled by the first interview"; "fear of what was proliferating"; "the need for antiproliferative treatments"; "and the most effective therapy" – these would all be stories to be written later, even if by way of the text on the worries concerning the proliferative disease (would this be treated in time?).

I managed to find time to bring forward the beginning of Rosa's analysis.

Laura and the degrees

In a very intense session, Laura asked about a perfume called "Fahrenheit" that she could smell in the room, thus allowing me to introduce the theme of "degrees" indicating temperature differences and hierarchies in a field that she would have liked to be uniform, undifferentiated, homoeothermic and homoeostatic. I interpreted accordingly.

The next session saw the appearance of a very passionate young friend, Giovanni, who was very handsome and physically well endowed – "one of those boys that any girl would be happy to have beside her even if only once a week".

The climate of the session seemed to me to be excited and vaguely false; I was left with a sense of dissatisfaction, of something that had remained hidden and unsaid, even if I tried to connect the presence of "Giovanni" with what I had told her on the previous day.

That night I dreamed of a little shark, with which I was playing, in spite of the danger; it then turned into a torpedo, but I went on playing with it although it was potentially explosive.

Laura turned up for the next session in a state of crisis: she had dreamt of a girl whose *mother had no womb* . . . a girl without an umbilical cord . . . indeed, instead of the mother, there was a man ♂ . . . the girl was starving to death . . . Laura added that she had thought a lot about suicide.

At this point I could see that although my "Fahrenheit" interventions – *degrees, gradients, differences, hierarchies* – had been centred and active, and although they had satisfied the more adult parts of the patient (as indicated by the entry of Giovanni), they had represented an overdose for the more infantile part, the little girl who still had fusional or foetal needs. That part had thus been deprived of what it needed in order to survive – namely, complete receptive emotional availability ♀ rather than precise interpretations that left the little girl/shark starving so that she explosively began to threaten suicide.

The first "Fahrenheit" interpretation might have been a good reverie-based one for another patient, but was premature in Laura's case, given her capacity at the time. As a result, by bringing out the difference between her and myself – between myself as an active thinker and herself as the recipient of an unexpected truth for which she was not prepared – I ultimately generated potentially explosive jealousy, rage and dissatisfaction.

The countertransference dream made me aware of the protoemotions kindled in her, which she had poured out into the field, guiding me and enabling me to assign meaning to the next day's communications and to attune myself to Laura's emotional capacity and needs, for she was still far from being able to tolerate interpretations that originated "too much" from me.

I therefore look upon the session from a vertex wholly internal to the session itself, as if nothing were being recounted but what was happening in the depths of psychic life within the field. *Other vertices*, oscillating with this one, were of course also kept in mind, so that the "shark", "Giovanni" and the "wombless mother" could be seen as belonging to Laura's internal world and her real external world.

Permeability of the field and the memory of new experiences

I should also like to emphasize the need for the field to be highly permeable, so that the most primitive aspects of the minds involved can enter into it and thereby be transformed. However, the appearance of a character is only a prelude to its transformation. In my view, as in Etchegoyen's famous example,[8] this transformation can lead to the construction of different memories of one and the same "fact" – or, I would add, to the possible "remembering" of facts that have never happened except in the emotional creation of the present,[9] whereby shreds of earlier experiences can be assigned new meaning.

Purely as an exercise, let us assume that, after an intervention by the analyst, a patient "recalls" the terror inspired in him by his father, a professional boxer – and how, as a child, this terribly violent father had never listened to him. How are we to think of this "find"? The boxer father is surely an important discovery that must include transference elements (as either repetition or externalization), but he is also something that takes shape there in the field at that particular time: he is the way certain parts of the patient have heard the intervention of the analyst-as-violent-boxer-father (who is no doubt an aggregate of the violence present in the field, even if it originates from the patient, producing projective identifications that enter into the field). Now this violent boxer father present in the field needs to be transformed by the working through of the analyst, by his capacity to manage and transform this violence through his own measured, containing interventions.

Of course, many appearances, involving months or years of work, will be necessary before this character, the "violent boxer", can be transformed into a father who also likes "to go fishing" or "to take the children to school", or "to be available to his friends after a good match/meeting".[10] Only then will we witness the structuring in the here and now of a father born in the here and now of the relational meeting, who will then come to inhabit the internal world and the history, thereby making possible the "memories of new experiences" that are one of the oddities of our mental lives. I am not referring here to the unblocking of other possible stories locked up in the prevailing story, which would imply that the subject had had positive experiences "elsewhere". Ignorant as I must necessarily remain about some things, I know for certain that, in the here and now, we witness the restructuring (or structuring?) of new characters and new narrations, which can then again (or perhaps, as the case may be, for the first time?) inhabit the patient's history and internal world. Analysis provides us with constant examples, if we refrain from listening to the patient's accounts solely as entities stripped of the veil of repression or removed from the distance of splitting, but instead remain open to their creative novelty.

Similarly, a character or feeling – let us say, the "fear of the violent father" – cannot first be understood in terms of the patient's fantasy when it takes the stage at the beginning of the session and then be seen later in the session as a transformation of the "competent father" born of the relationship.

These are realities from different worlds and readings. The "violent father" and, presumably, the "competent father" belong to all three aspects of the field. All three can be seen in the story, the fantasizing and the relationship. It is wrong to say that the positive figures belong to the relationship and the negative ones to the internal world or the history, for the violent father too originates from the relationship, from the previous sessions – let us say, from the analyst's lack of receptive capacity at a given time – and this too is a *relational reality of the field*. Alongside this is the reality of the internal world. And alongside the latter, in turn, is the historical reality.

The locus of knowledge is the reality of the internal world and of the history, while the locus of transformations is the emotional reality of the relationship in the field.

A competent analyst, in my opinion, will take charge of the "father's" violence. He will not do so outside the field by defending against it and displacing that emotion on to the patient's history or internal world, but will reflect on the vertex (be it strange, absurd or psychotic) from which, *for that patient at that time, he really is a father who arouses terror* (bearing in mind the overdetermination of his demeanour, which is influenced by the patient's projective identifications so that he may even assume particular roles). He will wonder, too, how he is to set about *transforming himself* so as to permit the transformation of that father into one sensitive to his son's emotional needs and able, let us say, to arouse affection or gratitude.

This relational transformation in the field will give rise to a new configuration of the "father" as a memory of a new fact in the story, who will come to be a new denizen of the *fantasy world*.

The range of potential examples is of course infinite, but it should now be clear that the locus of transformation is the here and now of the analytic situation, and, more precisely, that the place where every transformation begins is the analyst's mind.

A similar argument could in principle be applied to the appearance in a session of any character – let us say "Francesco". Of course, "Francesco" very likely has some real, external connection with the context in which he is summoned up; he probably "represents" certain aspects of the patient, associated with split-off forms of functioning or modalities of which the patient is not conscious, or he may be a kind of Conradian "secret companion" (Gaburri, 1986) – an inhabitant of the analyst's mental life. "Francesco" may well be all of these, but he *certainly* has to do with the emotional–linguistic–affective field within which he arose, or rather – which is the same thing – was named (Bezoari & Ferro, 1990a, 1991a, 1991b; Ferro, 1993f).

Next I must reflect on the emotional vectors of the field that have led to the aggregation of "Francesco" there, at that moment, in that narration, and consider what transformations of this "character from the field" and of "its relations" will then be possible.

This is significant and therapeutic because all these new aggregations will in turn inform the patient's internal world and the history.

This model obviously differs from others, also present in the field, in which the history is seen as a real external story and the fantasies are deemed to be a matter of the patient's "solo" mental functioning. Clearly, too, in this model knowledge and insight are replaced by transformation through the metabolization of β elements by the analyst and by the α function of the field.

Exhaustive interpretation ceases to be central, its place being taken by the analyst's mental work in the session, whereby he as far as possible allows a β → α gradient to arise in the field; the success or failure of this operation will be constantly renarrated by the patient through the stories, facts and characters he brings into the session.

This view of what happens in the field contrasts sharply with the concept of a *corrective emotional experience*, in that what is involved is not a new positive experience accruing from an affectionate or understanding attitude on the part of the analyst. It is rather a matter of bringing about *emotional experiences of transformation*, and this calls for the highest possible degree of permeability of the analyst, and of the field, to all aspects of the transference and of the patient's internal world, as conveyed by repetition and projective identifications (Tagliacozzo, 1982; Lussana, 1991). The central idea, therefore, is a dynamic conception of the unconscious as a place–space–modality in the throes of continuous formation and transformation: the contact barrier continuously "opens up" territories of consciousness, distinguishing and separating them from the territories of the unconscious (Bion, 1962).

In terms of the above example of the boxer father, a prerequisite for any change is that this "violence" must be able to enter the field through any "window" – the patient's words, emotions or acting out, or the analyst's interpretative violence.

The various aspects of the session (historical, relational, fantasy and field-related) are synchronic and distinguishable only in accordance with our chosen vertex; taken by itself, each is coherent, isotopic and self-confirming, and only the oscillation of listening vertices can allow a multidimensional view capable of lending substance to the history, the internal world, the relationship, the emotional field and the way the patient finds his way within these possible worlds (Ferro, 1992, 1993f).

Macrotransformations in the history

So far I have concentrated on describing the microtransformations occurring in the session, which are unstable and reversible and change with the instantaneous emotional attitude of the analytic couple. Of course, a no less important vertex is that of the stable and not readily reversible macrotransformations observed in the long-term evolution of the analytic process (Ferro, 1993f).

The history is of course a precipitate of possible narrations, which, as the retroactive process of *Nachträglichkeit* will confirm, is written only after the event, or rather, is invented and takes shape from what comes "after" – for if we construct reality itself (Glasersfeld, 1981), we surely do the same with the "story" (Baranger, Baranger & Mom, 1988).

Another exciting topic is transgenerational psychic transmission,[11] as discussed in the fundamental contributions of Faimberg (1988a, 1988b) and Kaës *et al.* (1993), as well as in the Italian studies of Neri (1993), Bonaminio *et al.* (1993) and Meotti & Meotti (1996).

Again, a sufficiently permeable field becomes the place-and-time where the patient's transgenerational fantasies too may experience transformation: they must "live" in the field before they can be identified and hence transformed.

In a functioning field, however, the same applies to the analyst's transgenerational fantasies – and to his theories, which should take the signals constantly generated by the field as an occasion for their own (sometimes radical) transformation.

Let me end this chapter with a quotation from Willy and Madeleine Baranger dating from 1964: "Perhaps Freud's greatest achievement was to have enabled his patients (Dora, the Wolf Man and Little Hans) to teach him something and to have passed on this knowledge to us."

Notes

1 In one story, the eponymous hero ["Quantestorie" means "Manystories"] is a *carabiniere*. However, *if* a different emotional tone had prevailed at a certain point, he might in the same story have been a robber; or, if his father or mother had behaved in a certain way, he might, again in that story, have played the part of the pilot or of the mathematics teacher whose hostess wife is deceiving him with the pilot.

2 See Eco's suggested reading of *Un drame bien parisien* in *Lector in Fabula* (1979).

3 Usually when one has to cancel a session, one would wait for the patient to ask to have it at a different time, and then accede or not according to one's schedule; in this case, however, because I already knew how much Claudia wanted to "recover" the session if possible, I myself had suggested postponing it.

4 [Translator's note: The Italian word basco means a beret; when spelt with a capital, however, it means a Basque.]

5 [Translator's note: The Italian word *ferro* means iron; with a capital, it is, of course, the author's surname.]

6 That is, in terms of what theory? What is the relevant topic (cf. Eco, 1979)?

7 I see this as a boundary function, as in the film *Dances with Wolves*, whose hero allows himself to get involved as a protagonist in the stories of the Indians, but then separates again, returning to his own story after a twofold transformation – of the Indians and of himself.

8 In this example the author shows how a memory is radically transformed as the analysis proceeds (Ferro & Meregnani, 1993).

9 We may ask what "objective" value we may assign to a memory if "produced" inside "the same place" where dreams arise, or in the transformation of β elements into α elements, which can be stored only in the latter form (Bion, 1962) – at least, if Bion's idea of an unconscious in a state of continuous formation is accepted. See also Sandler & Sandler (1984) on the present and past unconscious.

10 Provided that the analyst is capable of "fishing" for meanings, going with the patient on his journeys, being available for meetings/matches [translator's note: the Italian word *incontro* can mean both "meeting" and "match"], and so on.

11 Other possible references might be Bion on the myth of the cemetery of Ur and Schnitzler's story *Reichtum* [Wealth].

Chapter 4

Interpretative oscillation along the PS–D axis in the field of transformations

This chapter is intended as an expansion of Bion's suggestion about playing "psycho-analytic games as a part of the daily review of the analytic work" (Bion, 1965), whereby we imagine what other courses the session might have taken given different interpretations, bearing in mind that the "psycho-analyst's domain is that which lies between the point where a man receives sense impressions and the point where he gives expression to the transformation that has taken place" (ibid.).

This idea of Bion's seems to me to fit in well with the episode, in Ermanno Cavazzoni's *The Voice of the Moon*, of the Prefect who commissioned a geographer to draw up a map of his Prefecture: whatever technical stratagems the geographer deployed in his effort to map the region "in real time", the task proved impossible owing to the constant changes in the area's territory (Cavazzoni, 1990).

α Elements: narrative derivatives and compositional constructions

In *Learning from Experience*, Bion (1962) gives us a provisional, unsaturated model of the mind, a central aspect of which is the working up of senso-extero-proprioceptions (stimuli of all kinds and origins – so-called β elements – which, as such, are unknowable in themselves) into α elements, which are like visual pictograms that poetically syncretize every instant of relatedness to self and the outside world. There are also α elements that are not visual but acoustic or kinesic (audiograms or kinaesthesograms), which may, however, for the sake of simplicity be disregarded, because what applies to the visual type of α elements is also true of all the others. The α elements are then sequentially composed into waking dream thought, which accompanies us in all our daytime operations although we are unaware of it. The contact barrier between the conscious and the unconscious systems, which creates and distinguishes the two, is made up of sequences of α elements belonging to either the conscious or the unconscious system. These form the building blocks of unconscious waking thought and indeed of thoughts in general.

Thoughts are "narrative derivatives of the α elements", which retain varying degrees of "alphaness". Bion contends that, once thoughts have been formed (by the process β elements → α elements → unconscious waking thoughts → thoughts), there needs to be a system, an "apparatus for thinking thoughts", and that if this is lacking or its capacity is exceeded, thoughts are treated in the same way as evacuated β elements.

Night dreams, in this scheme of things, differ from "waking dream thought", which is basically a linear sum of the emotional pictograms, in that they presuppose the existence of a function whereby all the α elements produced and preserved in the conscious or unconscious system during waking life are reworked and/or organized.

Because there is relatively little need to make pictograms of real-time stimuli (i.e. ones from the outside world) during sleep, the dream work may be self-centred, so that it can also draw on undigested material, which, as such, has not been transformed into α.

I therefore postulate that there must be either an α function that works differently during sleep or – perhaps more consistently with the model and with experience – a *system for dreaming dreams* within the *apparatus for thinking thoughts*, alongside the PS–D and the ♀ ♂ systems.

In other words, I should like to make a radical distinction between, on the one hand, the *production* of α elements and their sequential ordering in waking life (which may be likened to a film cameraman constantly recording in images everything meaningful that happens), and, on the other, the organization, composition and reworking of this collected material, which is undertaken during sleep by the apparatus for thinking thoughts (the system for dreaming dreams) – like a film director or editor creatively selecting from thousands of frames the material of the final cut.

As we know, Bion distinguishes two types of pathology. The first and more serious concerns a deficiency of the α function, in which the inability to transform β into α elements is lacking, so that the former are evacuated, giving rise to hallucinatory and psychosomatic disorders, characteropathies, etc.; while the second, in which the α function is unimpaired, is observed when the apparatus for thinking thoughts is incapable of "handling" or using these thoughts.

The central issue here is pathology of the dream function. In the first case, as stated, undigested β elements are evacuated, giving rise to "hallucinations"; here we have the well-known characteristics of Bion's "bizarre objects", and the analytic situation conforms to Meltzer's description. The second case concerns the ostensibly similar phenomenon of "dream-like flashes in waking life", which, however, proves to be completely different in nature. These flashes result not from a pathology of the α function – of the dream pictogram (α element) production system – but from a deficiency of the system for dreaming dreams, which is responsible for the storage of α elements and their editing into meaningful sequences.

I have described elsewhere (Ferro, 1993b) situations in which the α function is seriously deficient, in connection with the long analysis of a preadolescent boy suffering from visual hallucinations (where the α function and hence the function of producing α elements were gradually restored). Here, however, I wish to focus on the common situation in which the α element formed lacks an adequate apparatus for thinking thoughts, and hence an adequate PS–D system – an adequate ♀ ♂ system, an adequate system for dreaming dreams. In these cases, the barely formed α element is evacuated "live" while the subject is awake.

My first clinical encounter with this phenomenon was in the analysis mentioned above, in which the visual flash was totally different from a hallucination (Ferro, 1993b). Hallucination completely tore the patient away from me and was utterly lacking in meaning; the patient could talk about it only in the past tense, once it had been completely evacuated: "I saw . . ." The visual flashes, on the other hand, were precious material, susceptible to investigation by analysis; they were consistent with the preservation of the relationship with me and describable in real time: "I see . . ."

I subsequently encountered more and more patients with non-serious pathology who had visual flashes that constituted incredibly rich and creative pictograms of the climate of the moment; it took me quite a long time to understand that these were *pure α elements*, seen in all their immediacy.

When I once announced to a female patient that I wished to increase her fees, she answered in confusion: "I *see* a chicken being plucked on the wall opposite." The α function did its work and produced the α element, but the apparatus for thinking thoughts (or for dreaming dreams) did not; the ♀ ♂ system failed and the α elements were evacuated. Thereupon came the visual flash, telling us that the α function was working but that the second-level apparatus (for thinking thoughts or dreaming dreams) was not doing its job properly.

In the analysis of the young man mentioned above, the apparatus for thinking thoughts and hence for dreaming dreams gradually equipped itself for its function and the visual flashes disappeared, to be superseded by night dreams. Gianluca described this as follows: a boy who lived in the flat below him used to vomit because of excessive tension in the head; this boy had undergone neurosurgery involving the insertion of a cannula (*tubicino = tu vicino*[1] perhaps, as pointed out to me by P. Lussana) to relieve the tension, which was discharged by means of a "little box" placed on his stomach.

The relationship – Gianluca seemed to be saying – also constructed a "little box" that could contain the α elements.

As stated in the first chapter, at a moment of high emotional tension when Gianluca already wished to terminate the analysis but I was holding him back because I was unsure that he had progressed sufficiently, the young man had another visual flash: "I see a pair of pliers holding me . . ."

Over the course of time, more and more clinical situations have put me in contact with such "visual flashes". In particular, however, I have realized their theoretical importance in providing me, as stated, with a direct channel to the α element.

In the absence of dream-like flashes, we can discern the α element's narrative derivatives in the patient's communications, especially at emotionally charged moments – such as in response to our interventions – or at times of particular insight.

In other words, in waking life we cannot normally come into contact with the α element except through its "narrative derivatives" or by the "grace" of reverie, which opens an internal vista on to the α element (Vallino, 1991).

These areas contain some clues to creativity, which, in my view, is closely bound up with a particular capacity for contact with waking dream thought and the α element.

Dreams are another matter, suggesting the need for an inquiry into the characteristics of the apparatus for thinking thoughts (or system for dreaming dreams), which could focus on its compositional and directorial functions; this subject is comprehensively discussed in Hautmann's excellent contribution (1995).

PS–D oscillations on the interpretative axis

Unsaturated interpretations

At the left-hand end of this axis, at PS, I place *unsaturated interpretations* – the ones Bezoari and I have previously called "weak interpretations"[2] (Bezoari & Ferro, 1989, 1994a) – which bear witness to the analyst's capacity both to endure doubt and uncertainty, and to tolerate the existence of worlds in which unforeseeable vistas open up. Such interpretations draw most strongly on the "analyst's negative capability" (Bion, 1970; Flegenheimer, 1989).

The teacher and the "exercises"

This is what Licia told me: "At school I gave the children an exercise that was quite easy, because some things had been done very well – big and small, long and short, parts of the body – but it actually went very badly. *Instead of getting angry, though, I tried to see if there was something wrong in my way of teaching*, and I think I realized I *was making them too passive, forestalling them and explaining everything to them*. Now if the children instead discovered something for themselves, that gave them more satisfaction; they felt it was something of their own and did not forget it again; of course I have to help them and guide them, but also give them the pleasure of discovering things for themselves, without being hurried. They are more active than you think, and then all you have to do is to wait a bit longer and leave them their space, and they will find the answers. If the children acquire confidence in themselves more easily, they will be better able to acknowledge their need of grown-ups."

The narrative construction made with the patient supplies unsaturated narremes (like multi-purpose Lego pieces that can be fitted together in a large number of different ways), whereby the patient's theme can be developed without excessively determining it or closing it off in too strong a sense. In this connection the following passage from Winnicott (1971) is very apt: "It appals me to think how much deep change I have prevented or delayed [. . .] by my personal need to interpret. If only we can wait, the patient arrives at understanding creatively and with immense joy, and I now enjoy this joy more than I used to enjoy the sense of having been clever." Some examples of situations where this capacity for unsaturation was lacking now follow.

The scientists and the egg

As I have already reported elsewhere (Ferro, 1993f), at a time when I was wont to give frequent saturated interpretations in the relationship with my little analysand Roberto, he told me he had seen a TV programme about scientists who took eggs, dissected them and studied them under the microscope – now this was a pity, because they did not realize that the chick could then never be born.

The suffocating bodice

After I had given a strictly transference interpretation, a female patient told me how her grandmother used to make her wear very tight bodices, which she would lace up almost to the point of suffocating her; for this reason she had often avoided spending time at her grandmother's house. It was not difficult to relate this to her frequent late arrival for her sessions.

Saturated interpretations

At the extreme right-hand end, at D, I place exhaustive *saturated interpretations* – those stemming from a "selected fact" involving mourning for all the possible expansions that existed in PS and for the formation of a *Gestalt* precluding all others. This operation entails the forgoing of everything "that is not"; the selected fact (Bion, 1962) derives from an indispensable emotion and not from the application of a code (Rocha Barros, 1992; De León De Bernardi, 1988). Saturated transference interpretations are of course the paradigm of this category.

The Mafia cemetery and the conspiracy of silence

The analysis of Carlo, who had been seriously ill at the beginning, had reached an advanced stage. Contrary to his usual practice, he did not pay at the end of the month, announcing that there would be a delay – because his mother, out of spite, would not give him the money. He said he had spent a large sum on lots of books with which to face the holidays. All this, he went on, had nothing to do with us, because there was a real problem with his mother; we just needed to be patient, until her rage subsided and everything was all right again.

I was not sure how to take all this – whether in terms of the announcement of the date of the holidays, or of the subsequent void to be filled with books, and hence of his rage and spite – but this was also Carlo's first gesture of autonomy towards his mother and towards myself. I decided to bide my time, leaving "the problem outside the field" for the moment. In the next session, Carlo told me about

Caravaggio's *Madonna and Child*, a painting with an idyllic atmosphere, adding that he would like a submissive girlfriend who would put up with anything from him and "suck his cock".[3] "Oh, no," I said to myself, "that is too much." I realized that he wanted me to be silent . . . that the penis in the mouth was not an erotic penis but the Mafia's "stone in the mouth" to make people keep quiet . . . It was a device to stop me talking and spoiling the idyll. I was also afraid to broach the subject of the delayed payment again, because I was familiar with Carlo's fits of anger and his drinking bouts resulting from mingled pain and rage; however, I decided that I could not remain silent and focused on what I felt to be unavoidable: the delay in payment and his wish for me to be silent and submissive. He lost his temper, telling me that what I had said was completely off the point, and the session ended with references to Pacciani, the "monster of Florence", and another famous murderer who had killed his wife with a hatchet. I was anxious and concerned, prepared for more fireworks in the following session.

Next time, Carlo lay down on the couch and immediately said that he felt very well and indeed quite calm, or rather, that he had left me on the previous day quite upset, but had had a dream that night that had restored his tranquillity and trust. It went as follows. The anti-Mafia police had plucked up the courage to go to a Mafia cemetery and exhume things that had been buried there. The cemetery was like the ones you saw in westerns. What they exhumed was a long black bird, perhaps called a "paradise weaver".[4] He had been terrified, but gradually regained his courage. Then the scene changed: a friend of his father's was using a grader to clear big blocks of stone from a road that was under construction, smoothing the way for the tar spreaders to move in . . . He associated with a painting of two capercaillies by the Sicilian artist Migneco.

Working with him, I found it easy to get to the root of the dream. By speaking to me, he had broken the conspiracy of silence and disobeyed the Mafia's injunction to keep quiet. The stone and the genitals in the mouth were precisely a part of Mafia rituals; we had smoothed out the field and removed the blocks to communication, even if he was afraid that this might involve exhuming the hatchet of war and unleashing a ferocious battle like a fight between capercaillies. He was relieved and pleased that previously inaccessible meanings could now be negotiated.

Narrative interpretations

So-called *narrative interpretations* occupy an intermediate position along the PS–D axis; they belong to PS by virtue of the unsaturated form of their presentation, but also have aspects of D, because they already define an image.

These are the interpretations most clearly assignable to row "C" of the grid; they often stem from α elements, as the fruit of reverie (or of relational dreams in the analyst's here and now), and most obviously partake of Bion's "extension in the domain of myth" (Bion, 1963), concerning which he was later to write: "Which story is one to tell? [. . .] This is where the analyst has to be an artist – he has to make constructions of what is going on" (Bion, 1987).

Mario's lifebuoys

Having had the traumatic experience of losing both parents in a car accident when she was a little girl, and not yet capable of affective cathexes because of the resulting terror, Lodovica was able to tell of all this, and other things too, through a character, "Mario" (with whom she had some kind of relationship), whose characteristic feature was that he had lots and lots of affective stories, none of which could become either prevalent or significant. One day she said that the people with whom Mario had these stories were for him like lifebuoys to cling to.

I responded: "So he is like a survivor of a shipwreck who is so afraid of risking another sinking that he prefers to keep his head above water – and paradoxically in safety – by a system with lots and lots of lifebuoys, rather than sailing off in a new ship."

On the one hand, this interpretation defined a possible story (a possible narration or transformation), so that it was saturated, but, on the other, it left the patient free to accept it, reject it, or accept part of it, perhaps in a way we might not expect.

Furthermore, it was the fruit of the relationship; arising like a reverie in the session, it was therefore the offspring of waking dream thought, drawing on a model created without memory or desire, and not resulting from the use of saturated theories in the session. It might be a prelude to transformations in "O".

Transformations

In this section I shall attempt an arbitrary extrapolation of the theses put forward in *Transformations* (Bion, 1965) and a description of their clinical applications from the vertex of the operations performed by the analyst in the session.

Rigid-motion transformations

The analyst may work in the field of *rigid-motion transformations* – those in which the starting figure is readily recognizable owing to its high level of invariance (Bion, 1965) – which are observed whenever, for example, we draw close to a split or bring some of the patient's communications into the transference. Such operations may in my view be very useful to the analyst, because they have the potential to generate a basic relationality comparable to a trapeze artist's safety net.

In *Transformations*, Bion gives the example of a patient's feelings of exclusion at the weekend, which he connects with exclusion from the primal scene, accompanied by all the associated emotions: "The feelings and ideas appropriate to infantile sexuality and the Oedipus complex and its off-shoots are *transferred*, with a wholeness and coherence that is characteristic, to the relationship with the analyst" (Bion, 1965).

Projective transformations

The analyst's operations of *projective transformation* are different again. Here there is less invariance, and they are less easily recognizable as transformations than the previous type. They often stem from reverie, from the opening up of new vistas of meaning; and they have their origins in an operational model in the field, rather than in a theory.

In Bion's famous example, a patient says "Ice-cream", the cold of which he interprets as keeping back the violent emotion of "I scream". In projective transformations, "Tp β appears to require two personalities, an object into which something is to be projected and an object responsible for the projection" (Bion, 1965).

"Signora" or "S'ignora"?[5]

This example is taken from a difficult juncture in Mauro's analysis, one of the problems being the preservation of the setting, because he would skip sessions on a variety of pretexts.

A "Signora" with whom he had embarked on a satisfying sexual relationship took the stage more and more frequently. He found this worrying because it distanced him from Marta, a girl with whom he had gradually built up a tender and constructive affective relationship.

For a long time I did not know how to "take" this Signora, whom I felt to be present alongside other possible vertices, as if connected with something inherent in the analysis, which had to be somewhere, in some form of relationship or non-relationship, inside the room. In our dialogues, I therefore always let her remain the "Signora", although I was increasingly struck by the fact that she was never called by her name.

I gradually became aware of the lack of direct responses to my communications about cancelled sessions and to the announcement of the dates of my summer holidays; and, meanwhile, the setting became more and more unstable, with sessions being skipped, although everything else was seemingly going well.

This went on until, one session, upon the *n*th entrance of the "Signora", it suddenly occurred to me that there was another way of hearing these syllables, namely "S'ignora" or "Si ignora" ["not knowing" or "he does not know himself"]. This reverie seemed to afford a way of organizing all the problems of this period – the appearance on the stage of his *not knowing* the feelings activated within him by some of my communications, the wounds to which these gave rise, the consequent rage and the underlying pain; it certainly all added up, but in subterranean form, for, although not known, these matters found expression in disturbances of the setting.

Mauro was very struck by the interpretation of "S'ignora/Signora" and immediately said that his "non s'ignora" ["not not knowing"] and "nossignora" ["no, madam" or "no way"] – i.e. his protests – had now multiplied; he then told me how he had recently begun to toy with the idea of breaking off the therapy; by "Signora-izing" everything, he could only have ended up with an "outburst" whereby he would no longer have come ... I think it important to listen to every single communication in the field, until we find the ones capable of organizing new directions of thought.

Sara's "down"

Sara was a young psychiatrist who brought narcissistic material. At a certain point I felt that I could clearly demonstrate her constantly hidden and disavowed needs to her. In one session she brought a dream, in which a haircut revealed splinters of glass or crystals on her head; then a girlfriend wanted to have a fifth session, but was afraid of giving birth to a Down's syndrome baby . . .

It was easy for me to tell her that this reminded me of the cutting of Samson's hair: without the strength of Samson, she would be put in touch with her fragility, which terrified her, making her fear that she might need a fifth session and be at risk of a breakdown.

She replied that, that morning, her daughter Maria had had a terrible fit of jealousy because her brother had successfully performed a task before her; she had slammed the door in fury, but had then managed it herself and been pleased. In the same way, "Sara" could now experience jealousy if I were to tell her things she had not yet thought – without any longer saying "I knew that already" or feeling bad, because she was now capable of experiencing and metabolizing an emotion.

Transformations in K

Transformations in K are ones that include a link of knowledge, albeit without activating catastrophic changes – for which they may, however, pave the way. "[. . .] transformations in K are feared when they threaten the emergence of transformations in O. This can be restated as fear when $T\alpha \to T\beta = K \to O$" (Bion, 1965).

The photograph of the ingredients

After a session in which I had interpreted some of a male patient's needs correctly but had not been sufficiently available for receiving and transforming his projective identifications, he dreamed that he had received a photograph which was of no use to him and which he certainly could not eat, whereas he had brought a lady some ingredients for a meal which were depicted in the photograph but had not been cleaned and cooked and were ultimately not usable (inappropriate interpretation).

Later, at the beginning of a session, the same patient said that his mother had been wearing the same clothes for quite a while, that she would not tolerate a puppy at home but was only prepared to accept a well-behaved big dog, and that his father had a detached retina. I felt it insufficient to interpret the patient's fear that I had for a while not been available to his more infantile parts, that I was saying the same things and had blind spots, but instead thought it necessary to allow myself to be helped by him – my "best colleague" – to understand in what respect, from *his point of view*, I was not functioning properly (Bezoari & Ferro, 1994b).

The missing dream

Erminia's analysis was difficult, based as it was for a long time on "official relations". I had for a while been reflecting on the lack of warmth and closeness in an analysis in which the patient seemed to me to be "defending herself" powerfully and in which everything was unclear, when Erminia brought a dream: as if in a western, settlers surrounded themselves with wagons to defend against an Indian attack. Then there was a girl in a darkish, rather cold room, looking in a mirror that cast a dim reflection of her.

The dreams seemed consistent with my feeling about the analysis, and I proceeded as follows. The first dream evidently hinted at a situation in which it was necessary to defend oneself, and the second to something unclear, with few connotations; above all, however, it seemed to me that a third dream was missing – one with a climate of warmth, of non-dangerous and non-detached involvement. Perhaps, I said, if a friend were to ask her what analysis was, she might answer: "It is a place where you have to defend yourself, where things are not very clear, and where someone casts back a dim image of you, but it is certainly not a place that is affectionate or warm."

"How strange," she answered, "that makes me think of my father, who often used to travel abroad, and what I liked most about him was that he always showed me that he was thinking of me and had me in his mind in a way that was entirely his own: he never used to buy me toys in Italy – after all, they were available here for the taking – but, whenever he crossed the border, he would unexpectedly bring me something that had not yet arrived in Italy, and in this way he used to show me that he was thinking of me even when we were not together."

Transformations in "O" and catastrophic change

These are the transformations that involve a sudden leap in mental growth, which is achieved by way of a crisis that may sometimes even include short periods of depersonalization. Characteristic features of catastrophic change are violence and subversion of the system or of the existing structure and invariance, as a process of transformation (Grinberg *et al.*, 1991) – and, for the analyst, awareness of the emotion of being unable to spare himself or his patient an experience of "catastrophic" truth. "Transformations in O contrast with other transformations in that the former are related to growth in becoming and the latter to growth in 'knowing about' growth" (Bion, 1965). Resistance to an interpretation is therefore resistance to the change from K to O. Such a change is "of particular concern to the analyst in his function of aiding maturation of the personalities of his patients" (Bion, 1965).

The world of Daniela

Carla had gone into analysis owing to "panic attacks". After a great deal of work, two characters took the stage. Together with her new boyfriend, "Francesco", whom she trusted and loved, there was a teenage girl, Daniela, whom she had met in hospital, befriended, and was increasingly taking care of, and who was gradually becoming more and more significant.

The panic attacks characteristically came out of the blue, disrupting Carla's normal activities, but she nevertheless resumed her studies, graduated, got officially engaged to Francesco and was planning to marry him. She also started working on a small scale. The panic attacks were always completely unexpected and involved terror, sweating, vertigo, fear of fainting, tachycardia and extrasystoles.

They began to make their appearance in the sessions too, increasingly taking the form of "panic attacks of the heart", which put her more in touch with emotions that had been unexpectedly activated. Any change in the setting – any slight difference, such as a new rug at the entrance, or an armchair or seat slightly out of place – would trigger a panic attack. This put me in mind of the agglutinated nucleus and its activation by the slightest departure from the normal conditions of the setting (Bleger, 1967).

In her old family house, Carla then found an "iron[6] key", thought by some antique dealers to be a few centuries old, which would probably unlock a door in some unexplored vaults underneath a wing of the property. She loved exploring with her boyfriend.

I noticed, too, that when Carla entered the consulting room, she would note every detail and smell, as if searching for traces of something. I managed to refrain from interpreting, sensing as I did that something important was taking shape. The focus of attention shifted to Daniela and her hospitalization for a brain operation. Carla described Daniela's pathology to me: she was a prey to constant panic and terror; she had to check everything; and she would resort to avoidance behaviour, because the slightest stimulus, or any unexpected change or emotion, would unleash unspeakable terror in her.

At this point I felt the time had come to draw all the threads together: now that she trusted me, as she did her boyfriend, she really could use the "iron [*ferro*] key" to explore her vaults, in which she could make contact with her most catastrophic anxieties – for "Daniela" was nothing other than the *way* she was able to tell both me and herself of her panic and terror.

Carla's response to my interpretation was extremely powerful: she had an experience of bodily transformation, for a few moments living and feeling herself to be Daniela, with Daniela's face, and discovered and recognized all Daniela's states to be her own.

This ushered in a fruitful period of work, during which Carla's life in the outside world rid itself of terrors and fears, which increasingly found their way into the analysis.

Note that there are infinite possible ways of combining the position of an interpretation along the PS–D axis with its position in the field of transformations.

Applying the grid to interpretations, we can undertake a large number of exercises involving all the other interpretations that could have been, or all the different ways of categorizing one and the same interpretation – but this we already know (Bion, 1965).

There is no one criterion for choosing among the various possible interpretations; what matters is the compositional aspect of the interpretation and the end-product of a fabric of dialogue and emotions that in turn stems from the intersection of several types of "points". This must lead to a narrative harmony (or disharmony) capable of giving rise to the following evolution: $\beta \rightarrow \alpha \rightarrow$ dream thoughts $\rightarrow$ thoughts. "Ideally the analyst should be in the state of mind presented by C3, C4, C5 and D3, D4, D5 [. . .]. Furthermore, the field in which he has to observe the relationship of one phenomenon to another is unlimited in extent, and yet none of the phenomena 'in' that field can be ignored because all interact" (Bion, 1965).

The motorcycle accident

At the end of a session Stefano brought a dream, in which he was riding a motorcycle dangerously, causing it to rear up and being very frightened in consequence. I had no time to think about the dream, but merely wondered whether it was a reference to the way he used me – a token of minor but recurring accidents in the setting.

In another session, not long before the summer holidays, Stefano was in a state of high anxiety, the panic attacks that had disappeared from the scene some time ago having returned. At the end of the session, after threatening suicide, he asked if he could have an extra session on the following day. I did not have a free hour, and in any case saw no point in this modification of the setting.

Stefano arrived for the next session very upset; refusing to enter the consulting room, he told me in the waiting room that his cousin's car had knocked down a young motorcyclist, who was at his last gasp in hospital . . . Perhaps some of his organs would be removed for transplantation. The cousin had a vertebral fracture and could have ended up paralysed, but this had fortunately not happened. It had not been his fault; he had had the right of way, but the motorcyclist, riding very dangerously, had blocked his path.

The patient's anxiety was manifest. He then attacked me for not giving him the extra session. I said that what he had told me was terrible and that I understood that he might feel that the "rules" of analysis were inhuman and fear that he did not matter to me.

At this point he agreed to enter the consulting room. As soon as I sat down in my armchair, I had an intuition, which I offered the patient: might his story be – partly – the continuation of the dream of the motorcyclist? Had he not felt himself die, upset as he was at my refusal to give him the extra session? Had he not thought of breaking off the analysis and letting other people have his sessions (the organ transplant)? And did he not think that it was basically he himself who caused accidents by his frequent attempts to break the setting?

In reply he brought a dream, in which a boy told him that he should have noticed that he had a nasty, belligerent character, adding that he had failed to tell me that the neurosurgeon at the hospital to which the accident victim had been taken had persuaded his family to allow him to operate; although this was a very risky undertaking, it seemed as though the young man's life might thereby be saved.

In the same way, it might be possible to save Stefano's analysis, as well as to reflect on his dangerous and rebellious forms of behaviour with me in the consulting room and in his relations with everyone else in the outside world.

A dream

A dream proved vital to the further metabolization of Mara's anxieties in the third year of her analysis. In it, as she was entering a peaceful room, all of a sudden monsters came out of cracks in the wall; although it turned out that they were made of foam rubber, they were still dangerous . . . They started shooting . . . and if you were hit, you were infected with a virus . . . You had to be kept in isolation . . . She had woken in terror, but fallen asleep again in the hope of coping with the situation . . . and, as soon as she was asleep, the dream had continued. She confronted the monsters; she could not remember how, but had done so together with her boyfriend, and the monsters dissolved. *After a short silence*, I was about to open my mouth when I saw that Mara's expression had changed and her face was contorted. I asked her what was happening. "Nothing . . . nothing . . . Or rather, it is like this . . . I thought I was really pleased to have told you the dream and to be here, so pleased that I would have liked to come into your arms . . . but that is not possible in analysis . . . I felt disappointed, wounded, humiliated and on the point of tears."

I told her that she had the opportunity here of experiencing the dream "live". Here there was peace and pleasure . . . But then the "monster" was activated: the "crack" of my short silence was enough to make her fear that her burst of communication was not being received and that I was keeping her at a distance. The monster was the fear of rejection by me . . . It was a "foam rubber" monster from her childhood . . . but by together confronting this terror of being rejected and not wanted, we could defeat it and make it disappear.

Mara then calmed down. In the rest of the session, it became possible for her to see other "monsters" that had been activated. We also understood how she had tried to ward off being "infected" by the monsters through avoidance behaviour or the magic annihilation of negative thoughts that came into her mind about me or the analysis; these had entered the analysis originally in the form of an account of a friend's avoidance behaviour, and later in the consulting room itself in the form of parts of the room with which Mara had to take care to avoid any contact, making strange detours in order to reach the couch. It was now possible to confront these monsters and discover their infantile roots.

A long period of work on the "monsters" – all the emotions aroused by any interruption of communication – thus ensued.

If anything sounded like a criticism to her, or if she thought she had criticized me, she was afraid that we might hate each other and tear one another to pieces, as in a drawing of two cats ripping each other apart that she brought me: all that was left was a tail, and that was the end of the story. Everything then had to be gone back over again.

So it was every time emotions were aroused: whether jealousy or hate, or indeed also love and passion, all were at first extremely dangerous monsters, feared not to have any "limits", except that, from time to time, she might discover that they could be confronted and metabolized.

Symbiosis – or rather, the old wish for symbiosis – was seen as a protection from these terrors: a dream demonstrated the need *to construct a stomach to digest fiery food*, to allow affects and feelings to emerge from the cracks instead of the former swirling vortices of emotion (Bezoari & Ferro, 1991b).

A convent or container for Marcella

Marcella began her session by saying that she was furious with her husband for behaving very badly with two female friends she had invited the night before. First he had remarked on the short stature of Maria, and then, disregarding the sensibilities of Franca, a "Lombard League"[7] type with a liking for "cold countries", who was very formal, modest and serious in her mode of speech and came from an extremely religious family, he had got over-familiar with Maria, even holding hands with her on the couch. She had been offended and then mortified by Franca's visible embarrassment.

I could not fail to remember the previous session, in which the patient had been in effect mortified by my "coming towards her",[8] at least on the level of speech, by acceding to her request for a "short" week until her son was bigger, after which we had lingered in a climate of greater warmth and closeness, which, it had seemed to me, the patient was now able to tolerate – but I had manifestly not allowed for "Franca", who was also there on the couch.

I had in fact made soft, narrative interpretations, based on television programmes, and even mentioned a joke to clarify the problem. She added that she had been very angry with her husband because "overdoing things was crippling"; he had been like a gardener who might have scorched a plant by giving it too much fertilizer. Of course, problems of technique arose – for example, how to understand "Maria" and "Franca". These were certainly split-off parts of the patient, but equally forms of functioning that might be assumed by the field. I could interpret direct, play with the characters, refer back to the previous day, or not. Since the analysis was at an advanced stage, I explained everything in transference terms, linking up with the previous session and the various ways in which I had felt my approach to be familiar – perhaps too much so.

After a moment's silence, the patient replied: "You know what? My husband has decided to ruin our holiday by taking his father and mother along. The holiday will be a real bore."

The transference-based intervention had given rise to the "mother and father" characters, who were boring and serious.

I said that I no longer knew how to dress: whatever clothes I chose, they were wrong. If I let myself go, she was outraged, but if I was serious, she got bored. She answered that I needed a striped suit, and immediately added: "I was just thinking that my in-laws might not come after all, and that Sicily is very beautiful, with lots of bright colours, and surely very lush."

The session went on – but my main concern was to demonstrate the formation in the field of the characters who told of the problems of the field itself: here the issues were affection, lack of self-control, a rigid container . . . and all this would have to be worked on by way of the transformations that would be activated in the field.

Transformations in hallucinosis

I have already (in Chapter 2) discussed the constant risk run by the analyst of unwittingly bringing about transformations of the patient's attempted communications in hallucinosis. "The realizations which form the background of hallucinosis differ from those that form the background in the domain of accepted frustration. [. . .] The conflict can be described as a disagreement on the respective virtues of a transformation in hallucinosis and a transformation in psycho-analysis" (Bion, 1965).

Narrative transformations

I discussed these in Chapter 3. Corrao (1991) described them in detail in a fundamental contribution in which he says that truth is intrinsic to the narrated construction rather than attributed to events; truth is the structure of subjective experience rather than the character of objective registrations. Corrao, too, emphasizes that epistemologies based on the principle of uncertainty may result from an ethical evolution of man whereby he is increasingly prepared to relinquish his hubris, his cognitive arrogance.

Notes

1 [Translator's note: This play on words appears in the section on Gianluca in Chapter 1: *tubicino* is a cannula and *tu vicino* means "you are near".]
2 By analogy with "weak thought" (Vattimo, 1983).
3 [Translator's note: Literally "bird".]
4 [Translator's note: Literally "paradise widow".]
5 [Translator's note: A play on words: "Signora" means "lady" and "S'ignora" means "not knowing" or "he does not know himself".]
6 [Translator's note: "Iron" is *ferro* in Italian, and Ferro is of course also the author's name.]
7 [Translator's note: A "cold northern" type.]
8 [Translator's note: That is, accommodating her.]

Chapter 5

The impasse
Hansel, Gretel and the witch in the oven

For the sake of brevity, I shall not consider the classical conceptions of the impasse, a full treatment of which may be found in the excellent survey by Etchegoyen (1986), who also discusses its similarities with and differences from the "negative therapeutic reaction" and "reversible perspective", but shall instead proceed immediately to examine the views closest to my own approach.

Baranger & Baranger (1961–62) and Baranger, Baranger & Mom (1983) deem a certain degree of impasse to be physiological; this is inherent in the concept of the "bulwark", or blind area of the couple that forms periodically, from which the analyst must stand back so that he can take a "second look" at it and hence identify, describe and resolve the phenomenon, which he himself has helped to bring about.

The result is a continuous, repeated cycle of oscillation of unimpeded developments in the couple's progression – bulwark – second look – new developments. If a bulwark goes unrecognized for a long time, it will ultimately give rise to an impasse situation (Baranger & Baranger, 1964).

Another interesting approach to the impasse is Steinert's (1987) notion of an "organization" that forms as a kind of redoubt in which the patient seeks refuge from excessively powerful persecutory or depressive anxieties which, if not recognized – something that may require prolonged countertransference suffering, as this author describes in detail – lead to situations of deadlock.

Personally, however, I am inclined to see the "organization" as a more explicitly couple-related problem, bearing witness to the formation of an area shared between patient and analyst which protects them from persecutory or depressive anxieties that cannot, at least at this juncture, be tolerated by either on the level of thought.

The Hansel and Gretel story in my view closely parallels what happens between two minds blocked in an impasse, which is actually protecting them from the risk of confronting over-violent emotions.

After Hansel and Gretel are captured, they are put in a cage and fattened up for the witch to devour. Hansel has the idea of presenting a chicken bone to the witch when she periodically reaches into the cage to test how much fat they have put on, to make her think they are still too lean for her to eat. Here we have a description of the avoidance of a danger, in which the claustrophilia of the cage saves those within from being devoured by uncontainable anxieties split off outside the cage (and hence rendered unthinkable and unshareable).

However, the story also includes the moment when it becomes possible to hurl the "witch" into the oven; applied to the impasse situation, this would mean that β elements feared incapable of metabolization can find an α function (oven) whereby they can be transformed into thoughts.

A mythological parallel to the impasse situation is the call to Ulysses to take up arms and depart for the Trojan war (this is also an example of pathomimia, in which the subject uses "illness" as a protection from excessive persecution feelings, as with a patient who would rather remain ill than confront the "depressive anxiety" that must be negotiated if healing is to be achieved (Money-Kyrle, 1977)). When the envoys of Menelaus arrive, they find Ulysses feigning madness by ploughing the sandy beach. The messengers decide to test his insanity by placing the infant Telemachus in the path of the plough. Ulysses has no choice but to stop ploughing, come to his senses and leave for the war.

Finally, "war", as the necessary consequence of (and condition for) release from the cage of any kind of impasse, features again in Thomas Mann's novel *The Magic Mountain*, which also describes the progressive espousal by the unforgettable main character, Hans Castorp, of the pleasure of being ill, and hence of being looked after and treated; my patient Carlo explicitly drew my attention to this aspect.

I contend that such behaviour, in the form of the mental functioning of the couple, is much more common in analysis than might at first be thought, and that it in fact puts a "full stop" to many analyses (although it may also become the point at which the analysis restarts). This is because the couple thereby constructs for itself a claustrophilic cage (Fachinelli, 1983), to avoid confronting mental aspects which are so primitive and split off that analyst and patient fear they are tantamount to "war" and being devoured (i.e. overwhelmed); hence the status quo of the cage, of ploughing infertile sand, of an idealized magic-mountain treatment, is preferred to conflict, to destructuring or, at least, to the terrifying encounter with archaic contents of the two minds (the witch).

The impasse could in these circumstances also be seen as a waiting time, during which the couple equip themselves to confront the risks entailed by explicit resumption of the work.

Responsibility for such events cannot therefore readily be assigned to either member of the couple, because both minds are in fact profoundly involved.

Any interpretation that holds the patient responsible for – if not indeed guilty of – creating the impasse (in terms of his masochism, guilt, attacks on growth, perversion, envy, etc.) will prove ineffective in resolving it. As someone says in one of Bion's *Discussions* (1978), "I haven't seen any studies about the overwhelming fear that may be operating in the therapist"; and it is only by recognizing and negotiating this terror (i.e. the terror in the analyst's mind – not only that resulting from his own archaic zones but also that induced by the patient) that a way out of the impasse can be found. In the process, it is important for us not to defend against these feelings of terror, panic and persecution by the use of over-rigid models.

In undertaking an analysis, we are, as Winnicott (1965) reminds us, entitled to remain alive; in other words, we cannot be required to expose ourselves to more than a certain degree of destructuring, anxiety and risk – including, on occasion, physical risk – but, equally, it is up to us not to resort "excessively" to false maps for representing these as yet unexplored lands.

Emergence from the cage, descent from the magic mountain, or stopping the plough of pseudo-sessions often exposes not only the patient but also ourselves to suffering, mourning and pain, and ultimately, if we – the analyst or the patient and the analysis – have survived, to a whole range of potential fruitful developments.

From this point of view, even an impasse may be positive if it is experienced as the "time" necessary for gaining access to underlying anxieties and terrors. In this way split-off anxieties that have remained outside the field may be transformed and rendered thinkable. The parallel in the Hansel and Gretel story is when the witch is cast into the oven, enabling these split-off anxieties from outside the field to be "cooked" – i.e. transformed – and made thinkable. If this is not possible, they may at least be circumvented (Sarno, 1989), as with Ulysses's "Nobody" idea, which allowed him to escape undevoured from the cave of the Cyclops Polyphemus.

It is often the patient who takes it upon himself to draw attention to the impasse. For example, when the nine-year-old Renato told me about a car he had seen parked with its engine running and lights on but with no one inside, I was led to reflect on an analysis that was seemingly in motion but in fact not getting anywhere.

I also recall a patient's image of a hamster in a cage toiling away to no effect (Maldonado, 1984); a similar image was brought by Stefania at a difficult point in her analysis, before a dream opened a vista on to a terrifying primitive territory represented by "Mongolia".

On other occasions, a countertransference dream may warn us that, despite appearances, something is wrong – for, in my view, the most serious impasse situations are ones that convey an impression of movement, and where interpretations of content suggest that something is being done, whereas in fact the couple are merely marking time, as Maldonado demonstrates in detail in his recent contributions (1984, 1987, 1989).

I should now like to present some clinical illustrations of different levels of impasse, some of which even have positive aspects (to paraphrase the title of a paper by Limentani (1981) on the negative therapeutic reaction).

The impasse as the time needed to metabolize "bulwarks"

It takes a long time – in some cases a very long time – for it to become possible to metabolize primitive mental states that must be owned and undergo subterranean transformations in order to become thinkable and expressible in words.

A 30-year-old male patient, Fabrizio, who was seemingly a paragon of efficiency, made me feel quite drowsy from the very beginning of the analysis; indeed, I must confess that my lethargy was so intense that I sometimes fell into a deep sleep, if only for a few seconds.

However, this realization was already a step along the road. It took time for me to become conscious of the explicit causation. I noticed first that I felt sleepy in Fabrizio's sessions, but, owing to the post-prandial hour, I attributed this sensation to my "digestive difficulties". Eventually I began to reflect on the nature of the "digestive difficulty"; in my soporific state, I started thinking about papers on the "living dead", "sleeping objects" and "zombies". Then I secretly gave Fabrizio the nickname of "Vim", because at home he obsessively cleaned everything with this product, just as he cleaned up any emotion that might develop in the sessions. It took me even more time to realize that the Vim used in the session was precisely the lethargy that Fabrizio induced in me, just as he managed the most primitive emotions inside himself by putting them to sleep, although he was totally unaware of doing so.

Gradually dreams began to tell us of this unthought world and of the terrible emotions, or rather emotional turbulences, within it. In one particular dream reminiscent of a Michael Jackson video, living-dead zombie figures emerged from the tarred road surface, apparently awakening to the sound of music and following him; this was paralleled by dream fragments of my own in the sessions, featuring dinosaurs, prehistoric animals and zombies.

Then came highly split-off emotions: the ghetto for handicapped people where he worked, in which everyone was crammed full of neuroleptic and hypnotic drugs; the "afternoons with psychotic children"; the violent, irrational feelings of a friend who virtually became the patient's double . . . And, one day, he brought a dream in which the net that had served as a wall in the path linking two houses was torn down, leaving only hedges, which, however, had some gaps that allowed the passage of small animals – dogs – from one side to the other . . .

From then on it gradually became possible to negotiate and verbalize recognizable and describable emotional states. In addition to the Godzilla and King Kong of some of his dreams, we had travellers' tales set in prehistoric worlds – showing that, as if in a science fiction story, we had built the time machine whereby we could voyage from the present of rationality and efficiency to the present of deeper emotional states.

The impasse and avoidance of mourning

I should now like to describe a period of impasse that preceded the termination of my first patient's analysis (Ferro, 1993e).

The woman patient concerned, Mariella, had had a major psychotic breakdown when, at the school where she worked, she had been called upon to look after a child severely disabled by encephalitis, so that she could no longer be with the other children, who meant a great deal to her. That was the situation as she initially presented it. Years of negotiation of persecutory and erotized delusions were followed by very painful but fertile insights that enabled her to gain access to suffering parts of herself that she had always looked after "in others".

She had given up work on commencing her analysis, but when she resumed, she no longer looked after special needs but instead taught "normal children". Mariella's relationship with her husband improved, and her dreams began to indicate that she was achieving her existential aims. However, the "handicapped child" of the early days of the analysis reappeared in her stories.

As stated, I was not yet ready to mourn for what could not be accomplished (following completion of the work that had enabled the patient to lead a satisfactory mental life) and wanted – if only unconsciously – the "handicapped child" too to be transformed, together with certain of Mariella's ways of managing her more primitive passions (which she sometimes "froze" instead of being inflamed by them). For this reason, I pressed on.

At this point "rejection" made its appearance ("I feel that you are rejecting me"; "My husband tells me: 'You must not be as you are, but as I want you to be'"), followed by tokens of the erotized transference. For a few months we continued to work on the theme of "rejection", which I tried to pick up in every way I could, but to no avail. Countertransference dreams helped me to perceive and "cook" the "rejection" we had run up against and to reconsider Mariella's initial situation of "wanting to stop" working with the encephalitis-disabled child so as to "leave space for other children".

At this point it was I who had to mourn for my therapeutic ambitions and accept the idea of terminating the analysis. My "throttling back" of the therapeutic thrust was quickly rewarded: the patient stopped feeling herself to be the "prisoner of a project of mine" and resumed work, in particular on the affects involved in her relationship with her "husband" (myself in the transference); and eventually she requested a date for termination. The actual termination was preceded by dreams indicating that she had introjected the analytic function, featuring "a lady" and then "a woman friend" who helped and advised her and showed her the way when there was no more analysis. The introjection, it seemed, was firmly established by a dream of an island with a "little iron[1] temple" that was solid and robust, with deep foundations capable of withstanding "perhaps even the most violent of flood tides".

The work done was in effect summarized and confirmed by the story of a cat, Mamy, from one of her last sessions. "At the end of the Second World War, Milan railway station was invaded by huge numbers of greedy mice that had consumed everything down to the electrical cables, causing short circuits and paralysing the station. The railwaymen had the idea of using cats to get rid of the mice. This enormous labour gradually succeeded, and as their work came to an end, the cats left the station one after another – all, that is, except for Mamy, who stayed in Cubicle C, keeping watch in case the mice returned. Many years later, after the railwaymen had grown very fond of Mamy, he died, but his memory remains alive to this day, because he had been awarded a certificate of merit, which is now displayed on the wall of the stationmaster's office."

In my view, this story revisits the psychotic breakdown (short circuits) caused by the irruption of the split-off parts (mice); the work of reclamation–digestion performed by the analysis (cats) under the responsibility of the analyst (Ferro-viere[2]); introjection of the analytic function with the necessary watchfulness (the cat Mamy); gratitude (the certificate); and mourning.

Reflecting on my doubts about ending this analysis, I realize that I failed to pick up the many signals reaching me from the patient: the dream in which she was tired of going to the dressmaker because she had learned to sew herself; the need to resign herself to the death of the aged grandmother who had lived and built things in her life; the dream of the washing machine that was liable to burn out if left on for too long, even if switching it off necessarily meant that the washing would not be perfectly clean; etc. However, another reason why I found it difficult to finish this first analysis of mine was, I believe, that I wanted a "complete analysis" rather than one that was "feasible"; on the other hand, in "my" suffering over this termination, I may perhaps have been caught up in the patient's projective identifications as she struggled to separate (this was suggested by a dream of drug addicts who had to have their "fix" at all costs).

The approach of the termination date gave rise to profound mourning for our separation, appreciation of the work done, and joy at the capacity to experience her own feelings. In her last session, Mariella told me that at first she had always come to Pavia by herself, but now she knew nearly everyone waiting for the train on the station platform, as well as many of the passengers in her compartment, with whom she spoke freely. This I took to mean that she had acquired both knowledge of herself and the freedom to allow internal communication between different parts of her mind.

It is of course with seriously ill patients (and the psychotic parts of every patient) that we are constantly exposed to the greatest difficulties; however, this does not mean that the "terror" of negotiating certain mental states can always be confronted. As an alternative, or pending the possibility of negotiating as yet dark and blind areas of our minds and of the relationship with the patient, we can rely on our ability to patiently experience apparent standstill situations, beneath which the minds concerned are often constantly toiling in an attempt to metabolize as yet excessively intense anxieties. The implication where the impasse is concerned might be the need to negotiate countertransference micropsychoses (cf. Baranger & Baranger).

The "organization", the "bulwark" and even the "countertransference" are ultimately not so inaccessible after all. This is because the patient constantly performs a certain function, namely that of drawing our attention at all times, from vertices unknown to us, to what is happening in the depths of the couple's functioning (Bion, 1983) through all the characters and narrations he may from time to time present, which we should think of not so much in historical terms or as split-off parts of one or other of the protagonists, but as explanatory syntheses of the functioning assumed by the couple and the field from a particular vertex (of which we are unaware) at that time (Bezoari & Ferro, 1991b; Ferro, 1992).

Hence it is not the right interpretation but our internal transformational suffering that will allow the metabolization of the projective identifications which paralyse us. This work may be slow, laborious and often painful: the "betaloma" (Barale & Ferro, 1992), or lumps of β elements inconsistent with thought, is here accepted, digested, transformed and where possible broken down into a narration that can be assimilated by the patient.

For the primitive parts of the personality, it is often insufficient to feel and interpret one's own needs. These must instead find a satisfactory "emotional realization" (♀ ♂), whereby we show the patient a model of mental functioning and relationship that he will be able to introject.

Attention must therefore be concentrated on the micro-process level of the sessions (Nissim, 1984), for the "micrometry" of the session is the significant locus of every transformation. In this model, pride of place is assumed by projective identifications, understood in the strong, relational sense (Bion, 1962; Ogden, 1979; Baranger & Baranger, 1961–62), for their interplay will allow a constant exchange of emotional elements, which, as they gradually become verbalizable, will thereby find a privileged channel for transformation and expression. Projective identifications establish the strong, subterranean status of the couple, which will then be enabled, through the medium of dreams, memories and anecdotes, to narrate what is occurring in the depths of the relational exchange (Di Chiara, 1992).

As Bion (1978) pointed out, thinking is a new function of living matter, so that not all the most primitive emotions of the minds concerned can be transformed into thought; moreover, any such transformation has a high cost in terms of psychic suffering (Lussana, 1992; Tagliacozzo, 1982). The primitive parts must gain access to symbolization there in the consulting room, and this task sometimes exceeds our emotional capacity (Gesué, 1995). What we perhaps share most with our patients is the avoidance of mental pain beyond a certain threshold and the search for acceptable defences or solutions; after all, as noted above, no one has made a study of the terror the analyst may feel when overtaxed (Bion, 1978).

Then there is the aspect of micro-impasses in the session and how they are overcome or, alternatively, clump together to produce total deadlock. "Why does someone wake up in the morning, switch on the light, strike a match, go to the window and jump?" Laura asked me half-way through a session. Her brother had put this riddle to her and then left. She would have no peace until she found the answer. I did not know the riddle. I evaded her questions with all the interpretations and dodges known to me, but Laura's anxiety only intensified. I did not know how to respond; I felt in the dark, desperate, devoid of answers. "Because the person was blind," I found myself saying, "just as you now feel deprived of light because I did not understand how worried you are about my being away shortly." Only then did Laura tell me of the suicide she had planned down to the smallest detail, convinced as she was of my failure to understand her anxiety; only now did she tell me dreams in which she was tied to the couch with mice gnawing at her brain, or in which she was being flayed, "losing her skin", and a kitten was being dismembered. The next day she brought another dream in which a boxer puppy found a place on the mummy boxer's belly: she had "never seen anything like it".

The following brief examples will further clarify what I mean by working in the micrometry of the session.

After several interpretations of mine that had exacted a high emotional price from her, a young woman patient – a doctor by profession – withdrew into herself, for a while not bringing any dreams or communications to which I was able to assign a meaning. I insisted on picking up the thread, and the patient told me first of a western and then of a woman with high levels of lead in her blood; finally, she referred to the absurdity of the proposed imposition by the government of a "tax on real property".

When I realized that my excess of interpretative "blows" had caused the level of lead in her blood to rise, and became aware of the significance of the tax on real property, I was able to desist. In the same way, I reduced the dose of interpretative activity when a female patient told me of the "retrolental fibroplasia" suffered by babies in an incubator if they received too much oxygen; and the same patient, fearing that I had still not understood, described how a premature baby fed too early and to excess had suffered intestinal necrosis. Interpretative modulation is the way to avoid the onset both of an impasse and, as I have pointed out elsewhere (Barale & Ferro, 1992), of a negative therapeutic reaction, by revealing their possible precursors. Both the negative therapeutic reaction and the impasse may in my view result from an accumulation of microfractures in communication, which explode in the former case, whereas in the latter they block the analytic process until their location and qualities are brought to light. A negative therapeutic reaction may also be a sign of a transference–countertransference collision (a "bulwark" in the sense of Baranger, Baranger & Mom); in other words, they may indicate the presence of an unrecognized impasse, whose crisis point they represent. Moreover, a negative therapeutic reaction may become established in inaccessible impasse situations. It should also be noted that the negative therapeutic reaction is often acute, explosive and critical, whereas the impasse tends to be chronic.

As stated at the beginning of this chapter, all these aspects are discussed in depth by Etchegoyen (1986). In field terms, a reorganization can ultimately – and will necessarily – be brought about through a change or transformation at any point in the field; the analyst's mind is the prime locus of any possible change. In other words, alongside the universally shared views of the impasse, I am suggesting here that we should try to see this phenomenon as a "necessity" of the analytic couple until the analyst, in his working through – the psychoanalytic function of his mind – and the patient, his "best colleague", are able to set the analytic work in motion again. This calls for the preservation of hope and patience, coupled with the ability to accept new, original and guilt-free conceptions of the impasse itself, which, as stated, may indicate levels of mental pain or terror requiring many slow, subterranean transformations before they can be confronted.

An earlier contribution (Barale & Ferro, 1992) presented a number of clinical examples of precursors of negative therapeutic reactions, which I shall now briefly recapitulate.

Problems of interpretative style

Sometimes the analyst's "interpretative style" gradually leads to a negative transference and hence, as Etchegoyen (1986) points out, to a negative therapeutic reaction, unless this situation is noticed and seen as a valuable clue to the functioning of the analyst–patient couple in the session.

Laura was a very gifted young woman psychologist with considerable experience of working with children. Her analysis seemed to be going well, although I sometimes felt that what I was doing with her was more supervision than analysis. In the very next session after this idea had occurred to me, Laura told me that she had visited a boy with a school phobia, who had considered packing his bags and running away from home or, on occasion, picking up a knife because of his fury at his elder brother who kept punching and hitting him, hurting him badly . . . She then added that she herself had been furious on arrival for her session because, in order to come, she had had to leave her own baby girl, just a few months old, at home. She also brought a dream in which Licia, a woman friend who always tried, at the earliest opportunity, to go to her mother's house for her holidays, was in a lift going up to the sixth floor; she could only see her feet, as if in one of Dario Argento's horror films. She associated to the feeling of a person grabbed by the shoulders and pulled up like a dead weight, like a child suddenly dragged out of a swimming pool . . .

If the analyst functions as a supervisor (brother) by addressing the more adult levels, he arouses rage, rivalry, jealousy and persecution, while, in particular, preventing access to the baby-girl part of the patient, who must be "left at home", terrified in case she is pulled up, like a dead weight, to an excessively height, instead of finding a truly available mother at ground level, who does not already know where to pull but is capable of sharing the swimming pool. A mother who is concerned with knowing and pulling up is of no use; what is actually needed is one with a taste for sharing discovery and growth, which can be achieved only through the experience of immersion in the fluidity of meanings with the patient.

Respect for the patient's text

These considerations are connected with the more general theme of the "patient's text", or the patient's need for an interlocutor to share his narrations – to which the interlocutor contributes, thereby playing a part in their development – rather than for an analyst who extracts meanings and substitutes the "official version of the truth" (Bollas, 1987) for the patient's text. "As Winnicott (1971) said, the analyst needs to play with the patient, to put forth an idea as an object that exists in that potential space between the patient and the analyst, an object that is meant to be passed back and forth between the two and, if it turns out to be of use to the patient, it will be stored away as that sort of objective object that has withstood a certain scrutiny" (Bollas, 1987).

Many microfractures of analytic communication have their roots in this problem. It is not, of course, merely a question of the "form" of the interpretation ("weak" or "strong", assertive or open to doubt, etc.): the analyst's intervention may obviously also be decisive, subversive and impassioned or biased (indeed, this may be the basis of its containing capacity); and it may imply the courage to adopt new points of view, as well as (hopefully) containing an element of surprise in addition to contact and recognition. However, at issue too is the relationship the analyst genuinely feels he has with the analytic truth as something somehow arising in the relationship rather than pre-existing it (recorded in the internal world or the history) and personally owned by him. In one of my analyses that had ground to a halt because of my univocal interpretations, the girl patient drew attention to this problem directly through a dream in which she was refused admission after her "own intervention". The "intervention" referred both to a surgical operation she was to undergo and to her own verbal interventions, which, she was afraid, were being excised interpretatively rather than received in all their rich textuality.

We must therefore interact with the patient's text in an encounter that respects its full potential semantic wealth, sets in train a process of alphabetization of β elements, allows the joint experiencing of formerly unthinkable emotional areas, and gradually organizes shared and shareable narrations that will always be substantially unsaturated, composed as it were in the form of a duet and issuing from the relationship (Robutti, 1992a).

Negative therapeutic reactions, "characters" in the session and functional aggregates

The "characters" who take the stage in the session of course constitute an important signal from patients to us within the microfractures of the analytic dialogue.

Before the Easter holidays, Marina, a young lawyer, dwelt at length on her worries about her daughter Carla, who was just a few months old and whom she was to take on a journey: it would be an upheaval for Carla, who would not have her own cushions and cot and all her familiar places . . . Following her in her text, I was ultimately unable to resist the urge to intervene with a rigid transference interpretation. After a moment's silence the patient responded: "Carla very much likes being held in the arms of all members of the family, but bursts out crying if my uncle's apprentice or a 12-year-old girl takes her in their arms." In other words, if the immature and non-containing parts of the analyst, "activated" by the narcissistic aspects of the patient, take the stage, they make children cry. Marina then asked whether analysts sometimes did not feel like "working".

An analyst who fails to "transform" the uncontainable anxiety of an abandoned little girl but instead acts it out by interpreting it is not "working", and an evacuative interpretation of this kind is ultimately the act of an "apprentice" (Manfredi Turillazzi, 1978).

The characters appearing in the session may therefore, as I have already pointed out, be thought of as syncretic narrations of the way the patient sees us in our functioning with him, from vertices unknown to us, which we must share for a moment in order to reach the patient.

By adopting this viewpoint, we can quickly put together the emotional facts of the field without resorting to "sense-closing" interpretations. Our aim, after all, is to construct a sense jointly with the patient (Corrao, 1987; Morpurgo, 1988; Gaburri,

1987), thereby "responding" to his feeding needs – without necessarily interpreting them – and modulating our intervention in accordance with the specific "hologram" of the analytic couple's mental functioning represented by the characters appearing in the patient's narration.

After a session in which I had provided correct "meanings", which, however, had been too dense and premature, Luisa told me that she had eaten a "ciabatta" on leaving the previous session. Having myself shared this experience, I replied: "Like the soldiers retreating from Russia" (thinking of the cold, explanatory climate of some of my interpretations). As if encouraged by the recovery of narrative attunement, Luisa then mentioned that a woman friend had telephoned her to ask for news of a premature baby girl born with an ependymal haemorrhage possibly involving hydrocephalus; both parents had placed all their hopes in the birth of this daughter . . . I drew attention to the "parents' disappointment". Luisa then referred to another baby, who was microcephalic and had macroglossia. I intervened again to say how painful it must be to have a child in that state (rather than seeing it as a part of the patient or of myself, I presented it as a shared entity characterized by "thinking little" – microcephaly – and "talking a lot" – macroglossia – and "prematurely" at that – hydrocephalus). Luisa now turned to the subject of parents of Down's syndrome babies: there was an association in Genoa that demanded so much from these children, teaching them too much too soon – cramming everything in by the age of ten, because after that atrophy set in . . . The patient then wondered why she was talking about such difficult situations in the analysis; perhaps it was because . . . and she advanced various highly theoretical hypotheses. I refrained from giving the suggested transference interpretation and answered that it was perhaps to have beside her someone to tell these things to and share them with. "Or else," she said, "to realize how fortunate I am to have a daughter like Paola and not like those children" (my narrative interventions had transformed the Down's syndrome baby /hydrocephalus /microcephaly/macroglossia into "Paola"). After other narrative interventions concerning mothers – who made their children feel like Down's syndrome babies if they overstimulated them – Luisa told me what a warm person her husband was: while he told their daughter fairy tales, she herself would listen. The best of the lot was the one about the white wolf cub whom no one wanted: in the winter snow, the black cubs were so conspicuous that they could not catch any prey . . . and then they were attacked by bears. But the white wolf, because its coat mimicked the landscape, was able to catch enough to feed all the others . . . I commented that this was a reversal of the classical situation. Luisa replied: "Yes, you are right. Usually there is the ugly duckling . . ." (that is how the patient often feels in the "classical" situation) ". . . my husband is a very warm person . . . At home he reads aloud from Orlando Furioso and the Divine Comedy, even to Paola, who certainly cannot understand the words; what she hears is more the sound and the musicality, whereas I also like the meaning . . . At home we have a matryoshka, a nest of Russian dolls one inside the other, each of which can still retain its individuality . . ." Her parting words were: "I certainly won't need to eat a ciabatta today!"

Univocal, over-saturated interpretations – black wolves – ultimately generate persecution, flight and aggression, whereas narration and use of the patient's text allow the white wolf to catch enough prey for the entire pack without triggering flight or persecution . . . Some readings are contained in the analyst's mind, while others can be made explicit on all levels; the "semantic haloes" can then find a place where they have the potential to create "new" stories, thus avoiding the terrible retreats of the frozen Russian campaign.

However, the analytic relationship is not symmetrical. Besides his "counter-transference availability", it is up to the analyst to be watchful and undertake self-analysis to ensure that the anti-evolutionary and anti-oedipal aspects of the field (both his own and the patient's) do not prevail and that sharing does not degenerate into a *folie à deux*. Nor must the theme of "realization", the precondition for any genuine development in the analysis, with its important inherent dimension of "acting out", be reduced to the mere orthopaedia of the corrective emotional experience and of "acting out" in the traditional sense, with its evacuative connotations. The analyst must therefore assume responsibility for keeping open the specifically analytic dialectic between our converse with the patient on the one hand and, on the other, a whole series of other components of the analyst's internal attitude and of the formal setting, such as abstinence, separateness and privacy, as well as pressure not only in the direction of thinkability but also towards the fundamental aspect of the psychoanalytic ethic, namely the sense of personal and individual responsibility for one's internal world.

This polarity is a constitutive element of the analytic space and the encounter that takes place within it; it keeps these in a state of non-saturation and non-coincidence, of opening and oscillation "between O and K", extending at one and the same time towards passion and sense and towards myth (as Bion might put it). This polarity includes the coexistence of and constant tension between extra-ordinarily intense involvements and separateness, real exchanges between people wholeheartedly committed with all their humanity and an inevitable aspect of "pretending", and sharing and solitude. It is the responsibility of the analyst, involved in the field as he is, to ensure that this dialectic does not become blocked (Barale & Ferro, 1992).

Notes

1   [Translator's note: Ferro in Italian; this is, of course, also the author's name.]
2   [Translator's note: Another play on words: ferroviere is the Italian for "railwayman", but the word also includes the author's name.]

Chapter 6

Sexuality and aggression

Relational vectors and narrations

This chapter is made up almost entirely of reflections that have yet to undergo "theoretical" organization.[1] I should like to begin by considering aggression and, in particular, sexuality not as referring to their manifest content but mainly in terms of their story-telling aspect, that is to say the particular "dialect" used primarily for speaking about relational vectors of the field, which reflect the patient's and analyst's forms of mental functioning in the session and all the associated emotional configurations (potential primal scenes of the field; Fornari, 1975) to which they give rise.

The abundant and well-known psychoanalytic literature on sexuality has been thoroughly revisited, and so I shall here mention only the central place that sexuality has occupied in psychoanalysis from the beginning. There has been a plethora of contributions on, in particular, female and child sexuality, as well as every possible sexual perversion and pathology. For a long time, patients' sexual themes were approached in literal terms and even subjected to highly sophisticated analysis. Attention later shifted from sexuality itself to the early fantasies preceding it, and often from the content of a communication to its form (Green, 1996).

However, when a patient brings sexual facts (regardless of the form of the telling – an anecdote, memory, dream, game, fantasy, etc.), the account cannot be considered solely in terms of the concrete facts presented, as a communication of the patient's problems concerning these facts, or even as the result of fantasies; we should instead see it as the patient's description to us of mental facts in the here and now.

In other words, we must be able to see a "sexual character" in terms of communication of the type of mental functioning assumed by the emotional field in the analyst's consulting room. After all, we are concerned in that room with mental facts, and – from a particular vertex – sexuality can stand only for *relationality*, so that any sexual disturbance will be the narration of those aspects of the analysis of which the patient is not yet sufficiently conscious to be able to express them more directly and in a form more in touch with his own emotional truths.

I mean this not on the obvious level that every sexual disturbance reflects a concomitant emotional disturbance but, I repeat, in the sense that any story pertaining to sexuality is itself a story that can be listened to and understood as an account of the relational and emotional problem current at that particular time in the consulting room; therapy here is a matter not so much of making this problem explicit as of being able to transform everything "upstream" of it.

Sexuality, then, is a character, or a link between characters, which can be thought of as relating to (a) a "before" (infantile sexuality) and an "elsewhere" (real external sexuality); (b) an "inside" (real internal sexuality/sexuality of internal objects); and (c) a narration *in* and *of* the field in one of the many "possible dialects" of the α element's narrative derivatives – that is, a literary genre which is neither more nor less meaningful than the science-fiction genre in which a patient might speak of *Star Trek*.

As Bion (1975) makes clear, the "mind [. . .] is too heavy a load for the sensuous beast [i.e. man] to carry".

Sexuality, digestion, respiration, and so on, are deemed in themselves to be firmly established phylogenetic accomplishments; the great drama of the species *Homo sapiens* is the importance of the mind, and the fact that "thinking" is a new function – the most recent in phylogenetic terms – of living matter (Bion).

It is our responsibility as analysts to concern ourselves at all times precisely with the "mind", or with the fundamental basis for existence that it affords, namely the emotional and affective relationship with the other (Faimberg, 1988b; Ferruta, 1996); this is what we are constantly renarrating to ourselves. The Freudian vertex of sublimation is here turned completely on its head: the mental "assumes concrete form" on the basis of the mental and refers back to it at all times.

When two minds are in close proximity, they constantly speak of themselves and their interaction, continuously drawing attention to the nodes and qualities of their mutual functioning through every possible narration, and utilizing every possible dialect and literary genre, including all forms of artistic expression.

For "me-as-analyst", therefore, sexuality is the "quality" and "form" of the encounter between the β element and the α function – the management of thoughts and their communication through the functions PS–D and ♀ ♂.

What Bion already describes so admirably in *Learning from Experience* (1962) is mainly the form of development of ♀, ♂ and ♀ ♂.

I therefore contend that the entire analytical session can be categorized along row C of the grid as a dream produced by the patient's mind about the functioning of the analyst's mind and of the field. Other categorizations are of course possible, but in my view often less useful for allowing transformations in "O". In this sense, psychoanalysis has a specific interest in "sexuality" as a narrative vertex. This firm conviction of mine is buttressed by Bion's discussion, at the end of the excellent fourth chapter of *Transformations* (1965), of "the mental counterpart of the reproductive system".

The right distance

After a session in which I had explicitly drawn attention to Marina's need for closer contact with me, she told me of the trouble she had had with her over-lively daughter and then brought a dream in which I placed the armchair opposite the couch and she was afraid that this was too direct a way of being in analysis; then I was right next to her and we embraced, but totally non-sexually, although she felt intense mental pleasure at the closeness.

I believe that neither sexuality nor erotization was involved here, but that the patient was describing a purely mental fact. On the one hand, the arousal of intense emotions was disturbing, but, on the other, it gave rise to an intensely pleasurable sensation of intimacy and closeness.

Sandra's dialect

Sandra brought a dream in which a man in a bathing costume was manifestly turned on, eventually exhibiting a big, long penis.

She claimed to be worried because she thought the idea that her husband had a small penis (which was not in fact true) prevented her from experiencing pleasure. I commented that she was actually afraid that I was not going deep enough: she really wanted me to display a greater capacity for penetration.

Yes, she replied immediately, that was true, and furthermore she did not know me very well and was not sure what to think about me; she wanted a deeper relationship, but did not know whether . . . or whether . . . She was ultimately asking to be helped to achieve the pleasure of a greater and deeper knowledge of herself, through the experience of an active and intense interest on my part.

The long penis was the measure of my interest in her, which she was afraid was meagre, although she saw it as her sole means of access to profound self-knowledge.

The reading of accounts of sessions or parts of sessions involving clinical material with sexual content is a useful way of "distinguishing" such an approach to this material from others (given the limitations imposed by the absence of the two protagonists, the analyst and patient concerned). A good example is the issue of the *International Journal of Psycho-Analysis* (1991) mentioned earlier, which includes a number of case histories discussed in accordance with different theoretical models.

Let us now consider some further examples.

The suffering of the "relationship"

Returning depressed from the Christmas holidays, during which she had mourned, Patrizia brought a dream in which she was having sex with two men, one "vertical" and the other "horizontal", like a cross in a cemetery, she added.

She had become aware that for her a bond, a relationship, also entailed mourning . . . particularly during holidays.

In a previous dream, she had six fingers, with which she was attacking her mother: the closer the bond she forged, the more intense was her mourning.

Giovanna's progression

In the first session of her analysis, Giovanna mentioned her dried-up, premenopausal genitals, and then told me how her mother had treated her very cautiously during her teens in case she exploded . . .

Giovanna, as one readily saw, had two forms of relating, one explosive and adolescent and the other desiccated and dried-up; that was precisely how she related to other people in order to deny and pseudo-contain the explosiveness of which she was so afraid. When I interpreted in these terms, she remembered all the exanthemas of her childhood, which she had contracted one after another – rubella, measles and scarlet fever – and indeed she flushed red all over.

Carla's eunuch

Carla introduced the "eunuch", as she called one of her workmates, to the session. There was no point in unmasking the eunuch in all its safe, present meanings within the relationship – from the analyst with his cautious interpretations . . . to a part of the patient who experienced her own female identity as castration . . . but also a part of herself that was incapable of emotional penetration, submissive and insincere . . . as well as a way in which the analyst felt vengefully castrated by her in his thinking activity . . . as well as other infinite modulations of the functioning of our two minds together, which the "eunuch" pointed out from time to time . . . but in addition there was the "*male friend of a girlfriend*" . . . "who breaks the cups while washing them up" . . . and this "male", too, stood on the one hand for the excessively penetrative activity of the analyst, but also, on the other, for an intrusive part of the patient herself, and hence other possible declensions of the functioning of our two minds together in the session; sometimes the mask (or puppet) was animated by aspects of the patient and sometimes by aspects of the analyst, and on other occasions by aspects that could not readily be assigned to either in the cut and thrust of the relationship. The same applied to the other characters who entered into, or rather were brought to life in, the session . . . the "institute director" . . . her "friend Laura" . . . her "petit bourgeois friend" . . . her "feminist friend" . . . or the "homosexual cousin" . . . in this way an entire world of present relationships was outlined between "forms of functioning" of the patient's and her analyst's minds, like masks fleshed out and brought to life, which were mortified if they were not allowed a free mutual exchange of parts and roles, circulation of affects and transformations, now instantaneous and now born of suffering and toil, but which a rigid transference interpretation would have closed off and suffocated in their continuous process of becoming, in their narration, and in their composition of ever new emotional situations . . . the analyst certainly listened in the conviction that the "facts" arriving in the session were also, and in particular for him, "consulting-room facts", born of the encounter and the relationship between two mental lives and their mutual projective identifications, but it would be an internal kind of listening for the analyst, whereby he followed the internal development –

a multi-voice dialogue of his internal group of supervisors . . . of analytic experiences . . . yet while the internal dialogue, as constantly activated and deactivated, would be the compass indicating the "north" of the communications in the relationship to prevent him from totally losing his way, the analyst would at the same time take part in the game without stripping the characters on the stage of their masks or subjecting them to customs checks . . . and of course, any modulation or intervention, however "weak", by the analyst would influence the field, altering the scenery and characters, because his "saying" would embody an idea conceived by the patient at that time about his analyst "saying something", to which he would give a name . . . and the patient would in turn add something . . . so the game continued with constant transformations, with seemingly insignificant interventions by the analyst, whereby he drew explicit attention to a transference meaning, but despite their apparent insignificance inducing transformations in the bipersonal field and also activity in the patient. At some point the analyst might certainly feel a momentary need to freeze the situation with a snapshot of the here and now of the relationship, to file it away in his collection . . . or the patient might have an insight . . . or a flash of inspiration on the part of the analyst might break up the configuration that had been forming, thus modifying the structure of the field, but the transformations would resume from this point on. I repeat all this in the conviction that our only sextant must be the relational sense of what is said . . . precisely because what the patient is constantly "saying" in the session is nothing but a drawing of explicit attention to affects concerning his own and our functioning when we are together, thereby drawing on his history, life and dreams . . . but always to say what is happening in the current interaction, although we are aware that history, childhood, "daddy" and "mummy" are necessary translations into the modes of time and space of what would otherwise remain unsayable in the emotional fire of two minds in close proximity, for which thinking is but a very recent function (Bion, 1978).

From this point of view, however, when Carla breathed life into her "homosexual cousin", not only would attention focus on the moment in the session when he appeared, but the analyst would also enquire of his own internal group as to the possible meaning of "homosexual" in that session and as to the type of relationship activated at that time between the forms of functioning of the two minds. A type of mating will occur in such situations. It may be unproductive (type $\male \male$), in the case, for example, of an analyst forcing interpretations into a "patient" who is not ready or prepared to listen to them, or a patient speaking to an unreceptive analyst; or it may be fusional (type $\female \female$), tending towards lack of differentiation, without penetration of the words (and of projective identifications on to the other), without the creation of anything new in the relationship, and without the birth of thoughts (or children of the primal scene). This is perhaps because $\female \male$ functioning of the two minds – i.e. the receptive analyst receiving the patient's words and projective identifications, transforming them and returning them "at a temperature and in a form" tolerable to the patient, who takes them in, in turn integrating them with other preconceptions or expectations and then giving them back to the analyst

– implies a mental mating, or primal scene, resulting in the birth of new thoughts whose mutual mating is not prevented by –K. All this cannot but remain present in the analyst's internal dialogue and his between-sessions working-through; and meanwhile he will continue to play with the "Lego piece" represented by the "homosexual cousin" in all the possible aggregations that develop in the session (Bezoari & Ferro, 1989, 1991b, 1994a).

The dream of the globe belly

Gabriella was a young woman terrified at the idea of the slightest change; her sessions were becoming difficult, as she always said the same things: "I go to the shops, but I never buy anything." I interpreted her few communications in transference terms.

This patient often complained that she wanted to be comforted, but that she then felt guilty. At this point I had a countertransference dream: a little girl desperate with jealousy came into my bed; I wanted to calm her down and she wanted to be comforted, but one of my hands slid down and started stroking her legs . . .

This was in fact exactly what was happening with Gabriella: what the patient was receiving from constant, excessively close transference interpretations was not consolation but masturbatory excitation, which then made her feel guilty. In this way I made contact with seduction fantasies and was able to time my interpretations in a manner more consistent with the patient's needs; she for her part could then get in touch with her own seduction fears and wishes and later have a dream in which a girl finally got her bearings on a globe, having been supplied with longitude and latitude, while an adult woman received a globe from the man she loved and placed it underneath her breast; the relationship now became fruitful again.

Marta's "pene"[2]

I recall another situation in which I was helped by a countertransference dream: Marta was in despair because her boyfriend did not want to make love . . . and then I saw myself in a toilet with Marta, who had a penis [pene] hardly smaller than my own and we were comparing them for size.

This dream showed me that, preoccupied as I was with an interpretative ideology of my own, I was not listening to my patient's needs, including her need for me to relate to her in a manner of which I was then capable; and it also made me aware of the risk of phallic–narcissistic rivalry with the patient. These realizations led me to alter my interpretative attitude, a change that was rewarded within a few sessions, when Marta had a dream expressing renunciation of her position of phallic demands: she was the donor in a "penis" [pene] transplant operation, after which it became possible for her to look after a suffering girl she had never before wished to bother herself with.

There were two aspects to this "pene" transplant: first, the recognition of "some-one" able to tolerate and transform her pain (the other sense of pene) and, second, acceptance of "someone" whose virility was acknowledged just at the time when she was owning her femininity. This too had long been disguised and concealed, either because of the painful renunciation of sexual omnipotence or out of fear of a "Snow White witch mother" who would have been mad with jealousy at the blossoming of her daughter's womanhood, just as the analyst would have been jealous of the development of Marta's capabilities and fertility.

Penetrable or impenetrable?

Gianni dreamed of a homosexual relationship with a male friend, of the penis [*pene*] to penis [*pene*] type. I rejected the first interpretation that occurred to me because I was afraid it had been dictated by what I was then working on (focusing on his fear that there might be a mutual opposition between us, due to each of us opposing his own pain [*pene*] to the other's – the pain had to do with the beginnings of a plan to terminate the analysis; that is, a mutual lack of availability for listening). I also rejected academic interpretations of the homosexuality and opted for a developmental approach, suggesting that he could basically no longer find what he was looking for within the analysis, which was becoming sterile and unproductive, whereas there was an outside world from which he could expect new things.

He responded with what amounted to a fit of panic in the session, having understood me to mean: "I have accompanied you thus far, but from now on you are on your own." Picking up his anxiety, I told him that he was afraid I was confusing talking about something with actually doing it; he then felt relieved.

He began the next session by telling me a dream: three girls came along to his office; one of them had an attack of angina and his friend Colombo[3] immediately attended to her. The girl recovered and his friend Colombo was then able to depart . . . he himself had to overcome a resistance to going to see what had happened and perhaps concerning himself with it . . . he also desired the girls sexually . . . he decided to go into the room and look after the girl who had been taken ill . . . then he approached the others . . .

I felt that the dream expressed a recovery of the ♀ ♂ relationship, which had already been blocked in the first dream by a ♂ ♂ type of functioning and then by my interpretation. Only when I recovered my own availability (♀) for experiencing his anxiety did the patient in turn become available for picking up what his friend Colombo had done, and in turn for being receptive towards his own affects, which he was able to tune into even in my absence.

The "homosexual character"

Combining the comments in Chapter 2 about how to understand the "characters" of the session with the ideas set out at the beginning of this chapter, we can listen in a particular way to the "homosexual character" who appears in the session as representing something that narrates to us the deep qualities of the mental functioning of the field.

In other words, interpretation in couple terms tends to bring out not so much "objects" or "parts" of the personality as "dynamic constellations" of relational potentialities of the mind (Manfredi Turillazzi, 1985), captured from the continuously evolving pattern of intrapersonal and interpersonal relations.

Homosexuality can be approached in the same way, disregarding the metapsychological or genetic aspect (Bronstein, 1995; Doery, 1995; Henningsen, 1995) and instead seeking to identify the unconscious forms of mental functioning of the couple that are being recounted by the manifest level of the communication.

Luigi's "other side"

PATIENT: I have a sexual problem . . . it's not that I have become impotent, but I don't fancy it as much as I used to, it doesn't attract me, I have not got the urge . . . there is a certain desire . . . I don't know how to bring it to a conclusion . . . I do it out of habit . . . but what was it you were telling me last time about the "sexual dialect"?

ANALYST: That you were using a sexual *dialect* to express more intelligibly feelings and thoughts you were afraid of not being able to accept within yourself.

PATIENT: And what might they be?

ANALYST: That you still want things that used to be very attractive to you, like the idea of "being held and . . . looked after", but not as much as in the past; that you are doing it out of habit, but that they are basically no longer so attractive – to put it in plain language.

PATIENT: I don't know if I believe that. I had a dream which I cannot remember very clearly: *I had a submachine gun and I was shooting at the walls.* It puts me in mind of my fear of *husbands* . . . I am tormented by the idea that I might like men.

ANALYST: What I said to you first made you angry; you are afraid that I might not be receptive to your point of view, and become a "wall", but then that I might be too active, a "husband" revealing to you different meanings from the ones you present, and you are afraid that you might basically not be averse to that.

PATIENT: I don't know, but I have had the offer of a job; I could work at a petrol station and earn money . . . but I am afraid.

ANALYST: You feel that what I am telling you gives you an opportunity to work, that it might fill you up with fuel so that you can move on.

PATIENT: But I am afraid of crossing over "to the other side", that I might fancy men, and all this is happening to me because I have got involved with that boy.

ANALYST: And you fear that if you get more involved in working with me, you might want to cross over to the other side – perhaps not in the sense of homosexuality, but that you might fancy the idea of being a man, and a man with his own independence at that.

The homosexual couple: affection or abuse?

I told Carla the dates of the Easter holidays: the break would last one week as usual, but would be a few days later than the patient had imagined from the previous year; however, she had already made her arrangements on that basis.

I felt intensely guilty (not realizing that this "guilt" resulted from my own assumption of the guilt feelings aroused in the patient by her violent rage towards me) and – acting out on the spot in the way that I myself found incomprehensible – I said that, if she liked, we could bring forward one of the two extra sessions she would be losing and have it after all.

After a moment's silence, the patient said: "Not long ago I saw two homosexuals in a bar; they were really nice and kind to each other, and seemed to understand each other and be in tune with each other's feelings and needs . . . but if I think of the sexual aspect . . . all that violence . . . actually, I imagine that my husband would also like to have anal intercourse with me."

I replied that perhaps she had felt that I too had been very available and close in offering to give her back the session . . . but, equally, I had done something she had experienced as violent, namely deciding on the holiday dates in a way that had put her out. The patient remarked: "Don't worry, don't worry, the rage will come." And indeed, in the next session the patient told of her last meeting with her "mother", full of rage at the memory of childhood bullying, when she had even been told how she had to dress.

Once the full negotiability of emotions had been recovered, the homosexuals left the stage, to be replaced by a more living and passionate relationship, like that of a mother and daughter.

The character as it were becomes an *affective hologram of a form of functioning of the couple* characterized by extreme variability. The couple's emotions supply colours and tones and their words serve for aggregation and organization, eventually allowing shapes and structures to be discerned; these narrative–affective representations, which change with the varying nature of the relationship, are the only way the minds have of describing to themselves what is happening between them.

The couple's narrations as mediated by the characters, rather than the decoding of material, will serve to transform the underlying emotions and allow new vistas of meaning to be opened up (Vallino, 1994).

Defence against aggression; aggression as defence

The theme of aggression is of its nature particularly dear to psychoanalysis, closely bound up as it is with the problem of the drives, instinctuality and the associated defences.

I do not propose to review the subject of "aggression" here, even in broad outline, in view of the abundant literature on the topic (e.g. Gaddini, 1972; Giannotti, 1988; Kernberg, 1993; Limentani, 1988a; Masciangelo, 1988). The excellent survey of the death instinct by Borgogno & Viola (1994) is also worth reading. I should merely like to point out that aggression is a basic constituent and a natural endowment of our species; after all, as Bion (1978) constantly reminds us, we as a species have subjected every other life form on the planet to our will except for viruses, and patient and analyst are like two wild and dangerous animals.

Aggression is of course a mainspring of development, competition, overcoming of the oedipal conflict, and so on. Prior to all these aspects (and to the way it affords access to the various "states of mind", which it then enables the subject to overcome), aggression is the instrument deployed by every family member to assert himself as an individual, as a reaction to avoid being caught up in an agglutinated group (Bleger, 1967). Apart from a digression on the psychoanalytic development of this concept (not only Freud but, in particular, Klein puts aggression at the point of divergence between the birth of symbolization and the constitution of the death instinct), it would be interesting to make a comparative study of aggression and defences in the human species on the one hand and aggression and defences in ethology on the other. I was in fact surprised to observe the incredible parallels between the chapter titles of a book on the ethology of aggression and aspects of human mental functioning.[4]

However, like all infantile protoemotions, aggression must be "treated" by the mother's[5] reverie and α function if it is to be made compatible with the environment and its dictates. Such aggression will be expressible and constitute the engine of growth without becoming destructive to self and others.

However, this process sometimes fails, leaving the child faced with the need to "manage" very high, untreated levels of "crude aggression" by deploying a wide range of defences, which often entail paralysis of aggression itself and of emotional development as a whole. Here again, I see aggression not as confined to the patient but as an entity that cannot be considered separately from the analyst's capacity for transformation and reverie.

Defences against aggression

The published studies on these defences are many and varied – one need only think of the work of Anna Freud – but I shall consider here only *splitting* and *lethargy*.

Let me add that, of course, it is unusual for a deficiency of the maternal–paternal α function to affect aggression only;[6] in most such cases aggression is combined with greed, jealousy and envy, sometimes even giving rise to dramatic situations such as Williams's (1983) "death constellation".

The problem is some form of relational failure in regard to the projective identifications that convey aggression, which have not succeeded in being received, transformed and returned "enriched" with frustration and rage.[7] It has thus been impossible for the subject to introject a container capable of transforming the levels of aggression which are always generated and which, "if treated", would have become a vital mainspring of mental growth and development.

The same thing happens in the analytic situation, so that it is a matter not so much of interpreting aggression as of allowing the introjection of a container capable of absorbing and transforming it. This can be done only by "apprenticing" the patient to the analyst, who will show him in the living situation how he is capable of containing and transforming the quantities of aggression that are gradually liberated. In other words, the essential point once again is to maximize the development of the patient's "apparatus for thinking thoughts", to enable him to handle even high levels of aggression (or, in more serious cases, to permit restoration of the α function itself).

Splitting

This subject is so familiar that I shall not dwell on its theoretical aspects; there have been a number of recent treatments by Italian authors such as De Simone & Fornari (1988) and Gaburri & Ferro (1988). I should merely like to recall Rosenfeld's (1987) comment that splitting must be approached with extreme caution and respect for the patient's capacity; indeed, even this may be unnecessary, because in my experience, as soon as the patient has a sufficiently robust container and the aggression has been adequately "treated" between the minds involved, he himself will re-own what he has split off. For example, he will no longer need to talk about the aggression of, say, his "boxer brother" or "violent brother" or "bad classmate", but will be able to re-enter into emotional possession of what are *his own* mental states and "primal scenes", with all the aggression and violence contained in them.

Of course, aggression and violence must enter the session for the purpose of being treated and transformed, and to supply the patient with a mental model in which his projective identifications, even if evacuative, are received, contained and transformed (Eskelinen de Folch, 1983, 1988; Torras de Beà, 1989; Tuckett, 1989). Again, a field model does not permit easy and immediate assignment of aggression to either the patient or the analyst, because even cautious interpretations may violate or overtax fragile α functions or containers, thereby unleashing a great deal of violence in the field. See Bezoari & Ferro (1992a) for a description of how a premature approach to splitting can give rise to hallucinatory phenomena.

The hot iron [ferro][8]

One of my female patients had a very disturbed brother who had needed to be restrained for a long time, and I had interpreted him as a violent, uncontainable part of herself. In the next session the patient told me a dream in which, while she was doing her ironing, someone burnt her hand by forcing her to touch the "hot iron" [*ferro*]. An interpretation of this burn as generated by the previous interpretation would have indicated a failure on my part to receive the patient's message about not yet being able to tolerate "feeling", because she as yet lacked a place suitably equipped to hold that part of herself.

The boxer and the dancer

A seriously ill patient once told me how, before a match, a very violent boxer was shown a girl who seduced him to make him less violent in the ring. It was this story that put me in touch with my fear of him and with the seduction I was resorting to in order to avoid "destruction" in my own encounter, or match, with him.

The boxer brother

I recall the trouble I had with a male patient because of my conviction that I had to interpret to him directly in the transference everything to do with his violence and aggression, which took the stage through the terrible misdeeds of his "boxer brother". For a long time I interpreted this brother as a part of himself, or by assuming this role myself, without understanding that there was a radically different approach open to me, involving toleration of the splitting off of this violence, which might after all have found a place in the relational field and been sufficiently transformable for the patient himself to accept it eventually. It took me a long time to venture my first narrative interpretation: one day when the tension could be cut with a knife, I told him that I felt as though I were with him in a western saloon just before a glass fell on the floor and all hell broke loose. He laughed, the tension relaxed, and for many months thereafter we were accompanied by the notes of *High Noon*, which, by an unbelievable coincidence, was the time of his session.

The cup from Beauty and the Beast

I once had a little girl patient who was so terrified of aggression that, playing *Beauty and the Beast* in the session, she could not only on no account take the part of the Beast but also found it impossible to be Beauty; she participated in the proceedings only on condition that she could be the "cup" in the Beast's house. This, then, is what we must be able to tolerate – that is, allowing patients to tell us how much aggression they can tolerate.

Stefano's savages

Stefano seemed the "perfect daytime" boy, who, however, suffered from terrible nightmares all night long. At our first meeting, he began by drawing a very stylized and even mannered little gosling, and then, on another piece of paper, "faces of fear", which he told me were his nightmares. The two experiences seemed very far apart, as if belonging to two different worlds. He then drew an island, above which the sun was shining, its rays darting upward from half behind a cloud, and then the island also had tufts of grass with a garish halo around them. I immediately linked the nocturnal figures – which were "open" because the skulls had no tops – to the sun and the tufts of grass, which were drawn in such a way that they appeared to complete the faces with seemingly feathered crania. Superimposing the drawings, I said: "But that looks just like the bit that is missing!" Stefano answered: "*Yes, the island is inhabited by savages, but they are in hiding*", and "behind the cloud is where the island's totem is hidden . . ." Needless to say, this island of savages then became a focus of our work, for a long time constituting the privileged setting for terrible stories.

The theme of the double

The problem of the double can be approached from two points of view, although it is always a token of a container unfit to hold very intense emotions.

In some situations of stable *splitting*, the other – the double, the persecutor – takes the stage as an "uncanny" presence by which the subject feels disturbed, attacked or talked about. It is usually manifested through some personification, the possibilities ranging from the "imaginary twin" (when the split is total; Bion, 1960) to the "secret companion" (in the case of an incipient capacity to take the double on board; Gaburri, 1986).

Sometimes, however, the double takes the form not of another persecutor (for example, Edgar Allan Poe's Williamson), but of a different, allosteric configuration, a component of the subject's own self.

This situation is exemplified by my patient Carlo, who for a long time described two emotional configurations of himself in a state of oscillation, or rather of unstable mutual equilibrium, the choice between which depended on the emotional climate of the field, acting as a kind of pH.

Ivory and the mirror

The beginning of Lodovica's analysis was characterized by her terror of university examinations, but in particular of the detailed examination to which she was afraid I was continuously subjecting everything she said or hid in the session and to which she in turn subjected everything I said – for this examination might reveal "something ugly and monstrous". This monstrous entity was to appear in a dream, together with the pain and anguish of realizing how destructive it was: "Something terrible called Ivory . . . like a tumour . . . when they hear what it has done, people die of pain." This was preceded by other dreams featuring "Caterina", a kind of android robot from a film, which had terrible fits of fury.

At the beginning of the analysis Lodovica was not in touch with her rage, but seemed preoccupied with the fear of her own objects' fragility, engaged as she was in omnipotent reparative activity and absorbed in the struggle to contain the violence of her feelings. A dream of this period presented a little girl on a rock trying to protect her parents from terrible waves that ultimately overwhelmed both them and herself. As the analysis progressed, this dream was repeated with modifications that bore witness to the gradual transformations that had taken place: the rock grew in size and became an island; it was equipped with jetties and reinforced concrete structures that protected the harbour from less violent seas;

and, finally, "a solid protecting coral reef" appeared. All this demonstrated the structuring of a solid ego, the reduction in the turbulence of her feelings, and her increased trust in objects.

At first, Lodovica was afraid that she needed to defend against the violence of her own feelings with me too, which she feared I would also not be capable of withstanding; the first of these feelings to enter the analysis was a terrible "jealousy", accompanied by a homicidal rage that was also triggered by my interpretations. I had to throttle my interventions back progressively, because Lodovica could not tolerate being touched directly in the here and now of the transference, and I realized the need for a slow and gradual approach to her emotions (which actually still constituted violent, uncontainable passions).

The examination problem was paralleled by the theme of "dysmorphophobia", in which Lodovica saw herself as "ugly and bloated" and wanted constantly to diet (in other words, to pay scant attention to what I told her!) in order not to grow fat (i.e. not to fill herself with rage, jealousy and the like) when she remembered a mother who had told her as a child: "You are too heavy for me to carry you in my arms" (fear of my inability to stand up to her).

I noticed how I was gradually becoming the mirror that returned an ugly, unacceptable image to her if I concentrated too much on her negative feelings (in particular, jealousy and envy), and how the "dysmorphophobia" declined if I succeeded in making her feel "an active part" of the psychoanalytic process and not merely someone "under examination", as well as allowing her the time to discover things for herself, accepting her own pace and not running on too far ahead of her.

Let me emphasize, too, how inappropriate interpretations often injure the patient's container, forcibly penetrating it and resulting (as we shall see later) in the use of aggression as a plug; such situations can readily give rise to negative therapeutic reactions and psychotic transferences, as shown in the previous chapter.

Lethargy

The other very primitive mechanism for defending against aggression is to "put it to sleep", thereby also putting to sleep whole areas of the mind and, often, any potential for creativity. In this way the patient succeeds in rendering entire parts of himself lethargic. This lethargy must enter the field in the form of a falling-asleep by the analyst himself; thereafter he will embark on the work of assuming the violent projective identifications that begin to circulate in the field, facilitating their eventual transformation and access to thinkability (Tagliacozzo, 1982).

From projective identification to narration: Marcella's downstairs apartment

Uppermost in the sessions with Marcella was the atmosphere of boredom that quickly pervaded the entire room, as well as my mind. This good-looking girl with bulimic tendencies had no interest in anything. Nothing attracted or involved her. She had come to analysis because her apathy and laziness made it very difficult for her to concentrate on her studies.

My countertransference emotions towards Marcella were characterized by the feeling of a heavy weight, an inability to make transference interpretations, "not wishing to touch her", and a desire to avoid any emotional contact; at the same time, after I had listened to her for a while, I felt myself becoming "disconnected" from my thoughts, to the point of losing the thread and being unable to follow what she was saying even on the manifest level. This went on until Marcella brought a dream in which she was opening drawers in her bedside table, which contained an enormous number of reels [*spolette*][9] of every colour, all mixed up together; terrified, she closed the drawers again, thinking how difficult it would have been, and how much *patience* she would have needed, to unravel this tangle of threads.

She recalled how, when she had been very small, she had gone to play at her dressmaker grandmother's house, but what was immediately *lit* in my mind was the other sense of the word *spoletta* (in addition to the patient's manifest meaning of a cotton reel), namely that of a "device for detonating the explosive in an artillery shell", and I suddenly remembered a little boy in analysis who had coated the wild animals that terrified him with a thick layer of plasticine until they were hidden; and I also understood why I had for so long been unable to "touch her" emotionally with my interpretations: precisely for fear that she might "explode".

From then on, it became possible for the patient and myself to "transfer ourselves" to the grandmother's workshop, as well as to discover her fear and terror of tangled, explosive emotions, which she kept firmly locked up in drawers with her boredom, and which she tried to put to sleep with bulimia . . . the *spolette* were to be the starting point for so many "stories".

The reconstruction of "*the downstairs apartment*" gradually became significant (builders had been refurbishing the apartment on the floor below my consulting room for a long time), as Marcella began to cast cautious glances into it. At this time I became aware that we were communicating on two levels, one superficial and terribly thin, and the other mediated by projective identifications whose effect in the sessions was to disable my capacity to listen to the manifest text, thereby – as stated earlier – disconnecting me from my thoughts and putting me in touch with utterly primitive (repressed? split-off? unthinkable?) emotions that were held in check by the boredom.

As stated, stories of the "downstairs apartment" now began to emerge. It became possible to tell of the "wall *pastina*"[10] (Italian slang for a kind of rough paint she had seen the "workmen downstairs" using): after I had commented that the pastina on the walls put me in mind of a very angry child, she rediscovered it in the memory of her explosions of rage as a little girl if the *temperature* of the *pastina* was not to her liking, when she would hurl the dish at the wall, *upsetting its contents*. (One can readily imagine the containing capacity needed by the analyst to tolerate backdating the problem to infancy and forgoing an easy explanation in relational terms; that is, of the patient's fury whenever an interpretation was too hot or too cold, causing her to *upset* – turn over – the contents of the interpretation itself in a reversal of perspective (Bion, 1962).)

Such an intervention had to be forgone because a relational truth of this kind was not yet negotiable in the present situation: it would have involved being in K (knowing about something) with the patient, whereas today the childhood "*pastina* on the walls" – which was basically less hot and as such more tolerable – was more in "O" (sharing an emotional experience).

The same applied to the *Turca*[11] she had in her room, which we were able to understand as a "couch with a back" that referred to the analytical couch, and not yet to aspects of herself whose language she did not know and which were foreign to her; and similarly the *centauri*,[12] which could be broached as mechanized motor-cyclists in a village festival, but not yet as inhabitants of a primitive mythical world with which she was getting in touch.

However, such meanings are not lost in a field approach; they are present in some form in the consulting room if they are there in the analyst's mind waiting to become part of a shared plot or pending the possibility of opening up new spaces to thinkability.

What appears as lethargy in such cases thus in fact turns out to be something different, albeit similar: a child's way of dumbing down aggression by means of an enveloping claustrum.

Carlo's plasticine

Carlo managed to envelop his rage in boring, repetitive questions; the mechanism was revealed one day when he took some prehistoric wild animals out of a box and wrapped them one by one in a thick layer of plasticine "to suffocate them so that they don't cause any trouble".

As stated earlier, I shall not be dealing with other possible defences here, although the claustrum would be worth discussing; however, it is described extraordinarily well in Meltzer (1992).

Aggression as a defence

Switching now to a different vertex, let us consider aggression, and particularly certain forms of cruelty and sadism – as well as of violence – in terms of their *function* of protecting the patient from uncontainable fragmentation anxieties and, to an even greater extent, from dissolution anxieties. I am thinking of the severe pathologies in which the patient's experience of having projective identifications received has been deficient, so that three-dimensional mental development is lacking; such a patient will have had to resort to adhesive identification (Bick, 1968), using aggression and cruelty as a second skin to provide some degree of containment.

In my view, subjects who function in this way often exhibit narcissistic behaviour.[13]

Serial killer, Raskolnikov or Cuvio magistrate?

After years of work with Carlo (Ferro, 1993e) had ultimately resulted in a more peaceful climate, I became aware of a countertransference feeling that his analysis had been surgical, very much in the head and very correct, but lacking the "negotiation" of emotions and fears; we had always spoken and interpreted, but never experienced emotional states at close quarters together.

Even in the days of his "killer's kitbag" and his plans to get rid of me or himself, we had talked about and understood everything in the form of the "anatomopathology" of a dream. We had had to defend ourselves in this way against unbearable involvement. I was suddenly assailed by waves of terror and panic, concomitant with an intensification of his symptoms – phobia of others, of contact and of encounters. A dream then portrayed him as suffering from "third-degree burns" after the removal of his protective gold plates.

I noticed that now every word of mine and every variation in my tone of voice gave rise to an emotional whirlwind; this was what currently terrified him in his relations with others. We could then retell his story and ours from a new vertex: he was no longer an "arch-criminal", the "Dracula" of a dream who was unable to leave the confines of his own castle (such was the terror he inspired in the local populace), but a suffering Dostoyevskyan character, a Raskolnikov. We could see the megalomania, the narcissism,[14] and even the "criminality" as defences, as *narcissistic* and indeed *autistic barriers* to an emotional contact whose turbulence terrified him.

Carlo brought a dream of a supermarket with marvellous toys – the kind of now completely useless automata, beautiful machines, that were made to amaze and amuse the royal courts of the seventeenth century – and there was his uncle, a practical man with his feet firmly on the ground, who would not let him play with them; so he had to forgo this pleasure, but had to put up with some live animals, some of which frightened him, in his room.

We had to give up not only the masturbatory toys of megalomania and criminality but also those now mechanical interpretations of parts of the patient that were already thoroughly known, and needed instead to work on the difficulty and tribulations of our emotional encounter (Norsa & Zavattini, 1988).

After a particularly good session (and after the realization that he would ask me if he could go to the toilet whenever I aroused excessive emotions in him, or that I would find the couch drenched in sweat if I made him work too hard), he told me that, in the bar opposite, he had heard that Piero, an old friend, had been talking about him; he had referred to him as "Carlo" and described an episode from their school-days in a pleasant and affectionate tone of voice. Could it be that people liked him?

At this point he had a fantasy, perhaps stemming partly from a dream: two books were lying side by side, and a "character" – someone like Piero Chiara's "Cuvio magistrate"[15] – had somehow ended up by mistake in a book by Dostoyevsky; just when he was given up for lost, the pages opened, the books touched, and the "Cuvio magistrate", no longer contaminated, was able to return to his tranquil lakeside idyll.

In another dream, Carlo spread his arms wide and tried to grasp all the good things around him; the "climate of Cambodia" that he used to feel inside was gone.

At the time of writing we are working on this phase, which I hope will be the last, namely the autistic defences against very primitive emotional turbulences[16] that were for so long necessary; aware of the inner seething aroused by every word I utter now that the "golden scales" that used to protect him are gone, I fully realize that I must change my technique from surgery to affectionate containment.

Dreams as the "locus" of aggression

A patient's dream may demonstrate how β elements can be transformed and protoemotions become shared thought, whereas in the past they were evacuated in violent or characteropathic behaviour, for an internal narrator has now come into being to handle what could not be coped with before.

Stefano's abscess

Stefano was a patient with a long history of serious characteropathy, often manifested in his behaviour. After the frustration of an unplanned separation, he had four dreams. In the first, he could see burns on his thigh, with two particularly badly ulcerated patches, "like children who scratch themselves when left alone". The second portrayed a painful experience with his wife, who seemed to want to leave him. He for his part loved her deeply and could not understand her intentions; she too evidently loved him, but at the same time needed autonomy so that she could go her own way. In the third dream, he was sitting in a car telling a friendly old woman about his own sufferings when a widow who had just been to her husband's funeral asked to be allowed inside and was admitted. In the fourth dream he was pursued by a not very dangerous black panther; he tried to close the door of the house, but knew that this non-terrifying panther would probably find a way in and "attack" him – an "attack" of rage?

Bion often reminds us that thinking is a new function of living matter, and the culmination of complex operations involving major mental suffering. What starts as a β element can become a protoemotion, a shared emotional turbulence, an affect and, finally, a "thought". Although the formation of thought may be regarded as a continuous miracle, it is at the same time no more than a thin film (Hautmann) constantly at risk of dissolution or falsification.

Countertransference dreams bear witness to the ways and means whereby the analyst's mind begins to transform patients' aggression, as well as the difficulty of this process. These dreams are often emergency attempts – which do not always succeed – to avoid "clogging" of the analyst's mind; they relieve mental suffering by the reconstruction of meaning and symbolic spaces, by "alphabetizing" scattered β elements.

I have frequently been struck by the sense of well-being that follows such dreams, to the point of waiting and hoping for them to come when I have felt mentally invaded by patients' violent projective identifications.

Here are some examples, originally published in a paper by Barale and myself (Barale & Ferro, 1993).

The planting spades and the entryphone

This illustration dates from a period of intense fatigue on my part, due partly to a heavy workload and partly to the activation of a massive psychotic transference in a seriously ill patient.

I dreamed that I was being ripped apart by patients with planting spades. Then, in a very violent town, there was a knock at my door; I was expecting a friend, the son of Gaspare the porter, but my father pressed the entryphone button to open the door before checking who was there. He now rashly threw the door wide open and waited, while I wondered anxiously: "Suppose it is someone dangerous and my father opens the door – how will I be able to defend myself?"

The dream warned me of my mental fatigue: the parental function was ready to resume its duties towards patients who, at this time, were experienced as dangerous by the tired, exposed and defenceless part of myself. This contact with my current difficulty enabled me to reflect on the problem of my tiredness and, in particular, of how to turn to account not what the patients were afraid of doing to me but what they were actually doing to me by their violent projective identifications (the planting spades that were ripping me apart). The availability with which I found myself opening the door (both of the consulting room and of my mind) to the patients may perhaps have been a function of the work of transformation that I was supposed to be capable of undertaking from day to day, from session to session and from week to week.

It seems to me that these dreams form a continuum with self-analysis dreams, which allow the resumption of useful work after the mapping of dark areas or old scars.

Arrows and boards

In another dream of the same period, I was in Africa; expecting an attack by savages, I had some wooden boards erected to protect me from their arrows. The boards did not seem very strong, but would probably suffice for the purpose, as they were tied together. Even so, fearing they might be too fragile, I felt it would be safer to have each board reinforced by a supporting post. I was in touch with the difficulties of my work; there was a protective, absorbent barrier, which also distinguished me from the patient. However, I also needed to be able to call upon a father function or combined object to guarantee my mental stability.

The shift towards elements of self-analysis is even more pronounced in a sequence of dreams that referred specifically to Giulio, the patient with a severe psychotic transference.

Giulio's telephone calls

For some time I had experienced Giulio as a "persecutory double" (Gaburri, 1986), until I had a dream that enabled me to "disentangle" my double from him and gradually to distinguish myself from it.

In the dream I had given my double a first name and a surname and had noticed certain of its peculiarities.

One big problem remaining in Giulio's analysis was that he would telephone unremittingly, thereby arousing anxiety in me. During the same period I noticed that I was tempted to collude with other patients too and to tolerate a degree of "letting things go", until, after reading an excellent paper by a colleague on the oedipal situation, I had another dream: on receiving a threatening telephone call in which someone with an almost unintelligible voice claimed to be allied to a general, I was overcome by panic; my good objects were present in the telephone call and I needed to protect them. I felt alone, despairing of the possibility of obtaining help from the police, but then a very dear friend's hand was affectionately placed on my shoulder.

The telephone call was from an intensely feared split-off primitive part that was holding my mature parts to ransom (in the same way as it was undermining the maintenance of the setting in Giulio's analysis) through the collusion of the general/parent who allowed himself to be corrupted by the tyrannical child. This realization enabled me to regain contact with my ego, which was alone and terrified at having to bow to the dictates of this archaic voice: I was afraid I might not be able to find help in my investigation of the patient, but discovered a firm and reliable friend in my analysis and my present self-analytical capacity.

Notes

1 This organization can be found in two papers to the São Paulo congress on Bion (Ferro, 1996a, 1996b).
2 [Translator's note: The Italian word *pene* can mean either "penis" (masculine singular) or "pain(s)" (feminine plural).]
3 This character of course has an almost infinite range of connotations, such as *colombo* [Italian for pigeon or dove], "Cristoforo Colombo" [Italian for Christopher Columbus], "Lieutenant Columbo", etc.
4 The book is *Tooth and Claw* (J.L. Cloudsley-Thompson, 1980, Dent, London), whose chapters have the following evocative titles: "Life in a hole", "Disguise", "Camouflage", "Spines", "Mimicry", "Predator–prey interaction", and so on.
5 The "mother" here is understood figuratively; she stands for a significant function within the relational field in which the child finds himself living.
6 Although one can imagine a mother with an efficient α function who has an unreceptive blind spot precisely for aggression.
7 Bion puts this as follows in *Elements of Psycho-Analysis*: "In the situation where the β-element [. . .] is projected by the infant and received by the container in such a way that it is 'detoxicated', that is, modified by the container so that the infant may take it back into its own personality in a tolerable form. [. . .] the β-element has had removed from it the excess of emotion that has impelled the growth of the restrictive and expulsive component" (Bion, 1963). The opposite situation applies in *hyperbole*: "the

emotion that cannot tolerate neglect grows in intensity, is exaggerated to ensure attention and the container reacts by more, and still more, violent evacuation" (Bion, 1965).

8 [Translator's note: *Ferro* means an iron, but is also, of course, the author's name.]
9 [Translator's note: The Italian word *spoletta* (plural *spolette*) can mean either a reel (as a cotton reel) or a fuse (for detonating an artillery shell).]
10 [Translator's note: *Pastina* refers to small items of pasta, but in a decorating context is presumably a kind of thick paint.]
11 [Translator's note: *Turca* is a kind of ottoman, but can also mean "Turkish woman".]
12 [Translator's note: *Centauri* can mean either "centaurs" or "racing motorcyclists".]
13 The same could be said to apply to the analyst's possible defensive use of interpretative aggression during the sessions.
14 The subject of narcissism really deserves a chapter of its own, but here I should merely like to emphasize two points. The first is the enormous *fragility* of the narcissistic patient. As stated in an earlier contribution (Ferro, 1993f), a little boy patient with severe narcissistic pathology told me while playing that a certain stone seemed to be a diamond, the hardest and most precious of stones, but if placed in a tray and immersed in a *special liquid*, it would actually turn out to be a very fragile crystal. The analyst must therefore ensure that his observing and his mind constitute that *special liquid*. To avoid shattering and allow survival, the fragile stone appears hardened, set like concrete. The narcissistic patient *cannot* – he lacks the capacity to – withstand for any length of time (without shattering) emotional states such as separation anxiety, need, dependence, jealousy, envy, exclusion, and so on. My patient lacked an "appropriate narrator" (see Chapter 7) – one who would seek confirmation in the child himself, rather than one capable of reverie on the child's primitive mental states – and so he had learned to defend against intolerable mental states by splitting them off, often causing others to experience them in his place. The narcissistic patient has a constant need for "porters" to experience intolerable emotional states on his behalf. Self-idealization, seeming self-sufficiency and superiority (contempt, in more serious cases) are the bandages that protect him from shattering. If the analyst succeeds in using the *special liquid*, these patients will take optimum advantage of the analysis if it is commensurate with their capacity to tolerate it – i.e. if it is based substantially, and for long periods, on the characters who serve as "porters", without making explicit the relational aspect of their communication and without prolonged emphasis on the envy and jealousy they have had to split off. One possibility is to start with "rage" and the wounds resulting from it, to continue with separation anxieties and then to move on gradually to other feelings the patient has never been able to experience, as the "apparatus for thinking thoughts" progressively grows stronger. These patients cause severe countertransference problems, which can be solved if seen in terms of emotions the patient is unable to experience but which he must induce in those close to him – for example, *irritation*, feelings of *exclusion* or a sense of *worthlessness*. Direct interpretations on the denial of dependence or of need are not only useless but also harmful. The requirement is simply to experience the emotions the patient has always split off and projected and to metabolize them into entities having a form acceptable to the patient in an sharable narration. The second point is the analyst's need to *be efficient at all times*; if the analyst is good at accepting projective identifications, he will soon be faced with this difficulty – and here again he must not interpret but instead "digest". A rather odd situation then arises in which interpretations (at least as commonly understood) lose much of their significance; the fundamental requirement, instead, is to accept the ungrateful task the patient imposes on the analyst through his projective identifications, lacking as he does the equipment to perform it himself – namely, the task of experiencing and gradually transforming certain emotions in the patient's place (Bion, 1987; Kancyper, 1989, 1990; Goijman, 1988, 1990).

15 [Translator's note: Piero Chiara is the author of gentle, everyday stories set in the Lombard countryside featuring "ordinary" characters in ordinary situations; his work contrasts starkly with Dostoyevsky's tales of passion.]

16 The problem of aggressive acting out in the session often corresponds, and draws attention, to a failure of the analyst's capacity to receive and transform: the patient then finds himself compelled to act out evacuatively the quantity of β elements not accepted and digested. Furthermore, when seriously ill patients have fits of smashing things to pieces, this is often their way – perhaps the only way they have – of coming into contact with, or causing other people to come into contact with, and representing their situation, in which they "smash everything to pieces because they are (or have been) broken to pieces inside". In other words, even the most serious instances of acting out (within the session) can be understood as communications, as these patients' only form of symbolization within the setting. In some situations, of course, analysis is not enough and the patient has to be given a safety net, such as a colleague to supply medication or have him admitted to hospital or support him during crises or holidays. As stated in Chapter 2, the analyst also has a "tolerability limit", beyond which he may even decide to terminate the patient's contract if the patient subverts the rules on which the "analytic game" depends. If the analyst is able to function as an elastic container, this will be indicated by dreams.

Chapter 7

The "narrator" and fear

Some ideas based on Freud's "The 'uncanny'"

In this chapter I should like to distinguish two approaches to the subject of fear. The first derives from a one-person psychology, as clearly embodied in Freud's theory, whereas the second, a two-person psychology, is perhaps best epitomized in the model developed by Bion and by Baranger & Baranger. The chapter's "bifocal" title places equal emphasis on fear and on the narrator, for reasons that will become evident later.

However, let us proceed in an orderly manner and commence our examination of fear by considering Freud's celebrated 1919 paper "The 'uncanny'" (Freud, 1919).

After a detailed investigation of the various possible meanings of the word *heimlich*, Freud (1919) notes that it belongs to "two sets of ideas, [. . .] what is familiar and agreeable, and [. . .] what is concealed and kept out of sight. [. . .] everything is *unheimlich* that ought to have remained secret and hidden but has come to light".

As if proving a theorem, he goes on to demonstrate his original conception step by step, extending his concepts, adding notes, and referring in particular to Hoffmann's tales *The Sand-Man* and *The Devil's Elixir*, the theme of the "double", "involuntary repetition" and the "omnipotence of thoughts". He concludes that the sense of the "uncanny" is aroused by the unexpected return of a repressed content, often due to an external stimulus.

The repressed material concerned, involving emotional and affective constellations, suddenly irrupts into consciousness; hence the feeling of something "familiar", because it has in fact always belonged and still does belong to us (and ought to have remained concealed).

In this connection, Freud of course assigned great importance to the fundamental instinctual drives and the associated defensive structures. In the lecture "Wir und der Tod" ["Death and ourselves"] delivered to the "Wien" Lodge of the Jewish B'nai B'rith in Vienna in 1915 (Freud, 1915), he told his audience that "primitive man was a very passionate being, crueller and more wicked than all the other beasts, who was not restrained by any instinct from killing and devouring members of his own species. [. . .] he liked to kill and taking life was a matter of course to him". Now it is precisely these instinctual impulses and their complexes that are repressed. There are abundant examples from contemporary literature and cinema that are closer to our own cultural experience than those presented by Freud. The most telling is perhaps Hitchcock's film *The Birds* (1963), in which something familiar in Bodega Bay turns into a nightmare after the arrival of the heroine, a possible partner for a widow's son. The widow is afraid that her son, with whom she has a fusional relationship, might abandon her, and in consequence hate, rage and jealousy are unleashed in persecutory fashion and flood the scene. In Don Segal's *Invasion of the Body Snatchers* (1956), every living being, by falling asleep, allows itself to be replaced by a double previously grown in a huge pod: now what could be more familiar than one's own repressed or split-off emotions or parts of oneself which are rediscovered in nascent form beside one? In McLeod Wilcox's film *Forbidden Planet* (1956), a spaceship lands on the heavenly body in question and the crew find the survivors of an earlier mission, Dr Morbius and his 20-year-old daughter. The doctor has been able to *read* the extraordinary inventions of the highly evolved and intelligent civilization that used to inhabit the planet but then mysteriously disappeared. The doctor's companions and spaceship have been destroyed by terrible monsters. When the doctor's daughter decides to leave the planet with the new mission's captain, with whom she has fallen in love, the monsters are reactivated. After many vicissitudes, they turn out to be "monsters from the id" of Dr Morbius, incarnated by machines invented by the vanished civilization – it had been destroyed by the repressed monsters of its own unconscious – and now restored to life by entering the electricity generators.

The plethora of possible examples range from Kafka and the tales of Dino Buzzati to the enormous number of variations on the theme of the double.

But let us reverse our perspective and, instead of considering how the narrator (the film director or novelist) can evoke the uncanny or fear, look at the idea of *fear* as the promoter and activator of stories in the narrator himself. The narrative transformation is a response to the narrator's own fears and anxieties, which are converted into "stories" (films, tales, paintings, etc.) instead of symptoms or behaviours. The *need to narrate* (or create) becomes a therapeutic factor in relation to anxieties, dreads and fears. However, delving beyond the genesis of the creative processes, I should like to discover the *primal matrix of the need to create*: could it be that "narration" is a fundamental need of the human species, in response to the fear and terror of something more primitive than and prior to the repressed?

Here we are assisted by Bion's model of the genesis of thought, which in his view arises out of the meeting of urgent needs – "nameless terror" – with the mother's capacity for reverie. In other words, the primitive fantasies, protoemotions and undifferentiated, confused bodily sensations from the infant (Bion's "β elements") are evacuated into the mother's mind, where, if received, they are transformed into something thinkable and tolerable.

This process is mediated by what Bion calls the mother's capacity for reverie, which transforms the crude β elements into α elements – i.e., in effect, the emotional pictograms or visual images that constitute the building blocks of thought. Put differently, every quantum of fear, terror and the like is transformed by the receiving mother's mind into "Lego pieces" (α elements), which the subject will subsequently be able to organize into dream thoughts and thoughts proper. However, in this early emotional relationship, not only are the β elements alphabetized, but the mother also gradually passes on the capacity to transform β into α (see Chapters 1 and 4).

Many of the most serious pathologies are, as we know, connected with dysfunctions of these basic operations. The α function, once introjected, remains with us as a transforming "mill to grind fears and terrors" into dreams, fantasies and narrations.

I believe that fairy tales are an excellent demonstration of this interaction between the narrator of the tale itself – which has to be told orally and not read or seen in a video – and the child, through this process of putting children's deepest fears into story form, usually with a happy ending (Ferro, 1985; Ferro & Meregnani, 1995).

We are now in a position to reformulate our ideas on the genesis of fear: we are afraid when alone and ill-equipped to confront over-intense emotional proto-experiences. This situation is commonly observed in children, in the form of fear of the dark (the condition for the fantasies most profoundly hidden by the light to emerge into the room), fear of falling asleep (and of entering the forest of dreams and the child's own internal world), and fear of nightmares (indigestion when the "dream" fails to digest excessive internal and external stimuli).

Hence the importance of the "narrator", whether of fables and fairy tales, or in the form of Virgil accompanying Dante in the circles of Hell, or of the special "narrating companion" represented by the analyst.

Fear arises whenever our "internal narrator" is overtaxed. The figure of the "internal narrator" was described by Bion in his discussion of the α function and of the "apparatus for thinking thoughts"; however, a better account had already been given by Robert Louis Stevenson in "A chapter on dreams" (Stevenson, 1892), when he wrote of the "Little People [. . .] my Brownies, [. . .] who do one-half my work for me while I am fast asleep, and in all human likelihood do the rest for me as well".

On the subject of fears, a brief mention of *phobias* is appropriate. Phobias can be imagined as occurring when the narrator has not been empowered to negotiate excessively dangerous and terrifying "clods" of emotion – or rather, when the external narrator has not been able to negotiate these and therefore not allowed the subject to introject an adequate narrator. True phobias must, of course, be distinguished from *socially shared* ones (which involve a collective overload with no specific individual meanings) and from infantile fears (which all children may experience in certain phases of growth).

A true phobia is to be understood as a motiveless, irrational fear of something, a fear that will not yield to any argument. There is no field that cannot be invested with and become an object of fear. The classical behaviour towards a phobia is *avoidance* of the phobic situation.

Phobias always represent some difficulty or "no through road" in the internal world; by displacing the entity concerned and projecting it outside himself, the subject not only liberates the internal world but also succeeds in "controlling" the problem in the external environment.

Failure of narration

Phobias can thus be thought of as a partial failure of the mental capacity to produce transformational narrations from the subject's own protofantasies. In some cases, however, the situation is even more serious, for example when the capacity to embody fantasies in mental representations fails still more drastically. Ray Bradbury's story "The Veld" offers a good example.

"The Veld"

A futuristic house has a nursery with a two-dimensional ceiling and walls, which, however, can become three-dimensional and assume depth, according to the children's mental contents. (So with the story and characters of Aladdin or Alice, or any other emotional reality.)

One day the parents of the two children featured begin to worry about the insistent images of ferocious lions on the nursery walls. They even decide to lock up the room, so intense is the fear aroused in them by these images. The children are very upset but are eventually allowed to play in the room one last time. They call their parents inside, and then: "Mr Hadley looked at his wife and they turned and looked back at the beasts edging slowly forward, crouching, tails stiff. Mr and Mrs Hadley screamed. [. . .] now the lions had done feeding [. . .]. The vultures were dropping down the blazing sky."

This in my view is an extraordinary description of the virtual becoming concrete, or of what happens when the field collapses, so that the patient's communications lose the status of virtuality and are "taken" as part of external reality instead of the "pretend" reality of the field.

Note that the events of the story take place in a fully automated house, in which the nursery walls constitute the only "primitive" space; furthermore, in their terror of the fantasies inspired by the virtual reality and despite having promised the children that they were "free to play" at will in the nursery, the parents had gone to the control panel and operated the "nursery destruct" lever.

In other words, when the automatic mechanism of the relationship, of interpretations or of theories in the session arouses very primitive images or gives rise to evacuations of β screens, that is the dangerous moment of potential collapse of the field. An analyst who loses the capacity to "virtualize" the patient's communication is caught up in a real game, resulting in the loss of the very characteristics that constitute the analytic game, in which everything is permitted *in terms of play*; and the penalty is loss of the nursery and of the analytic situation itself.

In the clinical situation, however, what happens when the mental function of making narrative pictograms of protoemotions fails? *Hic sunt leones*, as Bradbury might say.

What, we may now ask, is the fate of these lions, these masses of unthinkability? The answer is evacuation, which may be massive and destructive as in hallucination, or involve psychosomatic illness or behaviour devoid of the substance of thought, such as characteropathic acting out, delinquency or drug addiction.

Therapy in all these situations involves the weaving of a narrative plot out of what the patient has been unable to "digest"; this transformation may be effected in any of the analytic couple's dialects, such as historical reconstruction, fantasies of the internal world, and so on – but these are only examples of possible "cuisines".

Bion holds that every individual has a "psycho-analytic function of the personality" (1962) and that the analyst, in interpreting, does what a father and mother do when they understand their child through reverie. Incidentally, Kennedy (1978) also writes that parents influence their children's capacity for self-observation and insight in accordance with the way they teach them to handle their own impulses and feelings.

On the basis of the specific "theory of mind" due to Premack & Woodruff (1978) – who discuss the psychic processes underlying the progressive emergence of theories about the state of the subject's own mind and the minds of others – Fonagy & Moran (1991) write that, in circumstances where intolerable mental pain is anticipated, some borderline patients greatly curtail their own capacity to form an opinion of their own and others' mental states. This leads me to the matter of insight, as formulated by Bion (1970) in the subtitle to *Attention and Interpretation*, which is "A scientific approach to insight in psycho-analysis and groups". Bion notes that for some patients contact with reality presents most difficulty when that reality is their own mental state. Again, some people who cannot tolerate pain and frustration "feel the pain but will not suffer it". Observing also that the process of mental maturation is painful, he notes, after his famous "liars" example, that if "entertained, they [thoughts] are conducive to mental health; if not, they initiate disturbance".

Bion points out, too, that for the analyst any "attempt to cling to what he knows must be resisted for the sake of achieving a state of mind analogous to the paranoid-schizoid position". This is the state of mind of "negative capacity", of patience, of tolerating the frustration of not knowing, in the awareness that the "human animal has not ceased to be persecuted by his mind and the thoughts usually associated with it – whatever their origin might be".

Postscript
The quadrants of the setting

The setting constitutes the rules that must be observed if our game is to be playable and if it is to be the right game (analysis!). In this connection it is appropriate to consider in depth Bion's (1963) concept of "reversal of perspective", a situation in which the game the analyst thinks he is playing does not correspond to the one the patient is actually, albeit unconsciously, playing. It is, I believe, to some extent legitimate for the patient to try to play a game of his own, but it is up to the analyst to draw attention to the fact and to re-establish the rules of a game that can be shared.

At any rate, if transformational operations are to be possible, the setting must be a container with properties of elasticity and absorbency (Fiorentini *et al.*, 1993, 1995; Giuffrida, 1995; Quinodoz, 1992; Robutti, 1993; Bonasia, 1994a).

Bion (1965) points out that the "analytic situation" can merely approximate to what is desirable and that the "terrain" in which transformations take place calls for further study.

My own considerations on the setting follow. I analyse four of the main senses in which the term "setting" is used, which, because certain prevailing meanings are emphasized in each, I propose to call its four quadrants; however, it is their combination that makes up the setting as a whole.

The setting as a set of formal rules

This is the first quadrant. It comprises the set of rules or behaviours which, once established, prefigure the psychoanalytic situation. These rules and behaviours can in effect be seen as invariants that allow a process to take place (Meltzer, 1967).

The setting is a precipitate of experiences derived from the working methods – and personal requirements – built up by Freud over the years into a stable structure that proved most appropriate for the conduct of psychoanalytic psychotherapy.[1]

In this first sense, the components of the setting are the arrangement of the room, the form and conditions of the meeting between the protagonists, the regularity and length of sessions, and so on. The setting thus has a *physiology* of its own, which centres on the contract, subjective customs, fees, holidays, cancellation of sessions, and the regulation of what *happens or may happen* between analyst and patient. These aspects are described and specified in detail by Etchegoyen (1986).

One formal aspect of the setting to which I should like to draw particular attention is as follows. Whereas the setting protects the analyst from interference by the patient, it can conversely also be seen as a way of protecting the patient (and other patients). It limits the time for which the analyst is exposed to the patient's projective identifications and protects his existence outside the analysis. This problem assumes paramount importance with seriously ill patients, who would otherwise tend to invade the analyst's actual life; such patients often need other forms of protection and containment outside the analytic sessions, extending from the involvement of a psychiatrist who can prescribe drugs to possible hospitalization.

I am of course referring here to formal limitations on patients' intrusiveness. Quite a different problem is presented by patients who mentally invade the analyst and, as Bion notes, remain in his head, on account of their greed or the sheer volume of their projective identifications, for the metabolization of which the analyst needs a long period of time (Barale & Ferro, 1993).

The setting as the "analyst's mental attitude"

To regard this second quadrant as an invariant is surely illusory. The analyst's mental life has oscillations of its own, which stem from the play of his fantasies and the PS–D and ♀ ♂ oscillations of his mind; the very creativity of the analyst is a function of such oscillations. If the analyst is, as he must be, permeable to his patient's emotional states, it is not uncommon for his mental attitude to vary in accordance with the projective identifications he is called upon to receive and transform (Di Chiara, 1983; Brenman-Pick, 1985). In a field context, of course, these variables can be regarded as necessary and certainly as not something the analyst should feel guilty about, for he, after all, contributes to the structuring of the emotional field, of which he is a living part (Baranger & Baranger, 1961–62; Bion, 1962; Corrao, 1986).

The patient appears in one way or another as the guardian of the setting (in the first and second senses) (Preve, 1988), constantly pointing out both formal deficiencies and variations in the analyst's attitude, receptivity and availability; the patient will even draw attention to moments when the analyst is not on form or when the flow of projective identifications is actually reversed (Ferro, 1987).

Assuming that the analyst is permeable and receptive, his mental attitude will, if seen as a variable of the field to whose formation he in any case contributes, be *continuously disturbed and continuously refound* – that is, given an availability on his part for the patient's most primitive states of mind and protoemotions.

The setting as a target: breaches of the setting by the patient and the modulating and transforming activity of the analyst

Events in the analyst's consulting room are not as simple as the foregoing might suggest.

Instead of playing the game, the patient often commits "breaches of the setting"; these have long been interpreted as "attacks on the setting", which they certainly are. Indeed, nothing is more likely to induce a crisis in the analyst than the feeling that his ultimate certainties and "constitutional" guarantees have been called into question, based as many of them are on precise observance of the setting. However, such an approach has too often distracted us from realizing how extraordinarily rich in communication breaches of the setting by the patient can be – but we must then be sufficiently available to consider them in this light. Basically, as with any type of acting out, our ability to identify the disturbance, interference, danger or communicative aspect of these phenomena will depend on our level of toleration and capacity to assign (or, sometimes, suspend) meaning; the same, after all, applies to projective identifications. In my view, every analyst should have a clear notion of the extent of his ability to tolerate breaches of the setting, because this becomes *one of his criteria of analysability*.

The setting may be regarded as a claustrum (Meltzer, 1992) or as a container with properties of elasticity and robustness (Bion, 1962), but in any case the *target* to be aimed for must in my opinion be an absolutely rigorous setting.

In the analysis of seriously ill patients, this target will, I repeat, be attained only after both the formal setting and the analyst's internal setting have been subjected to every kind of turmoil.

Breaches of the setting may affect both the formal setting and the analyst's mental attitude, which may be disrupted by the patient's projective identifications. As stated above, precisely this *aspect of the "amount of internal disruption" the analyst can tolerate* will become one of his criteria of analysability, of which he must be conscious.

Use of the couch

Anna was a patient I shall refer to again; for this reason I shall say now only that, at the beginning of her analysis, she was intolerant of any kind of relationship that was not symbiotic and fusional. She had not managed to lie down on the couch, but sat on it (at first, in fact, she did not even dare to sit on it, but would very cautiously explore the entire room, as if staking out the territory with a view to discovering possible sources of danger). Here are some of this patient's dreams, dating from the time when, after several years of analysis, she finally succeeded in lying down on the couch (the dreams of course came after the first few occasions when she had lain down). (a) A kitten had an injured *back*, and when she stroked it, everything was contaminated. (b) Her friend Carla *separated* from her husband

and went to live in Iceland. (c) What was happening at a school? Was someone killing children? (d) She was in a room with a nun, with whom she had a very bad relationship because her daughter had died; then she met a woman friend with a 1930s overcoat.

These dreams highlighted and paved the way for the metabolization of what had been activated in the patient after the changes that had enabled her to assume a new spatial "position" in the consulting room – a new position that was to an even greater extent a mental position. Consider the suffering of the kitten with the injured back, an injury caused by contact with the analytical couch, and the feelings of *contamination* that invaded her on making contact with her own suffering; the mourning resulting from assuming a greater distance, which made her feel as if she were on an island and, into the bargain, one that was far away and cold; incipient thoughts of possible dependence within the analysis, and acceptance of an asymmetry ("school" as a place to learn); feeling the pain aroused by the end of an initial, infantile part of the analysis and the dawning recognition of herself as an adult approaching her thirties, rather than as the three-year-old girl she had thought she was and had needed to be seen as; and the projection of mourning on to the nun, saddened at the loss of a daughter who was growing up and going away. These, of course, are only some of the possible developments of these dreams.

Anna's "frustrating use of the couch" was of course characterized for a long time by forward thrusts and subsequent retreats; other dreams gradually drew attention to emotional movements connected with the possible acceptance of a greater distance and the progressive relinquishment of the need to control every posture or emotion of mine. Here are some more examples.

At the beginning of a session, Anna immediately lay down on the couch and began to speak about her frustrating mother (the patient was 26 years old!), who had decided to take away her cigarettes and chocolate. She then brought some dreams: she was riding a horse along an escarpment at speed . . . at a gallop . . . she fell . . . there was a green field . . . but she had not hurt herself and was not too upset . . . then there was a tank of little red fish (no longer the piranhas of previous dreams) swimming towards the water purifying unit, from which big bubbles were issuing . . . she took the fish in her hand for a while . . . the tank contained some algae and food for the fish . . .

The dreams clearly demonstrate the frustration and renunciation involved in lying down, the galloping feelings aroused, which unsaddled her, but then it was not so painful after all! These feelings could now finally be considered ("touched") and the new position proved not to be so terrible . . . the little fish had someone to care for them and were provided with food and an α function.

In a later session, Anna lay down on the couch and spoke of the difficulty of studying Spanish (there was a lithograph of Barcelona on the wall opposite the couch); she then remembered a trip to Spain, on which she had felt disgusted in a hotel where she had met a young married couple; she also remembered having had her first period on this trip, marking the transition from girlhood to young womanhood. Finally, she commented on her boyfriend's pride at having an office all of his own in the foreign section of a multinational corporation.

A whole series of progressive and regressive movements had thus got under way: the new language to be learned; the disgust at the new situation, but alongside it also the idea of a married couple and the analytic journey in motion; growth from girlhood to womanhood and its marking (by menstruation), and even the pride at the new position achieved (both physical and mental); the office in the foreign section and the various aspects of herself that were beginning to coexist.

I should like to emphasize that Anna won through to the use of the couch without my pushing her in any way. When I suggested at the beginning of the analysis that she might perhaps lie down, she brought a dream in the next session in which she was on a very long chute with knife blades sticking up at the bottom; she was thus sliding down these blades, bleeding and torn apart at the terror of ending up "squashed" against a wall. The cost of this emotional "laceration" obviously seemed excessive to me, and I was therefore able to allow Anna time to – let us say – "swim over to the couch".

There are *other possible places* for the patient in the room, each of which can be regarded as pertaining to a particular communication that must be received and understood on the basis of all the other components of the field (in a different language from the vicissitudes of the transference–countertransference axis). If one is used to working with small children and seriously ill patients, one is likely to find it much easier, when the patient takes up a particular position in the space of the room, to see the situation in terms of communication (as indeed with any form of acting in) rather than as a violation of or even an attack on the setting (Bonasia, 1994a; Conrotto, 1995).

I recall one woman patient who came into the room and ensconced herself on my writing desk; she would not budge from it until I told her that she reminded me of Italo Calvino's "Baron in the Trees", who was so alienated by his fellow men that he was no longer prepared to share the earth with them and took to the trees; I was then able to connect this angry reaction of the patient with what had happened in the previous session.

However, it was Laura who assumed the oddest position ever taken up by any of my patients: she came in and immediately settled in my armchair. I cannot recall ever having been so dumbfounded; it was something that "could not be happening", I said to myself indignantly, and was neither foreseen nor foreseeable. However, these countertransference experiences of mine enabled me to formulate the appropriate interpretation: my unforeseen (and unforeseeable) communication of the cancellation of two sessions had made her feel so ousted from her position and expropriated from her territory that she had to make me go through the same experience. Laura thereupon got up and went over to her couch.

There is of course no code for interpreting the (physical and emotional) positions the patient may assume in the consulting room, nor is the use of the couch precluded only by separation anxieties.

At the beginning of his analysis and for a long time thereafter, Marco would sit down in a small armchair opposite my own armchair in the other corner of the room; we were like two boxers in the corners of the ring. The boxer "brother" was the subject of the patient's first communications; Marco had to keep an explosive emotional situation carefully under control. It took years of work for this climate to be gradually transformed, so that Marco could move to a different position, at first "sitting" and ultimately lying down on the couch; these various positions in the physical space of the session of course corresponded to a range of differing emotional positions (Ferro, 1991a).

I would merely emphasize that, in all the varied breaches of the setting I have had to cope with and sometimes to confront, I have never moved from "my analyst's armchair", understood both in the physical sense and as the mental place from which to observe all the emotional and other facts of the analytic consulting room. Indeed, I believe that the "analytic mental attitude" and the emotional (and physical) position of the analyst in the room constitute a kind of "north", a fixed compass point from which to give a bearing to the patient and to the emotions of the room.

Missed sessions and late arrival for sessions

These are certainly meaningful occurrences, which can in turn be understood as attacks on the setting – and so indeed they are, because they in some way "disturb" the work in progress – but they can also be seen as valuable communications that facilitate reattunement with the patient and adjustment of one's timing or inter-pretative attitude; furthermore, viewed in this light, they are mostly early signs of a looming negative therapeutic reaction (Barale & Ferro, 1992). The first person to experience these situations as dangerous and to have guilt feelings about them is often the patient himself (before he has been helped to capture the communica-tive register and, instead of judging what is happening, to understand why it is happening). Here is how one patient experienced the missing of one of his sessions after a lapse of time: "My brother once made me feel very guilty because I had taken away a stone from a huge pile at Herculaneum; he told me that I might be preventing the reconstruction of an entire mosaic, because that one little piece would be missing." And later, in a similar situation: "I was touring the ruins of an ancient city, and allowed my little niece to play in one of the tombs, where she was amusing herself climbing up and down. The guard told me off because the little girl might spoil the reliefs, but I thought he was exaggerating; there was no risk, and apart from amusing herself, my niece was able to exercise her freedom by running about and climbing up and down."

The first example evinces guilt and the fear that skipping one of the sessions in the pile might ruin the analysis; although the guard's disapproval still features in the second, now the superego is seen in perspective, and there is a capacity to manage mourning and put something living in the place of what has been lost . . . involving also the exercise of creativity.

Here are some more clinical situations in which problems of this kind arose.

White Fang's bites

Sandra arrived a quarter of an hour late and began by telling me how her husband had taken her son and herself to see *White Fang*, a lovely adventure film, but difficult for the three-year-old boy to follow (the analysis too was three years old!), and, furthermore, it contained bloody scenes, in which White Fang used the eponymous organ to attack and was similarly attacked himself. She then spoke of the difficulty of reconciling the mother's *agnolotti*[2] with her working hours at the hospital . . . and mentioned that her son had several times shouted "Grandad, Grandad!" in the cinema . . . *After this she had cut down on her time at the hospital, where she had been overloaded with patient visits, and in this way she had slightly reduced her working hours.*

This session followed another in which I had given a large number of relational interpretations, on account of a particular figure who had then taken the stage, namely a supervisor who had said that it was important to explain to a child what was happening in a therapy in relationship terms. I had then considered it appropriate to offer transference interpretations of some of Sandra's communications; however, I had plainly exaggerated, so that many communications had been experienced as White Fang bites terrifying to the infantile part of the patient, who had been unable to reconcile the "agnolotti" with the "work" and, worn out, had cut a quarter of an hour from her attendance time in the session.

This is a good illustration of the need to form a sufficiently robust and capacious container ($♀$)[3] before interpreting, because even correct, true interpretations might give rise to excessive persecution and anxiety if forced into a container that has not yet acquired sufficient solidity and, in particular, availability. However, this subject has already been discussed in Chapters 2 and 3.

Mariella's broken tooth

It was the first session of the week. Interpreting in the last session of the previous week, I had used two of the patient's dreams to draw her attention to two ways she had of seeing myself, the analysis and reality: the first as a Mafia gangster like Coppola's *Godfather* – based on economic self-interest/economic narcissism – and the other affectionately, as in Scola's film *La famiglia*, involving the affects. Mariella arrived half an hour late, explaining that one of the "teeth" of her key had broken off in the lock. In particular, however, she had had a terrible row with her husband, who had accused her of excessive dependence and lack of autonomy in accepting the suggestion of her father, a wealthy landowner, to transfer only the formal ownership of his property to her but not to give her the use of it; he had done this to reduce his assets for accounting purposes, out of self-interest and not for the benefit of his daughter, considering that she did not have the use of the property for the time being.

My interpretation had therefore been experienced as evacuative, corresponding more to my need to divest myself of it than to an actual "gift"; it had originated too much "from me" and had not been enough of a two-person construction, thus giving rise "in the husband" (the part of the patient that was still intolerant of dependence) to high levels of persecution, rage and envy.

One possible view would, of course, be that everything that constitutes an attack on dependence must be explained and interpreted. That is not my way. In my opinion, a long period of joint construction is necessary, enabling the patient to feel himself to be an active part of the process and to develop his own creativity, rather than having his "*teeth broken*" by the analyst's interpretations, which compel the patient to build for himself, often at his own expense, the house in which to accommodate the analyst's already saturated interpretations (Winnicott, 1971).

Acting in

In these situations too there are, as stated, two possible approaches: either the evacuative, or attacking, element or the communicative aspect can be seized upon.

"Have you a toilet?" asked Carlo after a dream in which Ancelotti[4] was helping him to put a flower bed in order and teaching him what to do. In another dream he had at the same time, he was standing before a forbidding school-leaving examination commission. On returning from the toilet, he said: "It was very kind of you to make your toilet available to me."

The patient had discovered that the analyst's mind was available to function as a place in which to evacuate and discharge anxieties and tensions; on this level it would have been foolish to seize upon the aspect of narcissism or abuse.

I remember working with an autistic child for whom it was a great discovery to have the experience of a mind available to accept the evacuation of anxieties; for the first time he had discovered the potential three-dimensionality of the human mind, after having only ever experienced two-dimensional minds, which had never allowed him to effect projective identifications, so that his identifications had always been adhesive (Bick, 1968; Meltzer *et al.*, 1975; Gaburri & Ferro, 1988).

The computer and the womb

Laura had become pregnant to escape her boss's excessive work demands and was forced to miss a number of sessions. This could be seen as an attack on the setting or as a way of escaping the work of analysis, but it is also possible to "think of it" as her way of expressing her own female ($♀$) needs for receptivity and time, as her only possibility of rebelling against and escaping from the automatic functioning of her boss, the manager part of herself, who worked at the computer. Once this rebellion had been accepted and understood on the level of thought, it allowed the birth of a new way of thinking of the analysis on Laura's part, in addition to that of her second child.

Mariella's match

It was a difficult phase in Mariella's analysis, when her relationships with her analyst in the analysis and with her boyfriend outside it were undergoing a change from a "services-rendered", "utilitarian" mode to one involving acknowledgement and appreciation of the bond between them and of affective dependence. This transformation was punctuated by abrupt backward steps that put our relationship sorely to the test. Mariella constantly asked for changes and postponements of session times and took it for granted that I would accede to her demands. After I had said "no" to her nth attempt to disrupt the setting, she dreamed that her boyfriend had been nasty to her and her grandmother had organized a gang to kill him; she had felt sorry and then found a chopped-off horse's head in her bed.

During this session I felt quite blocked and had difficulty in following the patient's stories, which I found confused and muddled. (However, I had my own troubles at the time, involved as I was in mourning and in a development project.)

The patient began the next session by asking me for a match; because I do not respond to such requests in my usual setting situation, I refused. I then tried to work on the meaning of the request: was she asking for a service to be rendered or did she need a flash of light in the darkness? Meanwhile the patient was talking about her father, who could not keep up with the running of the business: he was so unable to cope with the normal course of events that he had "got meningitis". I gave a "rigid-motion" transference interpretation.

Apparently not listening, the patient went on talking about her "father's meningitis" in increasingly contemptuous terms; she then again asked for a match, saying: "Either you give me a match or I'll bash your face in." Next she headed towards my desk, as she had already threatened, with a view to opening drawers and looking for matches. I got up and in turn insisted: "No!" The patient shouted: "You are mad, mad, it is you who are my ruination", and took to her heels yelling at the top of her voice.

What had happened? The patient was admittedly going through a difficult time, having acknowledged the demands of her dependent and needy self, which were being counterattacked by her narcissistic self, but I *too* was in difficulties at the time, so that rather than receiving the patient's communications I was insisting on interpreting in terms of an attempt to establish a "services-rendered" type of relationship with regard to the request for a light – that is, clarity. Furthermore, the patient was guilt-ridden at the analyst's malfunctioning, feeling that she was the virus that had caused her father's meningitis (this was true, but only partly so). And it was true that this was a difficult time for me *too*, blocked as I was by my mourning and the development project; it therefore irritated me to see myself inside the patient ("No"), who, in opening "her" drawers, saw in this "mirror" response both her own illness and the fear of having damaged the analyst himself, so that she could only run away in horror.

The cigarette and AIDS

Luigi was experiencing for the first time something he had never been able to bring back, namely the agony of separation. After years of analysis, in which separations had always been met with fits of fury and rage that had sometimes even threatened my physical integrity, or with all kinds of acting out, he was beginning to own the separation "agony" (Winnicott, 1974) he had never experienced.

He acknowledged that he had also had good feelings towards me, and that the hate on which we had worked for years masked a need that he felt. Furthermore, he had been admitted to hospital for a short time, specifically to enable him to represent and re-own separation-related feelings that he had never experienced. At the same time, after showing me a deep cut in his finger, he told me that he was smoking so much that he was afraid of hurting himself badly. I of course mentioned the hurt caused by our cut (i.e. separation), and he then asked me if I would smoke at least one cigarette with him. I felt embarrassed and puzzled by this request and thought that if I could respond with a correct interpretation, that would solve the problem for me: I said it would be a mark of peace between us – overcoming hate and smoking a pipe of peace (he was a great fan of westerns, which had been our constant companions).

He nodded, but insisted on his request; taking the cigarette, I made use of a moment of inattention on his part to let a little ash fall into my ashtray. He commented: "Doctors want to stay healthy and do not smoke; I am the one who has to smoke so much."

Although terrified of acting out, of homosexual implications and of abuse, I felt that, in the absence of a valid, earth-shattering interpretation – and none occurred to me – I had to risk it, and was about to take a puff. I was immediately seized with panic. "Oh, no, I might catch AIDS," I thought, but then, beneath the homosexual anxiety, I was able, after being in "O" with the patient, to think of what he was asking of me: to share, "on the other side of the glass", in his most painful experience or, at least to a minimal extent, to have the courage and availability to allow myself to be infected – to run the risk, if only to a minor extent (*one puff compared with the patient's 40 cigarettes!*), of participating "live" in his terrible, agonizing experience. After I had interpreted to that effect, he said: "I have been wondering about that for years" (Bezoari & Ferro, 1991b).

Swimming along to thought: Eleonora's horse

In the clinical situation I shall now describe, melancholia and its opposite, mania, were in a state of unstable equilibrium.

I had never suspected the existence of this aspect in the woman patient concerned, who came along with other problems, namely the "fear of losing her wits", going mad and fainting in the street, as well as fits of anxiety and severe agoraphobia.

The well-organized bipolar nucleus entered the analysis when Eleonora brought a funny story that was to assume central importance for us, about a horse in despair.

A keeper of horses did not know what to do with one of his animals that spent the whole day in its stable, from morning until night, crying its eyes out in despair. He therefore organized a competition with a prize for anyone who could cure the horse. No one succeeded, until an unknown person asked to have a go, on condition that he was allowed to be alone with the horse. Suddenly the animal was heard to snigger. The happy owner gave the man the prize, but after a while the horse's constant hilarity became just as intolerable to him as its previous state – indeed, even more so. Summoning the unknown man again, he asked him to restore the former situation. Back he went to the horse, which, shortly afterwards, resumed its desperate crying. At this point the animal's owner was prepared to pay anything to find out how this could have happened, and the answer came by telegram: "The first time I told him: 'Mine is bigger than yours', and the horse started sniggering; the second time I showed it to him and he lapsed into despair again."

All of a sudden, Eleonora's problem appeared to concern the management of power towards the other: she would respond with despair when I said "No" and with excitement when I said "Yes". The setting became the locus of requests, modifications and adjustments, as if something structural were subtly being put in a state of crisis. The situation appeared hopeless, like that depicted in a drawing Eleonora brought me one day, of two people tied together by the neck: one or the other was bound to be throttled.

Whenever Eleonora felt that I was refusing her something or was unavailable to her, she was plunged into the blackest despair and would forge gloomy plans of suicide, involving – as in a dream that followed my being unable to give her the fifth session she so much wanted – nothing but vipers and other snakes, together with the terror of being bitten by them. If I adhered to the setting, for example by trying not to reply directly every time, somehow or other, to her questions but instead to interpret their meaning, she would immediately feel herself – as in various dreams – to be "the maid of all work, the one at the bottom of the pile, who did not matter to anyone", a latter-day Cinderella.

However, on the occasions when I acceded to a sensible request of hers, she was immediately at "a party with violins playing and champagne corks popping for her" – Cinderella at the ball indeed.

I soon managed to put these two modes of response side by side, telling her that the difficulty appeared to be a "Ferrarelle dimension", referring to the advertisement for Ferrarelle mineral water, which could be either still or fizzy; "Ferrarelle" was also, of course, a play on my surname.

Eleonora brought a dream that combined idealization and contempt: a university professor of whom she stood greatly in awe, because he was much more powerful than she was, had a son who was a worthless artisan. After I had interpreted the dream in terms of the above two aspects, emphasizing her contempt for me, the artisan working in her service, she remembered that since her infancy her father had called her the "princess on the pea", although she claimed never to have known either the reason for this nickname or the fairy-tale concerned, whose story I briefly told her.

All this triggered some dreams: a window was open and she felt cold; she wondered what position to take up in order not to be "uncovered", and then there was a giant running along, who was too intuitive but was fond of her.

She appreciated and even idealized my capacity for intuition, but if I opened a window with my interpretation, my words sounded cold to her, almost like a rebuke, and then what was she to do to prevent the exposure of her own triumph as the "princess on the pea"?

I was presented with a new problem by her requests concerning the dates of the summer break in the analysis: if I insisted on maintaining the setting, the dreams of dangerous vipers, suicide and catastrophe returned, whereas if I implied that modifications might be possible so that she could have a few more sessions, she would dream of a terrified homosexual bearing flowers.

I realized that I would have to extricate myself from this "binary computer logic" of a "yes" or "no" answer to all her requests and all the different kinds of questions she asked me. I understood that I would have to find a way of overcoming the fascination of a compulsory "yes" or "no", each of which caused the scales to tip giddily to one side or the other, and of telling her that I could not answer "yes" or "no", but that we could only think of these matters together.

In the next session she brought a dream in which she had been to the Festival of Unity or Friendship and had done so well – and indeed, the patient I had in front of me had changed radically: previously she had given the impression of being a little girl of five or six in a pastel-coloured playsuit, but now I saw a good-looking young woman of 25.

After a few sessions, we found ourselves "off balance" again, either to one side or the other, but we now had reliable reference points to rebalance the pans of the "emotional scales" featuring in a drawing she brought me.

The requests for modification of the setting, and the direct questions, were gone now, replaced session by session by a kind of *assay* of my emotional availability and tranquillity in relation to her emotional turbulence. Whenever I was slightly less or slightly more available, this would once again shake the "scales", which would thus shift imperceptibly towards a question of carefully controlling the relational *temperature* and *distance*: "In my room there is a washbasin with a cold-water tap from which freezing cold water comes out, and another tap with hot water, which is scalding. But my parents have a mixer tap in their bath."

Whereas it might be easy to modulate distance, variations in which were immediately signalled by dreams of glaciers that could not be climbed or of meat so overdone that it stuck to the grill (which was, of course, made of iron [Ferro][5]!), it was much harder for me to regulate my deep emotional *availability*, because it was constantly influenced both by the variation of my internal defensive attitude and, in particular, by my assumption of the patient's projective identifications, of which I could become aware only after the event.

In the case of Eleonora, I should like to mention two points.

1. For a long time I had accepted the patient's yes/no bipolar functioning, which lacked the three-dimensional "thickness" of thought, and made it my own, so

that this dipole entered the sessions (probably by way of projective identifications that caused me to assume a "role" within the field – cf. Sandler, 1976).

2.   One of the patient's dreams was particularly significant, containing as it did
     two scenes which summarized the two successive yes/no emotional situations
     of the session. In the first scene, Eleonora was in despair at finding herself
     once again in extreme danger, threatened by very long vipers and other snakes,
     but in the second, the snakes *became* the spokes of the wheels of an enormous
     bicycle that was so high that the patient could hardly control it.

I was struck by the absence of transformation, as if the moment of despair and
the moment of mania were simply two different ways of assembling the same
components, which remained untransformed.

With the achievement of more thought through the awareness of my having
taken on her two-dimensional yes/no functioning, and when the patient was able
to feel that instead of operating like a computer she could "think" the snakes and
serpents and transform them, they would become a thread [*filo*] (implying a certain
affective warmth, "*fare il filo*",[6] but no longer in a scalding, erotized situation
– meat/cooked/burning/getting burnt) woven by a witch – who was also a good
sorceress – into *elastic* garments (elasticity being characteristic of thought as
compared with the rigidity of yes/no).

Humour gradually became the binder that held opposing situations together: a
request to give me a kiss was followed by a dream of kissing a tube ("kissing the
tube" was to become the emblem of requests which she herself knew would never
be acceded to), a dried-up swamp, and so on . . . until eventually she dreamed of
a kitten that managed to stay on its feet despite *waves* that could have made it fall
from the sand where it was playing.

Another characteristic of the patient's inelastic bipolar thought appeared to be
the lack of communication between positive and negative, as illustrated by the
drawing of the scales, in which communication was prevented by the existence of
the central rod. This was illustrated in a dream in which the rod – also, of course,
understood in the sense of a rigid phallic defence against mutual access – was
equated with a wall between us that made it impossible for us to communicate;
once there was an opening, the scales too would cease to exist.

After a time, when it seemed to me that the "Ferrarelle position" had stabilized,
I accepted her request for replacement of a session I had had to cancel.

In the session before the postponement, she brought a dream in which she was
in a lift which, instead of going up and down on its vertical rails, was rushing about
horizontally like a very peppy car. The lift then resumed its vertical motion and
she pressed the button for the top floor. At this point her mother appeared and, the
lift being programmable, pressed the button for the lower basement floor. The lift
now started going up, and turned into a bag; she herself became very heavy, while
the bag got torn together with a cloth she found, and hurtled down to an even lower
level than her mother.

On the day of the postponed session, she began by telling me how she had had to search high and low for her father, who was a doctor, because of a young man who had been attacked and killed as soon as he opened the door, and a girl waiting for an organ transplant.

She went on to describe the customs of certain tribes where, after a child was born, it was the man who underwent cruel suffering, whereas there were other tribes whose menfolk were hung up by metal claws and still others in which the sons were not acknowledged to have been born from sexual intercourse but considered to have been "sent by the gods if one had been good".

"Laying hands" on the setting reactivated catastrophic anxieties; postponement to a different day had the effect of inducing mania, which already seemed to contain its opposite in the mother who died if the daughter "went up", after which the daughter, who had become very heavy (through guilt?) fell to an even lower level; meanwhile I died, struck down on opening the door, and there was an organ transplant, "vita sua *mors mea*". Out into the open came the tribes with their terrible customs to mark the fundamental events of life.

A new balance was found once the normal scansion of the sessions was resumed, until, with the holidays approaching, there came a new crop of dreams involving a challenge, competition, "which one of us had a bigger one", an "organ that had absolutely not been shown". I thought of Eleonora's family situation, as the only girl with three elder and two younger brothers, all of them just a year apart, and said to myself that, if she was not to go under, a girl in this situation would have to "show herself to have a big one". This idea made me more mentally disposed to accept Eleonora's "challenges".

My changed mental attitude bore immediate fruit in the sessions, in the form of a dream in which she was in a room where a boy (♂ ?), who might have been a girl (♀ ?), *approached* her affectionately and she felt that she was fond of him; she wanted to go home with him, and his brothers (♂) wanted to come as well, but she said no to them for the time being; she took the boy home, but meanwhile he had become a girl, a little girl in fact, *actually the one who lived downstairs*, who brought her oregano and basil; after they had eaten together, she was able to tell this friend, who had to go away, that she was very fond of her, that she would wait for her, and that she was very dear to her.

This brief account in my view demonstrates some of the many possible transformations and vicissitudes to which the development of ♀, ♂ and ♀ ♂ is subject, as Bion reminds us in *Learning from Experience* (Bion, 1962) and subsequent works.

Breaches of the setting by the analyst: the setting as the locus of the most primitive and institutional parts of the personality

The starting point for this section is Bleger's fundamental paper of 1967, in which the author contends that the most primitive part of the personality – the part prior to PS, which Bleger equates with the agglutinated nucleus – is as it were deposited in strata and is violently reactivated in the event of any disturbance, whether formal or substantial, of the setting by the analyst.

Bleger refers to a setting that must be actively guaranteed by the analyst. However, considering that the analyst is the only possible vehicle for the mobilization of the agglutinated nucleus, must the analyst breach the setting deliberately? He certainly must not, Bleger replies – and Etchegoyen (1986) agrees with him – as that would be tantamount to bringing on a disease so as to facilitate its treatment. All the same, in any analysis there are bound to be occasions when the analyst will be compelled to breach or modify the setting – for example owing to existential or professional needs, illness, and so on.

It is essential in such cases to devote all possible attention to what is activated in the analyst's consulting room, because it may then be possible to make closer contact with the agglutinated nucleus and its associated system of anxieties and defences.

Besides formal breaches, there are substantial ones – that is, all the situations in which the analyst's mental attitude is disturbed, so that he himself distorts the field to whose creation he contributes.

Breaches of the setting by the analyst must also be regarded as something *to be avoided at all costs*, but *equally as inevitable* in the prolonged course of an analysis. The analyst's mind cannot remain an invariant over a period of years; existential and fantasy events will modify his mental attitude, and the analyst's availability will change appreciably as a result of mourning, worries, illness, crises, depression or frustration.

The analyst *ought* to be able to split sufficiently to *prevent* such factors from entering the consulting room as far as possible; but if the analyst is not a "decoder of fantasies", the quality of his mental functioning on a given day will surely enter into the session as a constituent of the field. This ought never to happen, but, considering that its occurrence is inevitable, it is also held to be a valuable opportunity for metabolizing what is activated in the patient. Let us consider both situations.

Formal breaches of the setting

There now follow some examples of emotional situations activated in patients when I have had to cancel sessions, usually on account of short illnesses or some unforeseen contingency.

The "sister's" upset and the horse's two kicks

After I had informed her that I had to cancel two sessions, Mariella told me that her "sister", who had been expecting to start work in a "lawyer's office", had been very upset on being told that she could not begin until later; luckily, however, her husband had himself then offered her an opportunity of working and training in his own office, commencing in the near future. Her ailing mother had cried when her sister had told her about this.

She then brought a dream in which some children were to undergo major surgery after two terrible kicks from a horse had broken their legs.

Somebody else's cup

Carla had no difficulty in accepting the postponement of a session, but then spoke of the unexpected terror that overcame her if she found herself drinking from a cup that was not her own or touching earth without gloves.

Giuliana's torn-up thesis

I telephoned my patient Giuliana to cancel her Friday session. On the Monday, she began by mentioning her deep anxiety about her mother, who must, she was afraid, be ill because she was not working as usual.

Partly because of my knowledge of the patient, I decided to follow her text, considering that a purely transpositional rigid-motion transference interpretation would have contributed nothing new, and that it would be more useful to gather together the feelings she had had in connection with her worry (thereby potentially allowing the anxieties to be metabolized on the basis of the patient's text).

Suddenly, however, Giuliana mentioned a woman friend whom she looked after like a mother and who was in analysis with Dr X; this friend had complained of certain silences, particularly concerning the relationship.

After it had crossed my mind that I seemed to be violating some code of duty, I *felt under an obligation* to ask whether perhaps, here too, something was being passed over in silence – something to do with the meaning for us of the anxieties about her mother, connected with my telephone call cancelling the session. The patient said: "I don't think so, because . . . so and so . . . this and that . . . and so on" – a string of what she regarded as valid reasons for her concern "about her mother".

In the next session she brought a dream: she had gone to Professor Y with her thesis, hoping that it would be accepted, and it seemed that it would be. But then she was in a house under construction where there were some curtains intended to separate different spaces, and along came the professor, who had changed; he rejected the thesis, tearing it up and saying: "Now you must read this book of mine and learn it."

Further comment is surely superfluous, except to draw attention to the sense of debasement and profound injury (as well as, in many cases, the activation of envy) that may be caused if the patient's retina is wounded by flooding with inappropriate light.

Mourning impossible

After the cancellation of a session, Claudio dreamed that he had been informed of the death of a loved one, a loss he had painfully accepted. His sister, however, was unconvinced and decided to investigate the matter, imagining that the person had been murdered. Another dream followed, of a coffin that could not be closed and a mourning process that could not be undertaken.

The broken eardrum

I had a brief illness at a critical point in Carla's analysis when important developments were afoot.

When the sessions resumed, the patient brought the following dreams: she was beside a swimming pool . . . she dived in after me . . . she broke an eardrum . . . while still under water, she spat out air, which she then breathed in again; then there was a young woman with a case for which there was no room in her car . . . she tried to fit it in at all costs . . .

Carlo's "stand-in" job

Carlo's analysis was in a fertile phase; he had had his first job "standing in" for someone during the Christmas holidays, and in it he had made contact with an unexpectedly peaceful external reality.

I rang him on the Sunday to cancel the Monday session. On the Tuesday he brought the following dreams: he was in a boat plunging giddily along a river full of enormous fish that terrified him; he had to climb up some stairs that led into a kitchen, inside which he found a dead nobleman whose body had already begun to decompose; in fear and terror, he thought that it would have to be buried, and reflected on the obituary to be written. Then he was in a house from which he was about to depart for a short holiday; he said no to a little boy and an appealing puppy who wanted to accompany him, but whom he did not want to be with him, but then he changed his mind and took the puppy and the little boy on holiday after all.

These dreams can be read as tokens of affective movements whereby his innermost mental situation was undergoing a radical reconfiguration, as was his own view of them: going to the river to look for fish/feelings, which were no longer sequestered in the "affect hut" (from another dream); mourning for his former identity as a nobleman and coming into contact with the idea of death or, at any rate, of the termination of the analysis (having stood in for me and worked); and the "tamed" way of experiencing feelings of tenderness and affection in a homely climate resembling that of Alessandro Manzoni's "tailor".[7]

Another vertex is the linking of these emotional facts to my telephone call and the feelings thereby aroused, which he did not reject.

Yet another vertex is the transformation of emotional states, from contact with them via the resulting persecution and terror to working through and ultimate "taming", making them accessible for him to visit – whereas in the past he had had a phobia of his own land and the streets of his internal world.

The anxieties aroused in a given situation will of course depend on the quantity and quality of the anxieties that are as it were laid down in the form of geological strata in the setting itself. So if a sense of mourning or loss is aroused by the *missing of the session* or its postponement, anxieties activated by the analyst's breach of the setting – whether it be a minor "break-in" or a slight *delay* in ending a session – are more likely to return in the session.

Carlo's aneurysm

After a session I had allowed to overrun by several minutes, Carlo brought a dream in which the walls of someone's aorta were not smooth and straight as they should have been in a healthy person, but swollen with a dangerous aneurysm.

The disturbance caused by my allowing a session to go on over time was repeatedly brought home to me by a patient with whom it was always difficult to finish, and who did his utmost – sometimes successfully – to prolong his sessions, on occasion by several minutes; indeed, the only way I could bring some of his sessions to an end was by getting up and leaving the room.

Following these situations in which *he was the one* who prolonged our meetings, the problem always came back in the sessions in the form of leaking central heating systems or overheated oil in engines that had been running for too long, but always in a relatively mild form. However, on the few occasions when I was so invaded by his problem that I had not called time punctually, this was always brought to my attention dramatically by dreams of drunken, unreliable, weak fathers and of children with no one to depend on.

I recall one instance when I had detained a woman patient for a few minutes to allow her to finish bringing a dream: full of anxiety, she told me in the next session that she had been afraid her doctor might force her to undergo "compulsory medical treatment".[8]

Substantial breaches

I define substantial breaches as cases in which the analyst does not formally change the setting but modifies the emotional field by bringing a *different mental attitude* from his usual one. A distinction must be made between *reduced receptivity*, in which the patient's projective identifications are less readily received and transformed, and extreme situations in which *the flow of projective identifications is reversed* – something that ought never to happen, but is nevertheless not unknown. I have discussed this subject at length in earlier contributions (Ferro, 1987, 1993f); here I would merely repeat that such problems may arise in connection with particular phases in the analyst's mental life, or at times of particular anxiety and pain for the analyst, or when the analyst has been disturbed by a seriously ill patient in the previous session or sessions.

Patients immediately pick up the change in the analyst's mental functioning, draw attention to it and sometimes even take it upon themselves.

As Bion notes in the Italian seminars (Bion, 1983), the patient always knows what is going on in the analyst's mind, and recognizing this is the price we pay for authentically being analysts.

The patient can "dream" what is happening in the analyst's mind and indeed often does so in real time, treating the emotional climate of the session with his own α function and communicating it through the narrative derivatives of the pictograms of the contact barrier (Bion, 1962; Bezoari & Ferro, 1994b).

Here are some examples of the ways in which some of my patients have responded to a time of difficulty on my part, when I was profoundly invaded by a seriously ill psychotic patient.

Marcella

This patient seemed instantly to notice an alien presence in my mind, for she dreamed of arriving at school, going to the classroom bearing her name, and finding it occupied by another teacher with other pupils. She had enormous trouble getting them to vacate it.

I was not immediately able to grasp the obvious meaning of this dream, and, my mind still taken up with the disturbing presence of the previous session's patient (who, as stated, had a severe psychotic transference), I produced a credible interpretation without reverie.

Marcella now responded by "condensing" a dream: "I found a handbag belonging to one of my colleagues, opened it, and inside was a very nice purse, which I opened, but there was not a single coin inside it." I interpreted this dream as a comment on my previous interpretation, which Marcella had experienced as formally unexceptionable but empty.

In this way we were able to return to the first dream and grasp her concern at finding me unavailable in her session because my mind was clogged with other presences.

Next day Marcella said she had found it very difficult to come: "The weather was cold and wet and I was afraid to go out in it." Then she brought a dream: "There was a little bird, one of mine, which was ill; I revived it, but as soon as I went away, it immediately became ill again; that reminds me of another dream, in which the same little bird had a bad leg and could not stand on it; in fact I had hurt it while trying to feed it."

The patient was, I believe, here telling of her fear of damaging the analyst, who stood, in her history, for her mother – a very depressed woman on whom, as a little girl, she had been afraid she could not rely and whom, indeed, she had had to look after. However, I wondered whether it was mere coincidence that these emotional experiences had come at a time of reduced mental presence on my part owing to the "damage" done by another patient. Perhaps Marcella feared that she would not find a mind/house to shelter her from her own storms and that she herself might be responsible for my "mental damage" (in her history, the damage was inflicted on the mother by the patient's brother, who was quite probably severely psychotic – the brother as a part of the patient). In this case she might have felt that, turning the relationship on its head, it was up to her to take care of the analyst, whose interpretations were as lame as the little bird in her dream.

Here again, however, had there not been a reversal of the flow, which had enabled the patient to dream on my behalf once more? This sequence perhaps contained the entire issue in a gamut extending from reversed projective identifications – which were thus a problem of the analyst – to the restoration of the capacity for reverie in the analyst, who made the patient's problem his own and returned it to her after appropriate treatment.

Marta

The patient began her session with a dream in which some little dark-coloured creatures, processionary moths,[9] were devouring a house; next she spoke in a very sensualized way about sex, and then about pornography. I did not understand – until I managed to reflect on the sequence of the last few sessions: about half-way through the last session but three I had disappeared from the patient's emotional horizon, because something she had said had aroused a violent emotion on my part concerning a psychotic patient by whom I had at the time felt intensely "parasitized".

The patient then spoke to me about a hospital resuscitation unit, followed by sensuality and then pornography; these, I think, were drastic attempts to bring me back into contact with her, like the "heroic" manoeuvres sometimes observed when all seems to be lost. The dream was the key to understanding her fear that my mind was no longer available because it had been "devoured" by other thoughts which had disorganized it as a container for Marta (meanwhile, the psychotic patient referred to above had appeared in a dream representing precisely this attack on and disorganization of the container: her brother – her psychotic part – had attacked and destroyed a tank full of liquid pesticide of the kind used by wine-growers to protect their vines). In this way the pest, or "parasite", was able to invade me and prevent me from being available to Marta, who was in turn invaded by the "processionary moths".

However, once I had become aware of this situation, the relationship with the patient was restored. This material, of a strictly transferential nature, then also found a place in Marta's history, where this dream was revisited in the light of its successor (in which she was afraid that her mother, an au pair girl, might, through encounters with men, produce lots and lots of sons). That also explained the jealousy towards the processionary moths, which represented the brothers born as it were in procession, one linked to the other, taking the maternal container away from her.

The parasite, however, had been on a very long journey, from the psychotic patient to me, from me to Marta and from her, through the dream, back to me and our relationship, but also to her history and internal world – for the "parasite" was of course also a split-off part of Marta.

Evacuative interpretations

An excellent discussion of this subject is given by Manfredi Turillazzi (1994a), who points out that interpretation may be a form of acting out. Rather than venturing on to already well-trodden theoretical ground, I should like to give a brief clinical example.

Marcella was a very diligent patient. At this particular juncture, even the most suffering and primitive parts of her personality were entering into the analysis, splits were being healed, and her psychotic brother and his therapist – in effect doubles of the patient and her analyst – were now living presences in the sessions. I responded to a dream that might perhaps have touched upon a sore point in myself with a superficial, run-of-the-mill interpretation which might have passed muster some years before, having failed to grasp the dream's living, new vibrancy; I then tried to put things right again.

In the next session the patient told me of a very painful episode that had occurred at her school: the other teacher working with her had had to leave unexpectedly because the little boy she was holding had suddenly "done it in his pants". The patient had been left alone and, unnoticed by her, a very small disturbed girl had made a mess of her (Marcella's) plate and started eating from it, after which she herself had felt an aversion to eating.

Next day in school, the mere sight of the two children had aroused an aversion in her, which she had also felt when she came to her session. The only way I could interpret this was that she had experienced my interpretation of her dream as showing that I was unable either to think properly about what she had said to me or to contain myself; and although I had then noticed this, while I was trying to remedy the situation – like her colleague with the incontinent little boy – she had found herself alone and thus too close to, and not sufficiently distinct from, the neediest, most disturbed part of herself.

Considering the situation in field terms, there are of course many links between formal and substantial breaches of the setting: if the analyst is preoccupied with other things and his mental functioning is impaired beyond a certain threshold (for whatever reason), a breach – perhaps even a formal one – of the setting is bound to ensue, with all the associated consequences. What matters is to have the capacity and patience to recover what has been disturbing, indigestible and harmful, so as to arrive at new possibilities of transformation and thinkability.

Images supplied by the analyst

In some (pre-field) models, the introduction of images by the analyst into the fabric of the session was seen as a violation of the setting and a failure of neutrality on his part. With Bion, this view became obsolete for at least two reasons. Firstly, however the analyst behaves (Alvarez, 1985; Saraval, 1985; Renik, 1993; Berti Ceroni, 1993) – even if he comports himself as neutrally as possible – he will enter the field somehow, and his entry "in grey" is no less significant than it would be if he were to assume other hues. Secondly, the visual image used by the analyst – provided, of course, that it results from his reverie in the session – is the most meaningful and transformational contribution he can make to the construction of the session, operating along row "C" of the grid and fully achieving not only the extension in the field of meaning and passion but also the "extension in the domain of myth" referred to by Bion in *Elements of Psycho-Analysis* (1963).[10]

A third reason may also be adduced: the analyst can no longer be thought of as someone who decodes the patient's text, as it were furnishing a parallel account of its meanings from the sidelines, but is instead the co-author of the narrative fabric woven in the session with the creative contribution of both protagonists.

The image – which, I repeat, must be the fruit of reverie in the session – becomes the selected fact, the organizer whereby a new Gestalt can be defined and the field can be newly configured and thus "extended" to encompass the permanent possibility of assignment of new meaning.

Notes

1 Nissim (1987) gives an interesting and very graphic account based on the documented testimony of Freud's actual patients.
2 [Translator's note: A kind of ravioli filled with forcemeat.]
3 Or rather an apparatus for thinking thoughts made up of PS–D and ♀ ♂.
4 Carlo Ancelotti is a famous footballer who used to play for Milan.
5 [Translator's note: A play on the author's name, which means iron.]
6 [Translator's note: *Filo* means a thread or wire, and *fare il filo* is a colloquial expression meaning "trying to get into a person's good books".]
7 [Translator's note: The tailor appears in Manzoni's best known novel, *The Betrothed*, and epitomizes a poor but dignified and happy family.]
8 Just as the patient draws attention to microfractures on the part of the analyst, so, at least in my experience, do even the most seriously ill patients readily tolerate "necessary" breaches, such as a change of consulting room due to a move; interruption of a session due to some catastrophe (in my case, the collapse of Pavia's town hall tower a few dozen yards from my consulting room); the move on to the couch; or the move from the playroom to the adult consulting room on the cusp between childhood and adolescence. All these situations did of course return in subsequent sessions, but without any particular degree of disturbance.
9 Processionary moths are nocturnal Lepidoptera which move in a continuous column; voracious feeders, they can severely damage woodland.
10 Bion (1963) puts this as follows: "[. . .] when the analyst gives an interpretation it must be possible for analyst and analysand to see that what he is talking about is something that is either audible, visible, palpable or odoriferous at the time. [. . .] Suppose that a patient is angry. More meaning is given to a statement to that effect if it is added that his anger is like that of a 'child that wanted to hit his nanny because he has been told he is naughty.' [. . .] [they are] statements of a personal myth. [. . .] passion is evidence that two minds are linked and that there cannot possibly be fewer than two minds if passion is present."

Bibliography

Alvarez, A. (1985) "The problem of neutrality: Some reflections on the psychoanalytic attitude in the treatment of borderline and psychotic children". *Journal of Child Psychotherapy*, 11, p. 87.

Amati Mehler, J., Argentieri, S., Canestri, J. (1990) *La Babele dell'inconscio*. Raffaello Cortina Editore, Milan.

Ammanniti, M., Stern, D.N. (eds) (1991) *Rappresentazioni e narrazioni*. Laterza, Rome and Bari.

Badoni, M. (1994) "La clandestinità nell'organizzazione sociale e nella relazione analitica". *Atti del X Congresso Nazionale SPI*, Rimini.

Badoni, M. (1996) "Coppie al lavoro: intreccio di immagini e costruzioni". *Atti del III Convegno di Psicoanalisi infantile*, Rome, 18–19 May.

Barale, F., Ferro, A. (1992) "Negative therapeutic reactions and microfractures in analytic communication". In: Nissim Momigliano, L., Robutti, A. (eds) *Shared Experience: The Psychoanalytic Dialogue*. Karnac Books, London.

Barale, F., Ferro, A. (1993) "Sufrimiento mental en el analista y sueños de controtransferencia". *Revista de Psicoanálisis de Madrid*, 17, pp. 56–72.

Baranger, M. (1992) "La mente del analista: de la escucha a la interpretación". *Revista de Psicoanálisis*, 49 (2), p. 223.

Baranger, M., Baranger, W. (1961–62) "La situación analítica como campo dinámico". *Revista Uruguaya de Psicoanálisis*, IV, 1.

Baranger, M., Baranger, W. (1964) "El insight en la situación analítica". *Revista Uruguaya de Psicoanálisis*, IV, 1.

Baranger, M., Baranger, W. (1969) *Problemas del campo psicoanalítico*. Kargieman, Buenos Aires.

Baranger, M., Baranger, W., Mom, J. (1983) "Process and no-process in analytic work". *International Journal of Psycho-Analysis*, 64, pp. 1–15.

Baranger, M., Baranger, W., Mom, J. (1988) "The infantile psychic trauma from us to Freud: pure trauma, retroactivity and reconstruction". *International Journal of Psycho-Analysis*, 69, pp. 113–128.

Baranger, W. (1961–62) "El muerto vivo: estructura de los objetos en el duelo y los estados depresivos". *Revista Uruguaya de Psicoanálisis*, IV (4), pp. 217–229.

Baranger, W., Zac de Goldstein, R., Goldstein, N. (1994) *Artesanías psicoanalíticas*. Kargieman, Buenos Aires.

Baruzzi, A. (1987) "La fine dell'analisi". *Gruppo e Funzione Analitica*, 8 (3), p. 265.

Berti Ceroni, G. (1993) "Neutralità". *Rivista di Psicoanalisi*, 39 (2), pp. 275–290.

Bertolini, M. (1986) "La sofferenza mentale nella storia dello sviluppo infantile". *Atti del Congresso "La sofferenza mentale",* Rome.

Bezoari, M., Ferro, A. (1989) "Listening, interpretations and transformative functions in the analytic dialogue". *Rivista di Psicoanalisi,* 35, pp. 1015–1051.

Bezoari, M., Ferro, A. (1990a) "Elementos de un modelo del campo analítico: los agregados funcionales". *Revista de Psicoanálisis,* 47 (5/6), pp. 847–861.

Bezoari, M., Ferro, A. (1990b) "Mots, images, affects. L'aventure du sens dans la rencontre analytique". *Revue Canadienne de Psychanalyse,* 4, pp. 49–73 (1996).

Bezoari, M., Ferro, A. (1991a) "A oscilação dos significados afetos no trabalho da parelha analítica". *Revista Brasileira de Psicanálise,* 26 (3), pp. 365–374.

Bezoari, M., Ferro, A. (1991b) "From a play between parts to transformations in the couple: psychoanalysis in a bipersonal field". In: Nissim Momigliano, L., Robutti, A. (eds) *Shared Experience: The Psychoanalytic Dialogue.* Karnac Books, London.

Bezoari, M., Ferro, A. (1992a) "El sueño dentro de una teoría del campo: los agregados funcionales". *Revista de Psicoanálisis,* 49 (5/6), pp. 957–977.

Bezoari, M., Ferro, A. (1992b) "I personaggi della seduta come aggregati funzionali del campo analitico". *Notiziario SPI,* Supplemento 2, Borla, Rome.

Bezoari, M., Ferro, A. (1994a) "Listening, interpreting and psychic change in the analytic dialogue". *International Forum of Psychoanalysis,* 3, pp. 35–41.

Bezoari, M., Ferro, A. (1994b) "The dream within a field theory: functional aggregates and narrations". *International Journal of Melanie Klein and Object Relations* (1999), 17 (3), pp. 333–348.

Bezoari, M., Fiamminghi, A.M. (1995) "Funzione analitica e funzione genitoriale: alcuni modelli a confronto". *Rivista di Psicoanalisi,* 41 (2), pp. 211–235.

Bianchedi, E.T. (1991) "Psychic change: the 'becoming' of an inquiry". *International Journal of Psycho-Analysis,* 72, pp. 6–15.

Bianchedi, E.T. (1995) "Creative writers and dream-work-alpha". In: *On Freud's Creative Writers and Day-dreaming.* Yale University Press, London.

Bianchedi, E.T., Antar, R., Ferdinandez Bravo de Podetti, M.R., *et al.* (1983) "Beyond Freudian metapsychology: the metapsychological points of view of the Kleinian school". *International Journal of Psycho-Analysis,* 65, p. 389.

Bianchedi, E.T., *et al.* (1991) "Decisión de separación y terminación del análisis". In: *S. Freud: Análisis terminable y interminable, 40 años después.* Asociación Psicoanalítica Provisional de Buenos Aires.

Bick, E. (1968) "The experience of the skin in early object relations". *International Journal of Psycho-Analysis,* 49, pp. 484–486.

Bion, W.R. (1960) *Second Thoughts.* Heinemann, London.

Bion, W.R. (1962) *Learning from Experience.* Heinemann, London.

Bion, W.R. (1963) *Elements of Psycho-Analysis.* Heinemann, London.

Bion, W.R. (1965) *Transformations.* Heinemann, London.

Bion, W.R. (1970) *Attention and Interpretation.* Tavistock Publications, London.

Bion, W.R. (1975) *A Memoir of the Future. Book 1: The Dream.* Imago Editora, Rio de Janeiro.

Bion, W.R. (1978) *Four Discussions with W.R. Bion.* Clunie Press, Perth.

Bion, W.R. (1980) *Bion in New York and São Paulo.* Clunie Press, Perth.

Bion, W.R. (1983) *Bion in Rome* [Italian seminars]. The Estate of W.R. Bion.

Bion, W.R. (1987) *Clinical Seminars and Four Papers.* Fleetwood Press, Abingdon.

Bion, W.R. (1992) *Cogitations.* Karnac Books, London.

Bion Talamo, P. (1987) "Perché non possiamo dirci bioniani". *Gruppo e Funzione Analitica*, 3, p. 279.

Bion Talamo, P. (1991) "Modelli di base e modelli effimeri". Read to the Centro ricerche di gruppo, Rome, 9 March 1991.

Bleger, J. (1966) *Psicohigiene y psicología institucional*. Paidós, Buenos Aires.

Bleger, J. (1967) *Simbiosis y ambigüedad*. Paidós, Buenos Aires.

Bollas, C. (1987) *The Shadow of the Object: Psychoanalysis of the Unthought Known*. Free Association Books, London.

Bolognini, S. (1994) "Condivisione e fraintendimento". *Atti del X Congresso Nazionale SPI*, Rimini.

Bonaminio, V. (1993) "Del non interpretare". *Rivista di Psicoanalisi*, 39 (3), pp. 453–475.

Bonaminio, V. (1996) "Esiste ancora uno spazio per l'individualità del paziente". *Rivista di Psicoanalisi*, 42 (1), pp. 681–708.

Bonaminio, V., Di Renzo, M.A., Giannotti, A. (1993) "Le fantasie inconsce dei genitori come fattori Ego-alieni nelle identificazioni del bambino. Qualche riflessione su identità e falso Sé attraverso il materiale clinico dell'analisi infantile". *Rivista di Psicoanalisi*, 39 (4), pp. 681–708.

Bonasia, E. (1994a) "Dobbiamo ancora usare il lettino? Riflessioni sui modelli della mente e della tecnica". *Rivista di Psicoanalisi*, 40 (3), pp. 491–512.

Bonasia, E. (1994b) "Quale bastoncino usa lei per misurare la nevrosi?: il modello di campo analitico fra teorie pulsionali e teorie relazionali". *Atti del X Congresso Nazionale SPI*, Rimini.

Bon de Matte, L., Zavattini, C.G. (1990) "Dalle tenebre alla luce. Riflessioni sulla tecnica in psicoanalisi". *Rivista di Psicologia Clinica*, 2, pp. 12–27.

Bonfiglio, B. (1994) "Costruzione della relazione analitica e uso dell'interpretazione". *Rivista di Psicoanalisi*, 40 (3), p. 433.

Bordi, S. (1985) "Le prospettive tecniche della psicoanalisi contemporanea". *Rivista di Psicoanalisi*, 31, pp. 4–37.

Bordi, S. (1989) "La tecnica psicoanalitica: storia e mutamenti". *Rivista di Psicoanalisi*, 35 (2), p. 546.

Bordi, S. (1990) "Modelli a confronto in psicoanalisi". *Prospettive psicoanalitiche nel lavoro istituzionale*, 8, pp. 71–87.

Borgogno, F (1992) "Evoluzione della tecnica psicoanalitica". *Rivista di Psicoanalisi*, 38 (4), p. 1047.

Borgogno, F (1994a) "Eventi trasformativi del campo. Panel: "Notes magico – Predittività – Collasso del campo". *Atti del X Congresso Nazionale SPI*, Rimini.

Borgogno, F. (1994b) "Intorno a *Memoria del futuro di W.R. Bion*". *Rivista di Psicoanalisi*, 40 (1), p. 71.

Borgogno, F. (1994c) "Spoilt children. L'intrusione e l'estrazione parentale come fattore di distruttività". *Richard e Piggle*, II (2), p. 135.

Borgogno, F. (1995) "Perché gli Indipendenti". In: Rayner, E. (ed) *Gli indipendenti nella psicoanalisi Britannica*, pp. ix–xxiv. Cortina, Milan. (First published 1991 as *The Independent Mind in British Psychoanalysis*. Free Association Books, London.)

Borgogno, F., Viola, M. (1994) "Pulsione di morte". *Rivista di Psicoanalisi*, 40 (3), pp. 459–483.

Brenman-Pick, I. (1985) "Working-through in the counter-transference". *International Journal of Psycho-Analysis*, 66, pp. 157–166.

Bronstein, C. (1995) "Female homosexuality in adolescence: a clinical presentation". *Psychoanalysis in Europe*, 44, pp. 30–50.

Brutti, C., Parlani, R. (1983) "Sulla bugia". *Gruppo e Funzione Analitica*, 4 (1), pp. 51–53.

Calvino, I. (1973) *The Castle of Crossed Destinies*, trans. W. Weaver. Vintage, London (1977).

Cancrini, T., Giordo, G. (1995) *Una nave nella tempesta, le bottiglie nel mare: funzioni comunicative e creative del disegno infantile nel rapporto analitico*. Il Colloquio nazionale analisi infantile, Milan.

Carloni, G. (1984) "Tatto, contatto e tattica". *Rivista di Psicoanalisi*, 30, p. 191.

Catz de Katz, H. (1996) "Acerca de la ensoñación del analista, el campo analítico y sus transformaciones posibles". *Revista de Psicoanálisis*, 6, pp. 45–59.

Cavazzoni, E. (1990) *The Voice of the Moon*, trans. E. Emery. Serpent's Tail, London.

Conforto, C. (1996) "Nota sul transfert psicotico nella psicoanalisi di un paziente border-line". *Rivista di Psicoanalisi*, 42 (2), p. 299.

Conrotto, E. (1995) Qualche riflessione a proposito del lavoro di E. Bonasia: "Dobbiamo ancora usare il lettino? Riflessioni sui modelli della mente e della tecnica". *Rivista di Psicoanalisi*, 41 (1), pp. 105–107.

Contardi, R. (1994) "Il luogo della rappresentazione e i destini del simbolo". *Rivista di Psicoanalisi*, 40 (2), pp. 197–223.

Corradi Fiumara, G. (1980) *Funzione simbolica e filosofia del linguaggio*. Boringhieri, Turin.

Corradi Fiumara, G. (1994) "Processo metaforico e trasformazioni del campo analitico". *Atti del X Congresso Nazionale SPI*, Rimini.

Corrao, F. (1981) "Il modello trasformazionale del pensiero". *Rivista di Psicoanalisi*, 27 (4), p. 673.

Corrao, F. (1986) "Il concetto di campo come modello teorico". *Gruppo e Funzione Analitica*, 7, pp. 9–21.

Corrao, F. (1987) "Il narrativo come categoria psicoanalitica". In: Morpurgo, E., Egidi, V. (eds) *Psicoanalisi e narrazione*. Il Lavoro Editoriale, Ancona.

Corrao, F. (1991) "Trasformazioni narrative". In: Ammanniti, M., Stern, D.N. (eds) *Rappresentazioni e narrazioni*. Laterza, Rome and Bari.

Corrao, F. (1992) *Modelli psicoanalitici: mito, passione, memoria*. Laterza, Rome and Bari.

Correale, A., Rinaldi, L. (1996) (eds) *Quale psicoanalisi per le psicosi?* Cortina, Milan.

Costa, A. (1979) "L'insieme dei pazienti come oggetto interno. Il paziente come oggetto nel gruppo di lavoro". *Rivista di Psicoanalisi*, 25, pp. 117–126.

Costa, A. (1993) "Oltre il concetto di interpretazione in psicoanalisi". In: Di Chiara, G., Neri, C. (eds) *Psicoanalisi futura*. Borla, Rome.

Decorbet, S., Sacco, F. (1995) *Le dessin dans le travail psychanalytique avec l'enfant*. Erès, Toulouse.

De León de Bernardi, B. (1988) "Interpretación, acercamiento analítico y creatividad". *Revista Uruguaya de Psicoanálisis*, November, pp. 57–68.

De León de Bernardi, B. (1991) "Las teorías del analista y los cambios en la consideración de la dinámica del proceso analítico". *Revista de Psicoanálisis*, 47 (1), pp. 49–58.

De Martis, D. (1984) *Realtà e fantasma nella relazione terapeutica*. Il Pensiero Scientifico Editore, Rome.

De Masi, F. (1984) "On transference psychosis. Clinical perspectives in work with border-line patients". In: Nissim Momigliano, L., Robutti, A. (eds) *Shared Experience: The Psychoanalytic Dialogue*. Karnac Books, London.

De Masi, F. (1995) "Ciò che Abraham non poteva capire ..." *Rivista di Psicoanalisi*, 41 (3), pp. 489–499.

De Simone, G. (1994) *La conclusione dell'analisi. Teoria e tecnica*. Borla, Rome.

De Simone, G., Fornari, B. (1988) "Melanie Klein e la scuola inglese". In: Semi, A.A. (ed) *Trattato di Psicoanalisi*, vol. I. Raffaello Cortino Editore, Milan.

De Toffoli, C. (1991) "L'invenzione di un pensiero dal versante somatico della relazione transferale". *Rivista di Psicoanalisi*, 37, pp. 563–597.

Di Benedetto, A. (1992) "Il valore dei suoni nella relazione analitica e nell'ascolto dell'analista". Centro di psicoanalisi romano.

Di Chiara, G. (1983) "The Tale of the Green Hand: on projective identification". In: Nissim Momigliano, L., Robutti, A. (eds) *Shared Experience: The Psychoanalytic Dialogue*. Karnac Books, London.

Di Chiara, G. (1985) "Una prospettiva psicoanalitica del dopo Freud: un posto per l'altro". *Rivista di Psicoanalisi*, 31(4), p. 451.

Di Chiara, G. (1990) "La stupita meraviglia, l'autismo e la competenza difensiva". *Rivista di Psicoanalisi*, 36, p. 441.

Di Chiara, G. (1992) "Meeting, telling and parting. Three basic factors in the psychoanalytic experience". In: Nissim Momigliano, L., Robutti, A. (eds) *Shared Experience: The Psychoanalytic Dialogue*. Karnac Books, London.

Di Chiara, G., Flegenheimer, F. (1982) "Identificazione proiettiva". *Rivista di Psicoanalisi*, 28 (2), p. 233.

Doery, R. (1995) "The male homosexual organization: a structural approach". *Psychoanalysis in Europe*, 44, pp. 9–29.

Eco, U. (1962) *The Open Work*. Harvard University Press, Cambridge, MA (1989).

Eco, U. (1979) *The Role of the Reader*. Bloomington, Indiana University Press; Hutchinson (1981).

Eco, U. (1990) *The Limits of Interpretation*, Bloomington, Indiana University Press; Hutchinson.

Eizirik, C.L. (1996) "Psychic reality and clinical technique". *International Journal of Psycho-Analysis*, 77 (1), pp. 37–41.

Eskelinen de Folch, T. (1983) "We—versus I and you". *International Journal of Psycho-Analysis*, 64, p. 309.

Eskelinen de Folch, T. (1988) "Communication and containing in child analysis: towards terminability". *International Journal of Psycho-Analysis*, 69, p. 105.

Etchegoyen, R.H. (1983) "Fifty years after the mutative interpretation". *International Journal of Psycho-Analysis*, 64, p. 445.

Etchegoyen, R.H. (1986) *The Fundamentals of Psychoanalytic Technique*, trans. P. Pitchon. Karnac Books, London.

Etchegoyen, R.H. (1993) "Psychoanalysis today and tomorrow". *International Journal of Psycho-Analysis*, 74, p. 1109.

Etchegoyen, R.H. (1996) "Some views on psychic reality". *International Journal of Psycho-Analysis*, 77, pp. 1–14.

Fachinelli, E. (1983) *Claustrofilia*. Adelphi, Milan.

Faimberg, H. (1988a) "The telescoping of generations". *Contemporary Psychoanalysis*, 24, pp. 99–118.

Faimberg, H. (1988b) "A l'écoute du télescopage des générations: pertinence psychanalytique du concept". *Topique*, 42, pp. 223–238.

Faimberg, H. (1989) "Sans mémoire et sans désir: à qui s'adressait Bion". *Revue Française de Psychanalyse*, 53, p. 1453.

Faimberg, H. (1992) "The countertransference position and the countertransference". *International Journal of Psycho-Analysis*, 73, p. 541.

Faimberg, H., Corel, A. (1990) "Repetition and surprise: a clinical approach to the necessity of construction and its validation". *International Journal of Psycho-Analysis*, 71, pp. 411–420.

Falci, A. (1994) "Simmetria dello sguardo ed evoluzioni della teoria clinica in psicoanalisi". *Atti del X Congresso Nazionale SPI*, Rimini.

Ferrara, M.G. (1984) "Qualità della esperienza analitica e terminabilità in psicoanalisi infantile". *Rivista di Psicoanalisi*, 30 (3), pp. 368–382.

Ferraro, F., Garella, A. (1995) "Concessione dell'analisi". *Rivista di Psicoanalisi*, 41 (3), pp. 423–448.

Ferro, A. (1985) "Psicoanalisi e favole". *Rivista di Psicoanalisi*, 31 (2), pp. 216–230.

Ferro, A. (1987) "Il mondo alla rovescia. L'inversione del flusso delle identificazioni proiettive". *Rivista di Psicoanalisi*, 33, pp. 59–77.

Ferro, A. (1991a) "From Raging Bull to Theseus: the long path of a transformation". *International Journal of Psycho-Analysis*, 72, pp. 417–425.

Ferro, A. (1991b) "La mente del analista en su trabajo: problemas, riesgos, necesidades". *Revista de Psicoanálisis*, 48 (5/6), pp. 1159–1177.

Ferro, A. (1992) *The Bi-Personal Field: Experiences in Child Analysis*. Routledge, London (1999).

Ferro, A. (1993a) "Disegno, identificazione proiettiva e processi trasformativi". *Rivista di Psicoanalisi*, 39 (4), pp. 667–680.

Ferro, A. (1993b) "From hallucination to dream: from evacuation to the tolerability of pain in the analysis of a preadolescent". *Psychoanalytic Review*, 80 (3), pp. 389–404.

Ferro, A. (1993c) "Il disegno e le parole come 'disegno' all'interno di una teoria del campo". *Richard e Piggle*, I (1), p. 18.

Ferro, A. (1993d) "Mundos posibles y capacidades negativas del analista en su trabajo". Paper presented at the III Congreso Ibérico de Psicoanálisis, Barcelona, 30–31 October 1993. *Anuario Ibérico de Psicoanálisis*, III, p. 14.

Ferro, A. (1993e) "The impasse within a theory of the analytic field: possible vertices of observation". *International Journal of Psycho-Analysis*, 74, pp. 917–929.

Ferro, A. (1993f) "Zwei Autoren auf der Suche nach Personen: Die Beziehung, das Feld, die Geschichte". *Psyche* 10 (47), pp. 951–972.

Ferro, A. (1994a) "Criterios sobre la analizabilidad y el final del análisis dentro de una teoría del campo". *Revista de Psicoanálisis*, 3, p. 97.

Ferro, A. (1994b) "Del campo e dei suoi eventi". *Quaderni di Psicoterapia Infantile*, 30, pp. 39–50.

Ferro, A. (1994c) "Gruppalità interne, di relazione e di campo nell'analisi duale". *Gruppo e Funzione Analitica*, 5, pp. 32–45.

Ferro, A. (1994d) "Two authors in search of characters: the relationship, the field, the story". *Australian Journal of Psychotherapy*, 13, p. 1.

Ferro, A. (1995a) "El diálogo analítico: mundos posibles y transformaciones en el campo analítico". *Revista de Psicoanálisis*, 4, p. 773.

Ferro, A. (1995b) "Giocare e pensare". In: Noziglia, M. (ed) *Giocare e pensare*. Guerini & Associati, Milan.

Ferro, A. (1995c) "Il narratore e la paura". In: Noziglia, M. (ed) *Giocare e pensare*. Guerini & Associati, Milan.

Ferro, A. (1995d) "L'oscillazione tra capacità negative e fatto prescelto nel campo analitico". APA Conference, Buenos Aires.

Ferro, A. (1995e) "Ricordare, ripetere, trasformare". Paper presented at the APA Congress, Buenos Aires.

Ferro, A. (1995f) "Lo sviluppo del concetto di campo in Europa". Paper presented at the one-day meeting in honour of W. Baranger, Buenos Aires.

Ferro, A. (1996a) "Sexualidade como gênero narrativo, ou dialeto, na sala de análise". In: *Bion em São Paulo. Ressonâncias*. Sociedade Brasileira de Psicanálise de São Paulo.

Ferro, A. (1996b) "Elogio da fileira C: a psicanálise como forma particular de literatura". In: *Silêncios e Luzes*. Casa do Psicólogo, São Paulo.

Ferro, A. (1996c) "'Characters' and their precursors in depression: experiences and transformation in the course of therapy". *International Journal of Melanie Klein and Object Relations*, 17, pp. 119–133.

Ferro, A. (1996d) "Dessin et identification projective". Conference at the Institute of Psychoanalysis, Lisbon.

Ferro, A. (1996e) "Los personajes del cuarto de análisis: ¿Qué realidad?" *Revista de Psicoanálisis de la Asociación Psicoanalítica de Madrid*, 23, p. 133.

Ferro, A. (1996f) "Insight and transformations: When monsters come out of the cracks". *International Journal of Psycho-Analysis*, 77, pp. 997–1011.

Ferro, A. (1999) *The Bi-Personal Field – Experiences in Child Analysis*. Routledge, London.

Ferro, A., Meregnani, A. (1993) "Criteri di analizzabilità e assetto mentale dell'analista nelle interviste preliminari". Unpublished.

Ferro, A., Meregnani, A. (1994) "Listening and transformative functions in the psycho-analytical dialogue". *Psychoanalysis in Europe*, 42, pp. 19–27.

Ferro, A., Meregnani, A. (1995) "Psicoanalisi, favole e narrazione". *La dimensione estetica dell'esperienza*. F. Angeli, Milan.

Ferro, A., Meregnani, A. (1996) "The inversion of flow of projective identifications in the analyst at work". *Australian Journal of Psychotherapy*, 16, pp. 95–112.

Ferro, A., Pasquali, G., Tognoli, L., Viola, M. (1986a) "L'uso del simbolismo nel setting e il processo di simbolizzazione nella relazione analitica". *Rivista di Psicoanalisi*, 32 (4), pp. 539–553.

Ferro, A., Pasquali, G., Tognoli, L., Viola, M. (1986b) "Note sul processo di simbolizzazione nel pensiero psicoanalitico". *Rivista di Psicoanalisi*, 32 (4), pp. 521–538.

Ferruta, A. (1996) "L'altro. Note intorno a un caso di analisi con una paziente straniera". Read to the Centro milanese di psicoanalisi, 18 April.

Filippini, S., Ponsi, M. (1993) "Enactment". *Rivista di Psicoanalisi*, 39, p. 501.

Fiorentini, G., Frangini, G., Molone, P., *et al.* (1993) "Setting e modelli: confezione in serie o creazione su misura?" Read to the XXVII Convegno a seminari multipli della Società psicoanalitica italiana, Bologna. Unpublished.

Fiorentini, G., Frangini, G., Molone, P., *et al.* (1995) "Dalle regole del setting all'assetto mentale dell'analista". *Rivista di Psicoanalisi*, 41 (1), pp. 67–69.

Flegenheimer, F.A. (1983) "Divergenze e punti in comune tra psicoanalisi infantile e psicoanalisi degli adulti: alcune riflessioni". *Rivista di Psicoanalisi*, 29, pp. 196–205.

Flegenheimer, F.A. (1989) "Language and psychoanalysis". *International Review of Psycho-Analysis*, 16, pp. 337–384.

Folch-Mateu, P. (1986) "Identification and its vicissitudes as observed in the neurosis". *International Journal of Psycho-Analysis*, 67, p. 209.

Fonagy, P, Moran, G.S. (1991) "Understanding psychic change in child psychoanalysis". *IPA Congress Pre-published Papers*. Institute of Psycho-Analysis, London.

Fornari, F. (1963) *La vita affettiva originaria del bambino*. Feltrinelli, Milan.

Fornari, F. (1975) *Genitalità e cultura*. Feltrinelli, Milan.

Freni, S. (1996) "Gradienti di ostensione della clinica psicoanalitica: componenti teoretiche e pratiche". Read to the Centro milanese di psicoanalisi, June 1996.

Freud, S. (1905) *Three Essays on the Theory of Sexuality*, *SE*, 7, p. 125.

Freud, S. (1909) "Notes upon a case of obsessional neurosis". *SE*, 10, p. 155.

Freud, S. (1915) "Wir und der Tod". *Zweimonats-Bericht für die Mitglieder der österreichisch-israelitischen Humanitätsvereine B'nai B'rith*, vol. 18, 1, pp. 41–51.

Freud, S. (1919) "The 'uncanny'". *SE*, 17, p. 219.

Freud, S. (1925 [1924]) "A note upon the 'mystic writing-pad'". *SE*, 19, p. 227.

Freud, S. (1937) "Constructions in analysis". *SE*, 23, p. 257.

Gaburri, E. (1986) "Dal gemello immaginario al compagno segreto". *Rivista di Psicoanalisi*, 32 (4), pp. 509–520.

Gaburri, E. (1987) "Narrazione e interpretazione". In: Morpurgo, E., Egidi, V. (eds) *Psicoanalisi e narrazione*. Il Lavoro Editoriale, Ancona.

Gaburri, E. (1992) "Emozioni. Affetti. Personificazioni". In: Hautmann, G., Vergine, A. (eds) *Gli affetti nella psicoanalisi*. Borla, Rome.

Gaburri, E., Ferro, A. (1988) "Gli sviluppi kleiniani e Bion". In: Semi, A. (ed) *Trattato di psicoanalisi*, vol. I. Raffaello Cortina Editore, Milan.

Gaddini, E. (1972) "Aggression and the pleasure principle: towards a psychoanalytic theory of aggression". *International Journal of Psycho-Analysis*, 53, pp. 191–199.

Gagliardi Guidi, R. (1992) "Premature termination of analysis". In: Nissim Momigliano, L., Robutti, A. (eds) *Shared Experience: The Psychoanalytic Dialogue*. Karnac Books, London.

Galdo, A.M. (1991) "Ricordo e narrazione nella clinica psicoanalitica". In: Ammanniti, M., Stein, D.N. (eds) *Rappresentazioni e narrazioni*. Laterza, Rome and Bari.

Gesué, A. (1995) "Il 'muro del silenzio', il 'muro del corpo'. La mente dell'analista e alcune gravi impasse della comunicazione". *Rivista di Psicoanalisi*, 41 (3), pp. 391–409.

Giaconia, G. (1996) "Sulla fantasia inconscia oggi". Read to the Centro milanese di psico-analisi, May 1996.

Giaconia, G., Racalbuto, A. (1990) *I percorsi del simbolo*. Raffaello Cortina Editore, Milan.

Giannakoulas, A., Giannotti, A. (1985) "Il setting con la coppia genitoriale". In: *Il setting*. Borla, Rome.

Giannotti, A. (1988) "Le difese contro l'aggressività". In: *La relazione aggressiva*. Borla, Rome.

Giuffrida, A. (1995) "A proposito del setting". *Rivista di Psicoanalisi*, 41 (2), pp. 258–268.

Glasersfeld, E. von (1981) In: *Die erfundene Wirklichkeit*. Piper & Co. Verlag, Munich.

Goijman, L. (1988) "Obstáculos en el análisis: resistencia y narcisismo". *Revista de Psicoanálisis*, 45 (1), pp. 67–86.

Goijman, L. (1990) "Parricidio, exogamia y estructuración: cuestiones cruciales de la adolescencia". *Revista de Psicoanálisis*, 47 (4), pp. 623–632.

Goijman, L. (1992) "Escritura y lectura del texto psicoanalítico". *Revista de Psicoanálisis*, 49 (1), pp. 5–12.

Goldstein, N. (1996) "La transmisión y la enseñanza del psicoanálisis". Unpublished.

Gori, E.C. (1993) "Parola e parola". *Rivista di Psicoanalisi*, 39 (2), pp. 293–299.

Green, A. (1996) "Has sexuality anything to do with psychoanalysis?" *International Journal of Psycho-Analysis*, 76, p. 871.

Grinberg, L. (1957) "Perturbaciones en la interpretación motivadas por la contraidentificación proyectiva". *Revista de Psicoanálisis*, 14 (1–2), pp. 23–30.

Grinberg, L. (1981) *Psicoanálisis. Aspectos teóricos y clínicos*. Paidós, Barcelona, Buenos Aires.

Grinberg, L., Dario, S.O.R., Bianchedi, E.T. (1991) *Introduction to the Work of Bion: Groups, Knowledge, Psychosis, Thought, Transformations, Psychoanalytic Practice*. Clunie Press, Perth. (First edition 1975, The Roland Harris Educational Trust.)

Hautmann, G. (1977a) "La formazione del contenitore in una prima settimana di analisi". *Rivista di Psicoanalisi*, 23, pp. 408–430.

Hautmann, G. (1977b) "Pensiero onirico e realtà psichica". *Rivista di Psicoanalisi*, 23, pp. 62–127.

Hautmann, G. (1981) "Il mio debito con Bion: dalla psicoanalisi come teoria alla psicoanalisi come funzione della mente". *Rivista di Psicoanalisi*, 27, pp. 558–572.

Hautmann, G. (1995) "Il sogno tra clinica e teoria nel modello bioniano". Convegno a seminari multipli della Società psicoanalitica italiana, Bologna.

Henningsen, F. (1995) "Identification and the capacity to love. Two cases of male homosexuality". *Psychoanalysis in Europe*, 44, pp. 51–72.

Hinshelwood, R.D. (1989) *A Dictionary of Kleinian Thought*. Free Association Books, London.

Hinshelwood, R.D. (1993) *Clinical Klein*. Free Association Books, London.

Hunter, E. (1994) *Psychoanalysts Talk*. The Guilford Press, New York and London.

Isaacs, S. (1948) "The nature and function of phantasy". *International Journal of Psycho-Analysis*, 29, pp. 73–97.

Jarast, G. (1996) "El campo de la transferencia–contratransferencia: un nuevo acto psíquico". XXI Congreso Latino Americano de Psicoanálisis.

Joseph, B. (1984) "Projective identification". In: Spillius, E. Bott (ed) *Melanie Klein Today*. Routledge, London (1988).

Joseph, B. (1985) "Transference: the total situation". *International Journal of Psycho-Analysis*, 66, p. 447.

Junqueira de Mattos, J.A. (1995) "Pre-conception and transference". 39th IPA Congress, San Francisco.

Kaës, R. (1986) "Le groupe comme appareil de transformation". *Revue de psychothérapie psychanalytique de groupe*, 5–6, pp. 45–59.

Kaës, R., Faimberg, H., Enriquez, M., *et al.* (1993) *Transmission de la vie psychique entre générations*. Dunod, Paris.

Kancyper, L. (1989) *Jorge Luis Borges en el laberinto de Narciso*. Paidós, Buenos Aires.

Kancyper, L. (1990) "Narcisismo y pigmalionismo". *Revista de Psicoanálisis*, 48 (5/6), p. 1003.

Kancyper, L. (1992a) "La identificación reivindicatoria". *Revista Argentina de Psicopatología*, 3 (7), 28.

Kancyper, L. (1992b) *Resentimiento y remordimiento. Estudio psicoanalítico*. Paidós, Buenos Aires.

Kennedy, H. (1978) "The role of insight in child analysis: A developmental viewpoint". In: Blum, H.P. (ed) *Psychoanalytic Explorations of Technique. Discourse on the Theory of Therapy*. International Universities Press, New York.

Kernberg, O. (1992) *Aggression in Personality Disorders and Perversions*. Yale University Press, New Haven and London.

Kernberg, O. (1993) "Convergences and divergences in contemporary psychoanalytic technique". *International Journal of Psycho-Analysis*, 74, p. 659.

Klein, M. (1929) "Personification in the play of children". *International Journal of Psycho-Analysis*, 10, pp. 193–204.

Klein, M. (1930) "The importance of symbol formation in the development of the ego". *International Journal of Psycho-Analysis*, 11, pp. 24–39.

Klein, M. (1952) "The origins of transference". *International Journal of Psycho-Analysis*, 33, pp. 433–438.

Klein, M. (1961) *Narrative of a Child Analysis*. Hogarth Press, London.

Klein, M., Heimann, P., Money-Kyrle, R. (1955) *New Directions in Psychoanalysis*. Tavistock Publications, London.

Kluzer, G.P., Usuelli, A. (1983) "Suggestione e illusione nel percorso analitico". *Psicoanálisis*, XIXX, 3.

Langs, R. (1976) *The Bipersonal Field*. Jason Aronson, New York.

Lemlij, M. (ed) (1994) *Mujeres por mujeres*. Biblioteca Peruana de Psicoanálisis.

Leonardi, P. (1976) "Masturbazione anale". In: Gaburri, E. (ed) *Eros e onnipotenza*. Guaraldi, Rimini.

Liberman, D., *et al.* (1983) "Indicadores del final del análisis". In: *Homenaje a David Liberman*. Asociación Psicoanalítica de Buenos Aires, 7 (1–2), pp. 159–173.

Limentani, A. (1972) "The assessment of analysability: a major hazard in selection for psychoanalysis". *International Journal of Psycho-Analysis*, 53, pp. 352–361.

Limentani, A. (1981) "On some positive aspects of the negative therapeutic reaction". *International Journal of Psycho-Analysis*, 62, pp. 379–399.

Limentani, A. (1988a) "Le pulsioni: aggressività, sessualità e l'istinto di morte". In: *La relazione aggressiva*. Borla, Rome.

Limentani, A. (1988b) Postscript to "The assessment of analysability: a major hazard in selection for psychoanalysis". In: *Between Freud and Klein: The Psychoanalytic Quest for Knowledge and Truth*. Free Association Books, London.

Lussana, P. (1991) "Dall'interpretazione kleiniana all'interpretazione bioniana, attraverso l'osservazione dell'infante". Paper presented to the AIPPL, Rome, 2 June.

Lussana, P. (1992) *L'adolescente, lo psicoanalista, l'artista, una visione binoculare dell'adolescenza*. Borla, Rome.

Luzes, P. (1985) "Vers une nouvelle théorie psychanalytique des émotions". *Revue Française de Psychanalyse*, 49, pp. 327–353.

Luzes, P (1989) "Realidad psíquica: Su génesis a partir de lo biológico y de las relaciones objetales". *Anuario Ibérico del Psicoanálisis*, 1, pp. 23–57.

Maldonado, J.L. (1984) "Analyst involvement in the psychoanalytic impasse". *International Journal of Psycho-Analysis*, 65, p. 263.

Maldonado, J.L. (1987) "Narcissism and unconscious communication". *International Journal of Psycho-Analysis*, 68, pp. 379–387.

Maldonado, J.L. (1989) "On negative and positive therapeutic reaction". *International Journal of Psycho-Analysis*, 70, p. 327.

Mancia, M. (1987) *Il sogno come religione della mente*. Laterza, Rome and Bari.

Mancia, M. (1994) *Dall'Edipo al sogno*. Raffaello Cortina Editore, Milan.

Mancia, M. (1995) *Percorsi*. Bollati Boringhieri, Turin.

Manfredi Turillazzi, S. (1978) "Interpretazione dell'agire e interpretazione come agire". *Rivista di Psicoanalisi*, 24, pp. 223–240.

Manfredi Turillazzi, S. (1985) "L'unicorno. Saggio sulla fantasia e l'oggetto nel concetto di identificazione proiettiva". *Rivista di Psicoanalisi*, 31, pp. 462–477.

Manfredi Turillazzi, S. (1994a) *Le certezze perdute della psicoanalisi clinica*. Raffaello Cortina Editore, Milan.

Manfredi Turillazzi, S. (1994b) "Discussione al lavoro di A. Ferro". Congresso di Rimini. Unpublished.

Marinetti, M. (1996) "Impotenza, onnipotenza e narcisismo: alcuni problemi dell'analista con i pazienti gravi". In: Correale, A., Rinaldi, L. (1996) (eds) *Quale psicoanalisi per le psicosi?* Cortina, Milan.

Masciangelo, P.M. (1988) "La nascita dell'aggressività. Dall'esperienza psicoanalitica alla teoria". In: *La relazione aggressiva*. Borla, Rome.

Meltzer, D. (1967) *The Psycho-Analytic Process*. Heinemann, London.

Meltzer, D. (1973) *Sexual States of Mind*. Clunie Press, Perthshire.

Meltzer, D. (1982a) "Interventi in allucinazione e bugia". *Quaderni di Psicoterapia Infantile*, 13, pp. 161–187.

Meltzer, D. (1982b) "Una indagine sulle bugie. Loro genesi e relazione con l'allucinazione". *Quaderni di Psicoterapia Infantile*, 13, pp. 188–192.

Meltzer, D. (1982c) "Verità della mente e bugia nella vita del sogno". *Quaderni di Psicoterapia Infantile*, 13, pp. 139–161.

Meltzer, D. (1984) *Dream-life. A Re-examination of the Psycho-analytic Theory and Technique*. London: Karnac Books.

Meltzer, D. (1986) *Studies in Extended Metapsychology*. Karnac Books, London.

Meltzer, D. (1992) *The Claustrum*. The Roland Harris Education Trust.

Meltzer, D., Bremner, J., Hoxter, S., *et al.* (1975) *Explorations in Autism*. Clunie Press, Perthshire.

Meotti, A. (1984) "Di alcuni orientamenti della psicoanalisi italiana. Note e considerazioni su una recente raccolta di studi psicoanalitici". *Rivista di Psicoanalisi*, 30, pp. 109–121.

Meotti, A. (1987) "Appunti su funzione alfa, dolore sensoriale, dolore mentale, pensiero". In: Neri, C., Correale, A., Fadda, P. (eds) *Letture bioniane*. Borla, Rome.

Meotti, A., Meotti, F. (1983) "Su alcuni aspetti dei processi riparativi". *Rivista di Psicoanalisi*, 28, pp. 227–242.

Meotti, A., Meotti, F. (1996) "Gruppo interno, identificazioni multiple e trasmissione transgenerazionale: problemi di tecnica dell'interpretazione". Convegno a seminari multipli, Bologna.

Meotti, F. (1988) "Tecnica, transfert, realtà". *Rivista di Psicoanalisi*, 34 (1), p. 53.

Merleau-Ponty, M. (1945) *Phénoménologie de la perception*. Gallimard, Paris.

Micati, L. (1990) "Odio e distruttività in analisi. Funzione e utilità dell'odio dell'analista". *Rivista di Psicoanalisi*, 36, pp. 58–95.

Micati, L. (1993) "Quanta realtà può essere tollerata". *Rivista di Psicoanalisi*, 39 (1), pp. 153–163.

Milner, M. (1969) *The Hands of the Living God*. Hogarth Press, London.

Molinari Negrini, S. (1985) "Funzione di testimonianza e interpretazione di transfert". *Rivista di Psicoanalisi*, 30 (3), pp. 357–371.

Money-Kyrle, R. (1977) *The Collected Papers of Roger Money-Kyrle*. Clunie Press, Perthshire.

Morpurgo, E. (1988) *Fra tempo e parola*. Franco Angeli, Milan.

Morpurgo, E., Egidi, V. (eds) (1987) *Psicoanalisi e narrazione*. Il Lavoro Editoriale, Ancona.

Neri, C. (1982) "Ricordi di ciò di cui non si è fatta esperienza". *Rivista di Psicoanalisi*, 28, p. 3.

Neri, C. (1993) "Campo e fantasie transgenerazionali". *Rivista di Psicoanalisi*, 39 (1), pp. 43–64.

Neri, C. (1995) *Group.* J. Kingsley Publishers, London and Philadelphia (1998).

Neri, C., Correale, A., Fadda, P. (eds) (1987) *Letture bioniane.* Borla, Rome.

Nicolò, A.M. (1992) "Versioni del Sé e interazioni patologiche". *Interazioni*, 0, pp. 37–48.

Nicolò, A.M., Norsa, D. (1991) "Organizzazione degli affetti e significato dell'agire". In: *Gli affetti in psicoanalisi.* Borla, Rome.

Nissim Momigliano, L. (1974) "Come si originano le interpretazioni nello psicoanalista". *Rivista di Psicoanalisi*, 20, pp. 144–165.

Nissim Momigliano, L. (1984) "Due persone che parlano in una stanza (Una ricerca sul dialogo analitico)". *Rivista di Psicoanalisi*, 30 (1), pp. 1–17.

Nissim Momigliano, L. (1987) "A spell in Vienna: but was Freud a Freudian?" *International Review of Psycho-Analysis*, 14, pp. 373–389.

Nissim Momigliano, L. (1991) "The psychoanalyst in the mirror: doubts galore but few certainties". *International Journal of Psycho-Analysis*, 72, pp. 287–296.

Nissim Momigliano, L. (1992) *Continuity and Change in Psychoanalysis: Letters from Milan.* Karnac Books, London.

Norsa, D. (1993) "Modelli di identificazione genitoriale". *Interazioni*, 1, pp. 9–29.

Norsa, D., Zavattini, G.C. (1988) "La relazione perversa". *Psichiatria dell'Infanzia dell'Adolescenza*, 55 (6), p. 643.

Ogden, T.H. (1979) "On projective identification". *International Journal of Psycho-Analysis*, 60, pp. 357–373.

Ogden, T.H. (1982) *Projective Identification and Psychotherapeutic Technique.* Jason Aronson, New York.

Ogden, T. (1986) *The Matrix of the Mind: Object Relations and the Psychoanalytic Dialogue.* Jason Aronson, London.

Pavel, T.J. (1976) "Possible worlds in literary semantics". *Journal of Aesthetics and Art Criticism*, 34 (2), p. 165.

Perdigao, G. (1991) "Investigación, modelo de la mente y proceso psicoanalítico". *Revista de la Sociedad Colombiana de Psicoanálisis*, 16 (1), pp. 31–44.

Petofi, J.S. (1975) *Vers une théorie partielle du texte.* Buske, Hamburg.

Petrella, F. (1993a) "Percezione endopsichica/fenomeno funzionale". *Rivista di Psicoanalisi*, 39 (1), pp. 101–120.

Petrella, F. (1993b) *Turbamenti affettivi e alterazioni dell'esperienza.* Raffaello Cortina Editore, Milan.

Platinga, A. (1974) *The Nature of Necessity.* Oxford University Press, London.

Premack, D., Woodruff, G. (1978) "Does the chimpanzee have a theory of mind?" *Behavioral and Brain Sciences*, 4, pp. 515–526.

Preve, C. (1988) "Il paziente come guardiano del setting". Read to the Centro milanese di psicoanalisi.

Preve, C. (1994) "Considerazioni sulla fase conclusiva dell'analisi". *Rivista di Psicoanalisi*, 40 (1), p. 49.

Puget, J., Wender, S. (1987) "Aux limites de l'analysabilité. Tyrannie corporelle et sociale". *Revue Française de Psychanalyse*, 51 (3), pp. 869–898.

Quinodoz, J.M. (1991) *The Taming of Solitude*, trans. P. Slotkin. Routledge, London, 1993.

Quinodoz, D. (1992) "The psychoanalytic setting as the instrument of the container function". *International Journal of Psycho-Analysis*, 73, pp. 627–635.

Renik, O. (1990) "The concept of a transference neurosis and psychoanalytic methodology". *International Journal of Psycho-Analysis*, 71, p. 197.

Renik, O. (1993) "Analytic interaction: conceptualizing technique in the light of the analyst's irreducible subjectivity". *Psychoanalytic Quarterly*, 62 (4), p. 553.

Resnik, S. (1982) *The Theatre of the Dream*, trans. A. Sheridan. Tavistock Publications, London, 1987.

Resnik, S. (1994) *Mental Space*, trans. D. Alcorn. Karnac Books, London, 1995.

Riolo, F. (1986) "Dei soggetti del campo: un discorso sui 'limiti'". *Gruppo e Funzione Analitica*, 7, p. 3.

Riolo, F. (1989) "Teoria delle trasformazioni. Tre seminari su Bion". *Gruppo e Funzione Analitica*, 2, p. 7.

Robutti, A. (1992a) Introduction to: Nissim Momigliano, L., Robutti, A. (eds) *Shared Experience: The Psychoanalytic Dialogue*. Karnac Books, London.

Robutti, A. (1992b) "Cassandra: a myth for hypochondria". In: Nissim Momigliano, L., Robutti, A. (eds) *Shared Experience: The Psychoanalytic Dialogue*. Karnac Books, London.

Robutti, A. (1993) "Il setting e il modello interiore dell'analista". Convegno a seminari multipli, Bologna.

Rocha Barros, E.M. (1992) "Escrita psicanalítica e prática clínica". *Revista Brasileira de Psicanálise*, 26 (1–2), pp. 205–211.

Rocha Barros, E.M. (1994) "A interpretação: seus pressupostos teóricos". *Revista de Psicanálise*, SPPA, I (3), pp. 57–72.

Rocha Barros, E.M. (1996) "Addressing the psychic reality of the borderline child". *International Journal of Psycho-Analysis*, 77 (1), pp. 107–110.

Rosenfeld, H. (1983) "Primitive object relations and mechanisms". *International Journal of Psycho-Analysis*, 64, pp. 261–267.

Rosenfeld, H. (1987) *Impasse and Interpretation*. Tavistock Publications, London.

Rossi, P.L. (1992) "Relazione reale e comportamento dell'analista". *Rivista di Psicoanalisi*, 38, pp. 490–511.

Rossi, P.L. (1994) "Attività e passività dell'analista negli inizi difficili in psicoanalisi". *Atti del X Congresso Nazionale SPI*, Rimini.

Rothstein, A. (ed) (1985) *Models of the Mind. Their Relationship to Clinical Work*. International Universities Press, New York.

Sabbadini, A. (1996) "Psychic reality and creativity". *International Journal of Psycho-Analysis*, 77 (1), pp. 103–105.

Sacco, F. (1995a) "Bref parcours historique". In: *Le dessin dans la séance psychanalytique avec l'enfant*. Erès, Ramonville.

Sacco, F. (1995b) "De l'agir à la mise en forme ou le destin du figurable". In: *Le dessin dans la séance psychanalytique avec l'enfant*. Erès, Ramonville.

Sacco, F. (1996) "Destino della figurabilità". III Colloquio nazionale analisi infantile, Rome.

Sandler, J. (1976) "Countertransference and role responsiveness". *International Review of Psycho-Analysis*, 3, pp. 43–47.

Sandler, J., Sandler, A.M. (1984) "The past unconscious, the present unconscious and the vicissitudes of guilt". *International Journal of Psycho-Analysis*, 68, pp. 331–341.

Sandler, J., Sandler, A.M. (1992) "Phantasy and its transformations: a contemporary Freudian view". Weekend Conference for English-speaking Members of European Societies, 16–18 October 1992.

Saraval, A. (1985) "L'analista può essere neutrale?" *Rivista di Psicoanalisi*, 31 (3), pp. 343–356.

Sarno, L. (1984) "Il setting psicoanalitico fra costituzione interna e migrazioni istituzionali". *Prospettive analitiche nel lavoro istituzionale*, 2 (1), pp. 132–146.

Sarno, L. (1989) "Sull'interpretabilità analitica e sulla 'tecnica' della fine analisi". *Gruppo e Funzione Analitica*, 10 (3), pp. 15–28.

Sarno, L. (1994) "Transfert, controtransfert e campo psicoanalitico: ambiguità semantiche, variazioni di senso, trasformazioni". *Atti del X Congresso Nazionale SPI*, Rimini.

Schafer, R. (1994) "The contemporary Kleinians of London". *Psychoanalytic Quarterly*, 63 (3), p. 409.

Schlesinger, C. (1989) "Del Metroide". *Rivista di Psicoanalisi*, 35, pp. 141–169.

Segal, H. (1957) "Notes on symbol formation". *International Journal of Psycho-Analysis*, 38, pp. 391–397.

Segal, H. (1983) "Some clinical implications of Melanie Klein's work". *International Journal of Psycho-Analysis*, 64, p. 269.

Segal, H. (1985) "The Klein–Bion model". In: Rothstein, A. (ed) *Models of the Mind. Their Relationship to Clinical Work*. International Universities Press, New York.

Semi, A.A. (ed) (1988) *Trattato di psicoanalisi*. Raffaello Cortina Editore, Milan.

Semi, A.A. (1992) *Dal colloquio alla teoria*. Raffaello Cortina Editore, Milan.

Speziale Bagliacca, R. (1982) *Sulle spalle di Freud*. Astrolabio, Rome.

Speziale Bagliacca, R. (1991) "The capacity to contain: notes on its function in psychic change". *International Journal of Psycho-Analysis*, 72, p. 27.

Spillius, E. Bott (1983) "Some developments of the work of Melanie Klein". *International Journal of Psycho-Analysis*, 64, p. 321.

Spillius, E. Bott (1988) *Melanie Klein Today*. Routledge, London.

Steinert, J. (1987) "The interplay between pathological organizations and paranoid-schizoid and depressive positions". *International Journal of Psycho-Analysis*, 68, pp. 69–80.

Steinert, J. (1992) "Interpretações centradas no paciente e centradas no analista". *Revista Brasileira de Psicanálise*, 26 (3), pp. 409–424.

Stevenson, R.L. (1892) A chapter on dreams. In: *Across the Plains*. Books for Libraries Press, Freeport, 1972.

Tagliacozzo, R. (1982) "La pensabilità: una meta della psicoanalisi". In: Di Chiara, G. (ed) *Itinerari della psicoanalisi*. Loescher, Turin.

Tagliacozzo, R. (1990) "Cercando di pensare con Freud". *Rivista di Psicoanalisi*, 36, pp. 805–829.

Thomä, H., Kächele, H. (1985/1988) *Psychoanalytic Practice. Vol. 1. Principles. Vol. 2. Clinical Studies*. Vol. 1 trans. M. Wilson and D. Roseveare. Vol. 2 trans. M. Wilson. Springer-Verlag, Berlin and Heidelberg, 1987 (vol. 1); 1992 (vol. 2).

Torras de Beà, E. (1989) "Projective identification and differentiation". *International Journal of Psycho-Analysis.*, 70, p. 265.

Torras de Beà, E., Rallo Romero, J. (1986) "Past and present interpretation". *International Review of Psycho-Analysis*, 13, p. 309.

Tuckett, D. (1989) "A brief view of Herbert Rosenfeld's contribution to the theory of psychoanalytical technique". *International Journal of Psycho-Analysis*, 70, p. 619.

Tuckett, D. (1993) "Some thoughts on the presentation and discussion of the clinical material of psychoanalysis". *International Journal of Psycho-Analysis*, 74, p. 1175.

Usuelli, A. (1991) "La ilusión en la obra de Freud y de Winnicott: un valor controvertido". *Revista de Psicoanálisis*, 48, pp. 136–149.

Vallino Macciò, D. (1990) "Sulla consultazione: atmosfere emotive, sofferenza e sollievo nel bambino". *Analysis*, 1, pp. 1–32.

Vallino Macciò, D. (1991) "Il gioco delle parti nella rêverie dell'analista". Paper presented to the IX Congresso Nazionale SPI, Saint Vincent.

Vallino Macciò, D. (1992) "Surviving, existing, living. Notes on the analyst's anxiety". In: Nissim Momigliano, L., Robutti, A. (eds) *Shared Experience: The Psychoanalytic Dialogue*. Karnac Books, London.

Vallino Macciò, D. (1993) "Una storia, le storie, i sogni nell'analisi dei bambini". Read to the Centro milanese di psicoanalisi, 25 March.

Vallino Macciò, D. (1994) "Una storia che . . . ha degli imprevedibili sviluppi". *Quaderni di Psicoterapia Infantile*, 30, pp. 13–39.

Vallino Macciò, D. (1996) "Come va a finire la storia?" III Colloquio nazionale analisi infantile, Rome.

Van Dijk, T.A. (1976) "Pragmatics and poetics". In: *Pragmatics of Language and Literature*. North Holland, Amsterdam.

Vattimo, G. (1983) "Dialettica, differenza, pensiero debole". In: Vattimo, G., Rovatti, P.A. (eds) *Il pensiero debole*. Feltrinelli, Milan.

Vergine, A. (1990) "Riflessioni generali sul tema del Congresso". Paper presented at the IX Congresso Nazionale SPI, Saint Vincent.

Williams, A.H. (1983) *Nevrosi e delinquenza*. Borla, Rome.

Winnicott, D.W (1965) *The Maturational Process and the Facilitating Environment*. Hogarth Press, London.

Winnicott, D.W (1971) *Playing and Reality*. Tavistock Publications, London.

Winnicott, D.W (1972) "Holding and interpretation – fragment of an analysis". In: Giovacchini, P.L. (ed.) *Tactics and Techniques in Psychoanalytic Therapy*, Hogarth Press, London, pp. 455–693.

Winnicott, D.W (1974) "Fear of breakdown". *International Review of Psycho-Analysis*, 1, pp. 103–107.

Winnicott, D.W (1978) *The Piggle: An Account of the Psychoanalytic Treatment of a Little Girl*. Ed. I. Ranzy. Hogarth Press, London.

Zac de Goldstein, R. (1984) "The dark continent and its emigrants". *International Journal of Psycho-Analysis*, 65, p. 179

Zavattini, G.C. (1995) "Verità narrativa e storica in Freud: dalla teoria dell'evento alla teoria delle fantasie". *Atti dell'Accademia di Scienze Morali e Politiche*, 106, pp. 475–488.

Index

abstinence 92
abuse 101
acting in 127–33
acting out 90, 92; characteropathic 119
adhesive identification 16, 59, 108, 127
affection 54, 64, 101, 109, 110
affects 96, 97
aggregation 63, 98, 101
aggression 92; self-generation of 18;
    sexuality and 93–114; suffering
    concealed behind 18
agoraphobia 129
AIDS 129
alarm 4
"alphaness" 66
analysability 3–4, 17, 35
analyst's mind 9, 47, 96, 108, 110, 137;
    patient who damages 7; mind terror in
    82; transformational capacity of 59
anecdotes 1, 87
aneurysm 137
anger fits of 71
anguish 25
annihilation 78
antagonism 18
ants 26
anxieties 9, 15, 58, 77, 99, 112, 129;
    abandonment 18; castration 6;
    catastrophic 7, 76, 133, depressive 81,
    82; devouring 50; dissolution 108;
    fragmentation 108; intense 86, 87;
    metabolization of 78; narrator's own
    116; persecutory 81; primitive 7;
    psychotic 18; restricted availability for
    absorbing 42; separation 54; split-off
    83; uncontainable 82; underlying 83
apathy 107
Argento, Dario 89

assimilation 28
attitudes 92; affectionate or understanding
    64; emotional and defensive 38;
    interpretative 98; mental, analyst's 121
autistic barrier/defence 109, 110
autonomy 9, 10, 110
avoidance 81, 84–8

Barale, F. 88, 111, 125
Baranger, W. & M. 1, 5, 43, 47, 48, 65, 81,
    86, 88, 115
Basque terrorism 55–7
Beauty and the Beast 104
"betaloma" 86
Bezoari, M. 1, 55, 69, 103
Bianchedi, E. T. 9
Bick, E. 108
Bion, W. R. 1, 2, 5, 9, 13, 28, 35, 38, 41,
    43, 46, 47, 52, 57, 58, 64, 66–80, 82,
    86, 122, 133, 140; analytical situation
    120; bizarre objects 67; extension in the
    domain of myth 71, 141; genesis of
    thought 116; imaginary twin 105;
    internal narrator 117; mind too heavy a
    load 94; negative capability 6, 16, 22,
    32, 69; new function of living matter
    110; patient and analyst 102, 137;
    projective transformations 73; psycho-
    analytical function of the personality
    119; story of the liars 7; theory and
    model 8; thinking a new function of
    living matter 87; two-person
    psychology 115
Bleger, J. 4, 48, 133–4
bodily sensations 116
Bonaminio, V. 65
boredom 55, 106, 107
Borgogno, F. 102